READINGS ON

JOHN
STEINBECK

OTHER TITLES IN THE GREENHAVEN PRESS
LITERARY COMPANION SERIES:

AMERICAN AUTHORS

Nathaniel Hawthorne
Mark Twain

BRITISH AUTHORS

The Tragedies of William Shakespeare

THE GREENHAVEN PRESS
Literary Companion
TO AMERICAN AUTHORS

JOHN STEINBECK

David Bender, *Publisher*
Bruno Leone, *Executive Editor*
Scott Barbour, *Managing Editor*
Clarice Swisher, *Book Editor*

Greenhaven Press, San Diego, CA

Library of Congress Cataloging-in-Publication Data

Readings on John Steinbeck / Clarice Swisher, book editor.
    p.   cm. — (The Greenhaven Press literary companion
    to American authors)
  Includes bibliographical references and index.
  ISBN 1-56510-469-2 (lib. bdg. : alk. paper). —
  ISBN 1-56510-468-4 (pbk. : alk. paper)
  1. Steinbeck, John, 1902–1968—Criticism and
interpretation. 2. Western stories—History and criticism.
3. Mexican Americans in literature. 4. California—In
literature. 5. Naturalism in literature. I. Swisher, Clarice,
1933– . II. Series.
PS3537.T3234Z855   1996
813'.52–dc20   95-51243
                                                            CIP

Cover photo: UPI/Bettmann

Copyright ©1996 by Greenhaven Press, Inc.
PO Box 289009
San Diego, CA 92198-9009
Printed in the U.S.A.

" To finish this sadness to a writer—a little death. He puts the last word down and it is done. But it isn't really done. The story goes on and leaves the writer behind, for no story is ever done. "

—John Steinbeck

CONTENTS

Foreword   11

John Steinbeck: A Biography   13

How Six Short Novels Came to Be (1957)
by John Steinbeck   27

> Six of John Steinbeck's short novels—*The Red Pony, Tortilla Flat, Of Mice and Men, The Moon Is Down, Cannery Row,* and *The Pearl*—arose out of personal circumstances. Each of them contains a special, sometimes humorous, incident involving publishers, critics, or readers.

John Steinbeck's Authentic Characters (1957)
by Joseph Warren Beach   30

> In his early stories, John Steinbeck uses his literary talent to create realistic characters whose lives are plain and who live at an economically poor or near-subsistence level. Despite their sparse lives, they are individuals with souls, who have rich and diverse inner natures and who involve themselves with others in humorous and compassionate relationships.

John Steinbeck's Naturalism (1956)
by Charles Child Walcutt   40

> John Steinbeck explores two elements of American naturalism: the spirit, or the demands of the heart, and fact, or the demands of the mind. These opposing poles appear in nearly all of Steinbeck's novels. As a naturalistic writer, Steinbeck tries to describe human life precisely, but, unlike many naturalistic writers, he uses conventional forms, such as fable and epic, to explore these polarized elements in the lives of his characters.

Escape and Commitment in John Steinbeck's
Heroes (1970) *by Peter Lisca*   50

> In his early novels, John Steinbeck sympathizes with the heroes who escape from the demands of society. In later novels, he portrays heroes as martyrs committed to a cause or to others, as in *In Dubious Battle* and *The Grapes of Wrath.* In *The Pearl* and *The Wayward Bus* his heroes experience only disillusionment and escape, committed neither to the individual nor to society.

John Steinbeck: A Successful Failure (1959)
by R. W. B. Lewis   58

> John Steinbeck does the reading public a valuable service by making the realities and themes of his time visible. But he fails to probe deeply enough into these elements with the techniques available to the artist. Instead, Steinbeck remains political, focused on the group; he stops short of portraying the tragic fate of the individual and the flaws of the human heart.

John Steinbeck's *Paisano* Knights (1970)
by Charles R. Metzger 65

Of John Steinbeck's twenty volumes of work, half deal with Mexicans—Mexicans in Mexico, Mexican immigrants in California, and American descendants of Mexicans. Though he presents them in a variety of ways throughout his works, he focuses on one kind of Mexican American in *Tortilla Flat—paisanos.* These economically poor men have a knight-like pride in living by a code of dignified behavior similar to Arthurian knights of legend. Steinbeck's story of their macho world is a romantic and humorous treatment of real people.

John Steinbeck's Myth of Manhood (1961) *by Dan Vogel* 73

John Steinbeck's short story "Flight" is the story of a boy who kills a man while on an errand in town. As a result, he has to flee alone. But the story is more than a young man's adventure; it is a myth about the rite of passage from boyhood to manhood. Ironically, just when Pepé can stand alone as a man, he becomes the target of a posse. Like many myths, this one ends with violence.

John Steinbeck's Mature Style in *The Red Pony* (1939)
by Harry Thornton Moore 77

In his partly autobiographical story *The Red Pony*, John Steinbeck writes with a glowing style about ranch life in the Salinas Valley. This collection of four stories tells about young Jody's exposure to birth and death, hard experiences that initiate him into the realities of life. Steinbeck's style succeeds both in his creation of characters and in his depiction of the ranch and the valley.

Oneness and Mysticism in *The Red Pony* (1965)
by Arnold L. Goldsmith 80

Even though John Steinbeck's *The Red Pony* is composed of four stories, it has an underlying unity of time, place, and theme. The stories portray the development of a young boy named Jody as he experiences the realities of life and death— the life and death of horses and of men. Through the cycles of beginnings and endings, the stories create a mystical connection that unifies humans, animals, and nature.

Jody's Growing Awareness in *The Red Pony* (1961)
by Warren French 86

At the beginning of the first of the four stories in John Steinbeck's *The Red Pony*, the young Jody trusts and obeys adults implicitly. After the ranch hand fails to take care of his red pony, Jody learns step by step to realize the fallibility of both humans and nature. He is disappointed, angered, and saddened, but he emerges at the end of the fourth story as a compassionate, mature young man.

The Allegory of *The Pearl* (1963) *by Harry Morris* 93

John Steinbeck's short novel *The Pearl* is a special kind of allegory, one with an overlay of realism. The story portrays the allegorical journey of Kino, an ignorant, unsophisticated man, who confronts the injustices of a powerful society. Yet it also portrays a particular man of pride living in the real geographical places around La Paz, Mexico. As the allegory extends outward, *The Pearl* symbolizes the plight of all poor people and shows how they persevere.

The Parable of *The Pearl* (1974) *by Howard Levant*   100

John Steinbeck's *The Pearl* can be read as a carefully and artistically crafted parable about a pearl and its great price. Steinbeck tells the story of one family, which includes Kino, his wife, and his son. After Kino finds a large and valuable pearl, the family suffers many troubles. As the story progresses, the original microcosm of the single family expands into a wider and more complex world filled with violence and injustice. Through symbol, irony, and character development, Steinbeck elevates *The Pearl* beyond a simple moral tale about good and evil.

Symbolic Creatures in *The Pearl* (1974)
by Martha Heasley Cox   109

When John Steinbeck expanded a true story about an Indian boy into the novel *The Pearl*, he created characters that can be read as symbols, and he incorporated images from all parts of the animal kingdom. Some of the creatures are themselves symbols, like the scorpion that stings Coyotito. Other images from the animal kingdom serve as similes and metaphors. These images reinforce the message that Kino experiences moments when he has an animal-like existence.

Attitudes Toward the Poor in *Of Mice and Men* (1957)   117
by Edwin Berry Burgum

Novelists in the 1930s shifted attention from the middle class to the poor. John Steinbeck's many novels represent a wide range of attitudes toward struggling workers and vagabonds. In *Of Mice and Men*, a complex of sociological attitudes— some defined, some ambiguous—emerges from among the characters working on the ranch. Steinbeck leaves the reader at the end of the book pondering the moral dilemma that surrounds Lennie and George.

Patterns That Make Meaning in *Of Mice and Men* (1958)   122
by Peter Lisca

John Steinbeck intended to create a microcosm in *Of Mice and Men*, a world that portrays the yearnings of common people. This theme becomes apparent in the novel through the use of symbol, action, and language. Recurring motifs establish a pattern—George's retelling the story about a little farm with rabbits and Lennie's repeated destruction of soft things. This pattern raises hope and destroys it again. In spite of their slim chance of ever arriving at their safe place, George and Lennie continue on, strengthened by their need for one another.

Of Mice and Men: A Knight Dismounted and a
Dream Ended (1961) *by Warren French*   130
> *Of Mice and Men* is John Steinbeck's last novel to be influ-
> enced by the legends of King Arthur. Like the legendary
> knights, George is loyal and pure, on a quest for his dream
> farm. But romance falters in the unromantic world of the
> ranch and the bunkhouse. With Lennie's death, George gives
> up his quest for a farm of his own and faces his own short-
> comings and mediocrity. His heroism lies in his own survival.

Christian Symbolism in *The Grapes of Wrath* (1956)
by Martin Shockley   138
> John Steinbeck's novel *The Grapes of Wrath* contains lan-
> guage, events, and characters that relate to Christian theolo-
> gy and literature. Specifically, Jim Casy's dialogue and many
> of his actions parallel the words and actions of Jesus Christ.
> Tom Joad, who follows Casy's philosophy, acts like one of
> the disciples of Jesus. The novel's Christian philosophy, how-
> ever, is less like church doctrine and more like a direct illus-
> tration of Jesus' words. It is more like Unitarianism and the
> transcendentalist philosophy of Ralph Waldo Emerson and
> Walt Whitman than it is like strict, traditional Protestantism.

Artistic and Thematic Structure in *The Grapes
of Wrath* (1963) *by J. P. Hunter*   145
> John Steinbeck's *The Grapes of Wrath* has an artistic and
> thematic plan. Steinbeck parallels a wide sweep of Judeo-
> Christian history with the journey of a single family, the
> Joads. The family transforms from a self-centered collection
> of individuals into a solidified and devoted group. Jim Casy,
> whose initials are the same as Jesus Christ's, leads the Joads
> in this change. By the end, after a dismal journey, the grapes
> have ripened into regenerated hope.

Indestructible Women in *The Grapes of Wrath* (1988)
by Mimi Reisel Gladstein   156
> In *The Grapes of Wrath,* John Steinbeck creates in the char-
> acter of Ma Joad both a symbol and a realistic woman. As a
> symbol, she is the optimistic pioneer woman moving west to
> find a better life. She is the earth mother, who nourishes her
> own family and others. As goddess, she commands respect
> and holds power over those she leads. But as a realistic
> woman, she makes mistakes, shows her fears, and exhibits
> pride. In both roles, she is the indestructible woman who
> passes on the roles and responsibilities to her daughter Rose
> of Sharon.

John Steinbeck's Call to Conversion in *The Grapes
of Wrath* (1990) *by Stephen Railton*   165
> John Steinbeck's *The Grapes of Wrath* is about growing,
> moving, and transforming. It is a call for the reader to reject
> the conditions that bring on suffering and misery for the
> poor. By illustrating the conversion that takes place within

several members of the Joad family, Steinbeck clarifies the change he wants to enact in the reader. It involves inner concern and love for others *and* action on their behalf. Both, not just one or the other, are what Steinbeck's conversion requires.

John Steinbeck Awarded the Nobel Prize
in Literature (1987) *by Carl E. Rallyson Jr.*   174
John Steinbeck received the Nobel Prize in literature on December 10, 1962. The Swedish Academy selected Steinbeck primarily for his novels published before 1940, but cited two published in the 1960s. Most of the major American news and literary magazines ignored both the award and Steinbeck's acceptance speech delivered in Stockholm, Sweden.

Chronology   178

Works by John Steinbeck   182

For Further Research   185

Index   187

FOREWORD

*"'Tis the good reader that
makes the good book."*

Ralph Waldo Emerson

The story's bare facts are simple: The captain, an old and scarred seafarer, walks with a peg leg made of whale ivory. He relentlessly drives his crew to hunt the world's oceans for the great white whale that crippled him. After a long search, the ship encounters the whale and a fierce battle ensues. Finally the captain drives his harpoon into the whale, but the harpoon line catches the captain about the neck and drags him to his death.

A simple story, a straightforward plot—yet, since the 1851 publication of Herman Melville's *Moby-Dick*, readers and critics have found many meanings in the struggle between Captain Ahab and the whale. To some, the novel is a cautionary tale that depicts how Ahab's obsession with revenge leads to his insanity and death. Others believe that the whale represents the unknowable secrets of the universe and that Ahab is a tragic hero who dares to challenge fate by attempting to discover this knowledge. Perhaps Melville intended Ahab as a criticism of Americans' tendency to become involved in well-intentioned but irrational causes. Or did Melville model Ahab after himself, letting his fictional character express his anger at what he perceived as a cruel and distant god?

Although literary critics disagree over the meaning of *Moby-Dick*, readers do not need to choose one particular interpretation in order to gain an understanding of Melville's novel. Instead, by examining various analyses, they can gain numerous insights into the issues that lie under the surface of the basic plot. Studying the writings of literary critics can also aid readers in making their own assessments of *Moby-Dick* and other literary works and in developing analytical thinking skills.

The Greenhaven Literary Companion Series was created with these goals in mind. Designed for young adults, this unique anthology series provides an engaging and comprehensive introduction to literary analysis and criticism. The essays included in the Literary Companion Series are chosen for their accessibility to a young adult audience and are expertly edited in consideration of both the reading and comprehension levels of this audience. In addition, each essay is introduced by a concise summation that presents the contributing writer's main themes and insights. Every anthology in the Literary Companion Series contains a varied selection of critical essays that cover a wide time span and express diverse views. Wherever possible, primary sources are represented through excerpts from authors' notebooks, letters, and journals and through contemporary criticism.

Each title in the Literary Companion Series pays careful consideration to the historical context of the particular author or literary work. In-depth biographies and detailed chronologies reveal important aspects of authors' lives and emphasize the historical events and social milieu that influenced their writings. To facilitate further research, every anthology includes primary and secondary source bibliographies of articles and/or books selected for their suitability for young adults. These engaging features make the Greenhaven Literary Companion Series ideal for introducing students to literary analysis in the classroom or as a library resource for young adults researching the world's great authors and literature.

Exceptional in its focus on young adults, the Greenhaven Literary Companion Series strives to present literary criticism in a compelling and accessible format. Every title in the series is intended to spark readers' interest in leading American and world authors, to help them broaden their understanding of literature, and to encourage them to formulate their own analyses of the literary works that they read. It is the editors' hope that young adult readers will find these anthologies to be true companions in their study of literature.

JOHN STEINBECK: A BIOGRAPHY

Salinas, California, and the nearby Pacific coast, was home to John Steinbeck. In this area, about a hundred miles south of San Francisco, John Steinbeck developed his personality and wrote his best novels. Salinas, a shipping center near lettuce and celery farms, lies at the north end of a long valley that runs parallel to the coast. Only a few miles away from Salinas are the coastal town of Monterey and the village of Pacific Grove, where the Steinbecks had a summer cottage.

John Ernst Steinbeck was born on February 27, 1902, in Salinas; he was the third child of John Ernst Sr. and Olivia Hamilton Steinbeck. When John was born, his sister Esther was ten and his sister Elizabeth was eight. The Steinbecks, though they had a middle-class income, appeared to be upper class in Salinas because they lived in a large Victorian house and took an active part in community and cultural life. Steinbeck's father managed a flour mill, and his mother had taught in a one-room rural school.

EARLY CULTURAL AND INTELLECTUAL TRAINING

After two daughters, Olivia (called Olive) Steinbeck wanted a son to raise because she knew that men had more opportunity for adult achievement than women. In his book *The Intricate Music, A Biography of John Steinbeck*, Thomas Kiernan says:

> Olive had promised herself that if she were blessed with a son, she would mold him into a man of broad intellectual capacity, a man who might one day be a great university professor, scientist or scholar. Thus her disappointment when she first beheld her newborn child. "He has the looks of a businessman," she is said to have remarked sourly to a visitor a few days after John's birth.

Olive Steinbeck did her best to raise a cultured and intellectual son. She read to him: fairy tales at two, Bible and animal stories at three, *Robin Hood* and Robert Louis Stevenson's *Treasure Island* at four. Young John liked the sounds of words and the rhythms of sentences and learned to read when he was five.

John became timid and shy before he entered school. The turbulence of Steinbeck's adult life had an early beginning. In 1906, when he was four, he saw a store destroyed to a pile of ruins by an earthquake, an experience that frightened him. Children teased him about his physical features, especially his large ears, and his behavior, so he withdrew into books and daydreams. His mother, who responded by coddling him, did not help him build his confidence. Then his father took over and spent time with his son every day to expose him to the realities of farm animals, gardening, and country life. He bought John a pony named Jill and expected his son to care for it.

During the years of primary school, called Baby School in Salinas, John achieved well. For a time each summer, John was sent to visit Aunt Molly, Olive's sister, for further exposure to literature and music. As he grew older, John wanted to roam the hills and fields and felt confined by the lessons. His Aunt Molly gave John a book as a gift. Though he resented it, the book had a great influence on his works. Years later he wrote about the gift:

> One day, an aunt gave me a book and fatuously ignored my resentment. I stared at the black print with hatred, and then gradually the pages opened and let me in. The magic happened. The Bible and Shakespeare and *Pilgrim's Progress* belonged to everyone. But this was mine—secretly mine. It was a cut version of the Caxton "Morte d'Arthur" of Thomas Malory. I loved the old spelling of the words—and the words no longer used. Perhaps a passionate love for the English language opened to me from this one book. I was delighted to find out paradoxes— that "cleave" means both to stick together and to cut apart. . . . For a long time, I had a secret language.

John and Mary, his younger sister born in 1909, read the Arthurian tales together, acted them out, and with the pony searched for the Grail.

SHYNESS AND REBELLION

During his West End Grammar School years from fourth through eighth grades, John explored and made friends. As a fourth grader, he spent his days disrupting the class; by fifth grade, he had accepted the proper behavior expected of him, but he was still shy and often a loner. He made two good friends, Glenn Graves and Max Wagner, and found he could gain power over them by telling stories. He had a paper route and went exploring alone on his bicycle to Salinas's Chinatown, the Mexican neighborhoods, and the outlying ranches and pastures. On these trips he gathered in sights and sounds to use in his stories.

In 1915, John began ninth grade in Salinas High School, where he followed a regular college-preparatory program of English, mathematics, science, history, and foreign languages. He was neither popular with other students nor remarkable as a student. Classmates found him erratic, either very friendly or hostile, and teachers, who thought his features gave him a stupid look, made fun of him in front of their classes. John reacted with silent, burning shame. Secretly during his junior year, he began writing stories and sending them anonymously to magazines. Near the end of his junior year, John got pneumonia and pleurisy. Since antibiotics had yet to be discovered, the illness was serious, and doctors operated and removed a rib and the infection. The illness helped him mature and take his senior year seriously. He studied, became president of the student body, joined the science and drama clubs, and was editor of the yearbook. He graduated in a class of twenty-four students.

Steinbeck entered Stanford University in 1919, registered as a liberal arts student. With new surroundings and in competition with Stanford students, John's feelings of ineptness and timidity arose again; he coped by withdrawing instead of trying, by acting disruptive, and by taking on eccentric roles. His roommate and good friend, George Mors, was a self-directed engineering student who tried to persuade John to attend to his studies. John left Stanford with an illness before the spring term of his first year ended; he had earned three credits for the year. He attended Stanford on and off for six years between 1919 and 1925, but he never earned a degree. He had terms in 1923 and 1924, however, when he studied, took his classes seriously, and made good grades.

During summers and times away from Stanford, Steinbeck worked as a laborer. He worked for a sugar-beet company, Spreckels Sugar, sometimes laboring with migrants in the harvest field and living with them in the bunkhouse. Other times he worked for thirty-two and a half cents an hour as a bench chemist, where he ran routine tests on the sugar harvest. One summer he hung around the Hopkins Marine Station in Pacific Grove, Stanford's laboratory for the study of marine life. Though Steinbeck appeared aimless during these years, he was thinking and writing, trying to work out a style of expression for the stories he wanted to write. He wanted a method to express the unique qualities of people he met on the streets and people from his past. All the while, he was absorbing impressions of people and places that later became characters and settings in stories.

SEARCHING FOR A VOICE AND A STYLE

Although his years at Stanford never gained him a degree, the time there had several favorable outcomes for Steinbeck.

During his sophomore year, he wrote five or six stories about college life. Before he left, the *Spectator*, the college literary magazine, published two of his stories. When he enrolled in 1924 after a term away, he was older and more confident than his classmates. He took on the image of diligent scholar with pipe and cloth book bag. He came to know three people who influenced him. He and Duke Sheffield, who also wanted to be a writer, became friends, read each other's work, and offered support. John took a short-story class from Edith Mirrielees, who liked the form of his stories and taught him how to develop characters more effectively. At the English Club, an organization for literature students, Steinbeck met Elizabeth Smith, a faculty member who had published stories. She liked Steinbeck's stories and encouraged him to expand "A Lady in Infra-Red" into a novel. Both Mirrielees and Smith urged Steinbeck to stay in school.

After dropping out finally in 1925, Steinbeck lived in the family cottage in Pacific Grove and tried to make progress on a work he called *A Pot of Gold*. When he found he was getting nothing done on the book, he took a job on a freighter and went, via the Panama Canal, to New York, where his sister Elizabeth lived with her husband. In New York City, he worked first as a construction worker and later as a reporter for a Hearst newspaper, the *American*, for twenty-five dollars a week. A former Stanford friend, Ted Miller, offered to show Steinbeck's stories to publishers, one of whom was interested. Steinbeck wrote nine other stories while in New York, but by the time he had them ready, none of the publishers would look at them.

Steinbeck returned to California by freighter and worked as caretaker on the estate of Mrs. Alice Brigham in the Sierra Nevada near Lake Tahoe. Living alone in the caretaker's cottage, he wrote short stories, and in 1927 *Smoker's Companion* published a story called "The Gifts of Ivan" under the pseudonym John Stein. By February 1928 Steinbeck had finished *A Pot of Gold*, but he was twenty-six and feeling like a failure for having accomplished nothing in his life. In April he bought an old car for forty dollars and brought his manuscript of *A Pot of Gold* to Elizabeth Smith and Edith Mirrielees at Stanford, who encouraged him to send it to publishers. Smith suggested changing the title to *Cup of Gold*. He changed the title and sent the handwritten manuscript to Ted Miller in New York, but publishers refused to read a manuscript that was not typed. By this time Steinbeck was back at Lake Tahoe, where he had met a vacationing secretary named Carol Henning, who offered to type for him. *Cup of Gold* was accepted in January 1929 and brought Steinbeck four hundred dollars.

In the decade from 1929 to 1939 Steinbeck's personal life became more satisfying, he became more confident, and he produced his best work. During the first half of the decade he continued to struggle with large philosophical questions he had begun to think about earlier. He tried to write stories with grand actions and bigger-than-life characters, on the order of the Arthurian stories he had loved in his youth. He struggled with the place of humans as individuals and how they were forced to comply with a powerful social order. He wondered if humans were trapped between their animal impulses and the rules imposed on them by their minds. And he was bothered by the poor and hungry people he had seen in the American land of plenty. These issues occupied his thoughts and formed the structures around which he tried to write stories.

FRIENDS AND A WIFE

Steinbeck left Lake Tahoe late in 1929 to visit Carol Henning in San Francisco, where she had returned after her vacation. A former Stanford writing friend, Carl Wilhelmson, had a small apartment there and let Steinbeck stay with him. The two writing hopefuls had opposite interests. Wilhelmson read William Faulkner and Ernest Hemingway and preferred naturalism. Steinbeck read Henry David Thoreau, Ralph Waldo Emerson, and Walt Whitman and preferred idealism. Steinbeck was having trouble with a book called *To an Unknown God* and was also working on a book about poor farmers. During this writing period, his parents provided him an income of twenty-five dollars a month.

Shortly after arriving in San Francisco, he and Carol fell in love and declared their devotion to one another. They married in Glendale, near Los Angeles, on January 14, 1930, bought a Belgian sheepdog puppy, and soon settled in Pacific Grove, where Carol took a job with the Chamber of Commerce. Since Steinbeck was getting nothing but rejection slips from publishers, they needed her income and the monthly gift from the Steinbecks. Book sales were down because the depression had already hit New York.

Just when his work needed inspiration, Steinbeck met Edward F. Ricketts, a marine biologist who operated a laboratory and biological-supply company in Monterey near the docks. Both Steinbeck and Ricketts were witty, cynical risk-takers and became good friends. Ricketts was a confident, intelligent man who could zero in on a confusion of ideas and find order, a skill Steinbeck did not have. The two men frequented the saloons along the docks in an area of Monterey called Cannery Row, spending long hours discussing philosophical and literary ideas and observing the dockworkers. Ricketts advocated a scientific approach to writing; a writer, he told Steinbeck, must be "a scientist of the imagination."

By 1932, Steinbeck's financial situation had worsened. Carol had tried two business ventures that failed, she needed emotional support, and Steinbeck was feeling guilty about his failure as a provider. His friend Carl Wilhelmson suggested that Steinbeck hire a New York agent to sell his manuscripts and recommended Mavis McIntosh and Elizabeth Otis, who agreed to sell Steinbeck's work. Soon they sold *Pastures of Heaven*, the story of a family living under a curse, to an American subsidiary of a prestigious British firm; with the sale came a contract for two more novels. Steinbeck set to work to rewrite *To an Unknown God* and changed the title to *To a God Unknown* at Ricketts's suggestion. Reviews of *Pastures of Heaven* were bad and sales limited, a disappointment that meant Steinbeck would receive no further royalties. At the same time, the publisher withdrew his contract for two novels because of the company's financial trouble.

CHANGES IN STEINBECK'S FORTUNE

In May 1932 Steinbeck's mother had a stroke and had to be hospitalized. While caring for his ailing parents, Steinbeck began work on two new titles. Conversations with his father gave him the idea for a collection of stories that became *The Red Pony*. Stories from Susan Gregory, a Monterey high school teacher interested in poor Mexicans called *paisanos*, gave him the idea for *Tortilla Flat*. By 1933 the publishing company had recovered enough financial stability to publish *To a God Unknown*, and in the same year the *North American Review*, a respected literary magazine, published two of the pony stories. In 1934 the *North American Review* published "The Murder," for which Steinbeck won the O. Henry Award for the best story of the year. His writing career seemed to be improving, but he was also sad about his mother, who had died on February 19, 1934.

Steinbeck's writing style changed as he incorporated Ricketts's suggestions and as he became interested in the social protest theme. He based *Tortilla Flat* on the Arthurian legends, but at the same time took an approach closer to naturalism; that is, he treated his subject more as a scientist treats his evidence, the approach suggested by Ricketts. He sent the manuscript to McIntosh and Otis. Wasting no time, Steinbeck wrote "The Raid" about labor organizers and a longer work on the same subject, *In Dubious Battle*. A surprise came to Steinbeck when he heard from a man named Ben Abramson, a bookseller in Chicago. Abramson liked the red pony stories and had bought *To a God Unknown* and *Pastures from Heaven* to promote with readers.

Steinbeck's best news came when he heard from Pascal Covici, a New York publisher, in January 1935. Covici offered to publish *Tortilla Flat*, asked to be Steinbeck's permanent publisher, and wanted to reissue Steinbeck's previous books. *Tortilla Flat* came out in May 1935, a few days after his father's death. Covici published *Tortilla Flat* with fine line drawings and effective advanced publicity. American readers liked the story and identified with its underdog characters. Soon it was on the best-seller list, and Steinbeck became famous. The book was nominated for the California Commonwealth Club's gold medal for the best book about California. At first the Monterey Chamber of Commerce disapproved of the book because they thought it ridiculed their city, but when tourists and media people arrived and put Monterey on the map, the chamber members changed their minds. While John and Carol were on a trip to Mexico, Otis sold the movie rights for *Tortilla Flat* for four thousand dollars.

Meanwhile, Steinbeck sold "The White Quail" to the *North American Review* and worked on the book about labor organizers, *In Dubious Battle*. Otis convinced Covici to publish it in 1936. As soon as it appeared, it caused a political uproar both from the left and the right. In the spring of 1936, Steinbeck wrote *Of Mice and Men*, a title suggested by his friend Ricketts; Steinbeck structured this story about two migrants, Lennie and George, as a play in novel form. Published in February 1937, *Of Mice and Men* sold 100,000 copies, became an immediate best-seller, and was the Book-of-the-Month Club's choice. Playwright-director George S. Kaufman wanted to direct a play version of the book, so Steinbeck converted the novel into a play script and it won the Drama Critics Award for 1937.

DUST BOWL MIGRANTS

While Steinbeck was finishing the revisions for *Of Mice and Men*, the chief editor from the *San Francisco News*, George

West, asked him to do a series of articles on migrant farm labor in California, particularly on migrants who had come from the dust bowl in the Midwest. Steinbeck did field research by traveling to the migrant camps in an old bakery delivery truck equipped for camping. He and Eric H. Thomsen, director in charge of management of the migrant camps in the region, toured the San Joaquin Valley. Steinbeck had seen the slum outside Salinas, called "Little Oklahoma," and the labor camps called "Hoovervilles," but the poverty and filth of the squatters' camps shocked him. He saw a three-year-old boy with a potbelly caused by malnutrition wearing only a burlap sack tied around his middle. He also saw the contrasting conditions of the government camps, which were clean, well run, and offered inhabitants modest quarters. After completing the articles for the *San Francisco News*, he condensed the information for an article in the *Nation*. This research project gave Steinbeck an idea for a major book about migrant workers.

The Steinbecks went to New York to complete work on the script for *Of Mice and Men*. While they were in New York, Steinbeck discovered what it was like to be a celebrity; he was not used to all the attention, and he hated it. Since he was identified as a friend of the poor, groups wanted support and money. To escape, he and Carol bought a car and drove to Chicago to visit Steinbeck's uncle Joe Hamilton. The main purpose of the auto trip, however, was to travel the route that the migrants took when they left the Oklahoma dust bowl and migrated to California.

When the Steinbecks arrived back in California, they bought a fifty-acre ranch that Carol wanted. She was uncomfortable with her husband's fame and wanted to settle into quiet living. Carol wanted to decorate the house, and Steinbeck wanted to work on his book about migrants. Their interests clashed, and tensions arose between them. During the summer of 1938, Steinbeck got control of his book about Oklahoma migrant workers. Carol came up with the title, *The Grapes of Wrath*, from a line in the lyrics of "The Battle Hymn of the Republic." He finished the manuscript in October 1938, and dedicated it to Carol and Tom Collins, the manager of the well-run government camp. By this time Covici was bankrupt and had gone to work for Viking Press, taking all of the Steinbeck works with him. Viking published *The Grapes of Wrath* just as Steinbeck wanted it even though the editors recommended changes in the ending. They also published it with the complete lyrics of the song from which the title came.

The Grapes of Wrath came out in March 1939 and moved quickly to the top of the best-seller list where it remained until months into the next year. This book established Steinbeck as one of the country's most serious novelists, and it won attention both as a literary work and as a political document. Most of the reviews praised the book, some in glowing terms, but a few criticized certain chapters and many were confused about its ending. Some readers criticized Steinbeck's language and realism as shocking. Steinbeck was particularly pleased when First Lady Eleanor Roosevelt toured the migrant camps and told the press that she had read Steinbeck's book and found it to be an accurate portrayal of these camps.

FAME, FILMS, AND FAILED MARRIAGES

John and Carol made many trips to Hollywood as his books were made into films. Steinbeck became friends with Henry Fonda, who played Tom Joad in *The Grapes of Wrath*, and with Spencer Tracy, who starred in *The Red Pony*. Later *Of Mice and Men* came out in a film version. Steinbeck grew to like Hollywood and the people and activity connected with filming, but Carol did not. On one of the trips, tensions mounted between them, and Carol returned to the ranch. On that trip, John met a woman named Gwendolyn Conger, an attractive woman who wanted to be a singer and an actress. He was attracted to her, but kept his feelings secret.

The decade of the 1940s brought travel, strife, and upheaval to Steinbeck's personal life. The decade began with a research trip with Ricketts in 1940 to the Gulf of California, called the Sea of Cortez in Mexico. Because Carol insisted, she went with them, hoping the trip would save a faltering marriage. On the voyage, Ricketts and Steinbeck discussed science, philosophy, and literature, and Steinbeck took notes. At a stop at La Paz, Steinbeck heard the story about a boy and a giant pearl, the story that formed the basis for a later book, *The Pearl*. When they returned, Steinbeck discovered that he had been awarded the Pulitzer Prize for *The Grapes of Wrath*. Steinbeck began immediately to write *Sea of Cortez: A Leisurely Journal of Travel and Research*, which he published with Ricketts as the coauthor. The trip did not restore the Steinbecks' marriage, and Steinbeck began seeing Gwen Conger.

Steinbeck made many trips throughout the decade of the 1940s to do research and to work on films. He went to Mexico City for the filming of *The Forgotten Village*. He went to Hollywood for the filming of *Tortilla Flat*. In April 1945, he was back in Mexico City and Cuernavaca for the filming of *The Pearl*. Twice he worked on propaganda films for the American government. He wrote the script for *Bombs Away: The Story of a Bomber Team* and *Lifeboat*, a film he made with Alfred Hitchcock. In New York there was a musical play version of *Burning Bright*, which failed. Later there was a film entitled *Viva Zapata!*, starring Marlon Brando, the story of Emiliano Zapata, a Mexican who led a revolt for agrarian reform.

Amid writing, traveling to work on films, and moving between New York and California, Steinbeck's personal life was in upheaval. When he and Carol separated, she moved to New York, and Gwen Conger lived with Steinbeck until the two of them traveled to New York, where there was a public scene with Carol. The divorce from Carol was final in March 1943, and John and Gwen were married. Gwen, who was more vehement about settling down than Carol, was discontented when Steinbeck made several trips, sometimes alone. To please her, Steinbeck tried moving back to California in 1944 and then back to New York. They had two sons: Thom, born in 1944, and John, born in 1946.

At the beginning of 1948, Steinbeck went to Salinas and Monterey alone to do research for a book on the valley. After he returned to New York in April, he had surgery for an accident injury. A few days later his friend Ricketts was killed in a car accident. Ricketts's death was devastating to Steinbeck because he had lost a friend and teacher. Gwen accused him of overdependence on Ricketts. She told him, "Without him you are nothing. You will now be the failure you were before you met him, and I don't want to be married to a failure!" Steinbeck took a short trip to Mexico, then returned to Pacific Grove; Gwen took the boys and went to be with her family in Los Angeles. Their divorce followed shortly.

THE BOOKS OF THE 1940s

War occupied Steinbeck's attention off and on throughout the 1940s. He wrote *The Moon Is Down*, a story about Nazi invaders that could have taken place in any location. He finished the manuscript in November 1941, just before the Japanese invasion of Pearl Harbor in December 1941. The book came out in February 1942 and outsold *The Grapes of Wrath* in the first few weeks. It was made into a play, which opened in April. The war inspired Steinbeck to write scripts for propaganda films and to work as a war correspondent. In June 1943, he went to London as a reporter for the New York

Herald Tribune, and in August he went to North Africa to cover the invasion of Italy. After the war, Steinbeck traveled with war photographer Robert Capa to Russia to do articles for the *Herald Tribune* about the changes the war had brought to common people. Steinbeck developed these articles into a book entitled *A Russian Journal*.

In addition to all of his trips and moves from one coast to the other, Steinbeck wrote several books during the decade. After *The Moon Is Down*, he worked next on *Cannery Row* in 1944 after he and Gwen had temporarily moved back to California. They bought a house in Monterey, and Steinbeck wrote about the dockworkers he had met with Ricketts. The story revolves around planning and giving a party for Doc, the main character Steinbeck modeled after Ricketts. *Cannery Row* was published in 1945. In 1947, Steinbeck published *The Pearl*, the short novel he developed from the story he had heard on the trip to the Sea of Cortez, about a boy who finds a large pearl, but throws it back into the sea because it causes him trouble. Also in 1947, he published *The Wayward Bus*, a symbolic story about people traveling. Although *The Wayward Bus* sold well, it got poor reviews from the critics. *A Russian Journal* came out in 1948, and *Burning Bright* in 1950.

During the 1950s Steinbeck enjoyed a more settled personal life, but his writing career declined with each book he published. In 1949 Steinbeck had met Elaine Scott, wife of the film star Zachary Scott. When her divorce was final in 1950, she and Steinbeck married. He continued to have his sons living with him during the summer, and after his marriage to Elaine, her daughter Waverly lived with them. The family spent several summers in Nantucket, an island near Cape Cod, until John and Elaine bought a house in Sag Harbor on Long Island, New York. Since Steinbeck wrote most of the time during the summers, Elaine had to manage the three children, a difficult arrangement for her. Steinbeck and Elaine made two long trips to Europe, one in 1952 and another to Paris in 1954. With Elaine, Steinbeck felt he had finally found the woman who was right for him, and she was as happy as he.

A CAREER IN DECLINE

In February 1951, shortly after his marriage to Elaine, Steinbeck began work on the big novel he had wanted to write about the Salinas Valley. It was the saga of a family, beginning with his grandfather Samuel Hamilton. By April he realized that the story of one family was insufficient to carry his theme, and he created a second family, hoping to fuse the two. *East of Eden*, as he called it, became a novel of 250,000 words, covering a period from the Civil War to the end of World War I. The editors at Viking recommended many cuts and changes, but Steinbeck refused to change any of it, and Viking published it in the fall of 1952. The book sold well, but the critics were harsh, declaring that Steinbeck's creative talent was nearing its end. Then he revised *Cannery Row* and gave it a new title, *Sweet Thursday*, which was published in 1954. The reviews were worse, one suggesting that Steinbeck had lost his ability to write. But he did not give up. In the spring of 1956, he experimented with a new form of novel, a fable set in France about a man named Pippin. It was published in 1957 as *The Short Reign of Pippin IV, A Fabrication*; Steinbeck was now described by critics as self-deluded.

At the beginning of the 1960s, Steinbeck told Elaine that he thought he should bow out, but he did not. He wrote *Winter of Our Discontent* hastily and sent it to Covici, who published it in June 1961. He had barely finished *Winter of Our Discontent* because he had been planning to travel around America in a camper with Elaine's French poodle Charley. He kept a log of his trip, which he wrote into a book called *Travels with Charley in Search of America*. It was published in 1962 and received decent reviews as a travelogue. His greatest honor came in October 1962, when the announcement came from Sweden that Steinbeck had been awarded the Nobel Prize for literature. Only five other Americans had received this prize: Sinclair Lewis, Eugene O'Neill, Pearl Buck, William Faulkner, and Ernest Hemingway.

During the remainder of the 1960s, Steinbeck spent his energy on politics. He was invited to John F. Kennedy's presidential inauguration in January 1961. After Kennedy's assassination, Steinbeck became friends with Lyndon Johnson and spent many evenings in the White House. He went to Vietnam in 1967 to report on the war for *Newsday*, a Long Island newspaper. After his return, he wrote to Elizabeth Otis, saying, "I have nothing I can or want to communicate—a dry-as-dust, worked out feeling." In the year that followed, he had back surgery, a stroke, and a series of heart attacks. He died of a massive heart attack on December 20, 1968, and was buried in Salinas, California. He was sixty-six years old.

ABOUT THIS BOOK

The brief biography of John Steinbeck is designed to provide students with the basic facts about Steinbeck's life: when and where he lived, a record of his writing and publishing, and a few factors that influenced him and his writing career. More attention has been given to the years from his birth through 1939, when he published *The Grapes of Wrath*, and to *The Pearl*, which he published in 1947. These years cover his early development as a writer and the publication of tales and novels considered his best work and the ones students study first.

The essays and reviews selected for the Greenhaven Literary Companion to John Steinbeck provide teachers and students with a wide range of information and opinion about Steinbeck and his works. Some of the essays and reviews offer insight into the way Steinbeck's personal life contributed to his works. Some analyze the philosophical outlook Steinbeck presents through his fiction. A few essayists and reviewers rate the quality of Steinbeck's art and rank him as a literary artist. Several essays analyze the characters, themes, and literary techniques of particular works. Students doing research papers and oral presentations will find in this collection abundant material from which they may generate topics.

The essays for this collection were chosen and organized with the beginning Steinbeck reader in mind. Collectively they show that Steinbeck's works can be studied from a variety of approaches—biographical, historical, didactic, artistic, and philosophical. The first six essays in this collection focus on general ideas that apply to a number of works. The fifteen essays that follow focus on works frequently studied by beginning students and which received critical acclaim: the short story "Flight," *The Red Pony*, *The Pearl*, *Of Mice and Men*, and *The Grapes of Wrath*. A few works, such as *The Short Reign of Pippin IV*, *The Winter of Our Discontent*, *East of Eden*, and *Travels with Charley in Search of America*, are mentioned only briefly, if at all, because they have received less critical acclaim and because they are seldom part of the canon studied by beginning Steinbeck students. The final essay tells about the Nobel Prize in literature, which Steinbeck received in 1962.

Most of the authors of the essays and reviews in this collection are mid-twentieth-century writers. Beginning in the early 1950s, many commentators focused on Steinbeck and published their criticism. But by the time Steinbeck won the Nobel

Prize, many experts had begun to think Steinbeck had been overrated in the early years, and the number of articles about him began to decline. Of the critics, Peter Lisca and Warren French seem to have studied Steinbeck most thoroughly and have remained committed to finding quality in his works.

This companion to Steinbeck has several special features. Most of the essays explain a single, focused topic, either a single idea or a single approach to a particular work. The introduction to each essay sums up the main points so that the reader knows what to expect. Interspersed within the essays, the reader will find inserts that add authenticity, supplementary information, or interesting anecdotes. Inserts come from sources such as Steinbeck's journals and works, magazine articles from the 1930s, and literary history.

How Six Short Novels Came to Be

John Steinbeck

For the preface to a collection of his short novels—*The Red Pony, Tortilla Flat, Of Mice and Men, The Moon Is Down, Cannery Row,* and *The Pearl*—John Steinbeck explains the circumstances out of which each novel arose. Besides telling his personal reasons for writing each of them, he relates with each one a special incident involving his dog, the critics, the publishers, or the residents of Monterey, California.

I have never written a preface to one of my books before, believing that the work should stand on its own feet, even if the ankles were slightly wobbly. When I was asked to comment on the six short novels of this volume, my first impulse was to refuse. And then, thinking over the things that have happened to these stories since they were written, I was taken with the idea that what happens to a book is very like what happens to a man.

These stories cover a long period of my life. As each was finished, that part of me was finished. It is true that while a work is in progress, the writer and his book are one. When a book is finished, it is a kind of death, a matter of pain and sorrow to the writer. Then he starts a new book, and a new life, and if he is growing and changing, a whole new life starts. The writer, like a fickle lover, forgets his old love. It is no longer his own: the intimacy and the surprise are gone. So much I knew, but I had not thought of the little stories thrust out into an unfriendly world to make their way. They have experiences, too—they grow and change or wane and die, just as everyone does. They make friends or enemies, and sometimes they waste away from neglect.

The Red Pony was written a long time ago, when there was desolation in my family. The first death had occurred. And the family, which every child believes to be immortal, was shattered. Perhaps this is the first adulthood of any man or woman. The first tortured question "Why?" and then acceptance, and then the child becomes a man. *The Red Pony* was an attempt, an experiment if you wish, to set down this loss and acceptance and growth. At that time I had had three books published and none of them had come anywhere near selling their first editions. *The Red Pony* could not find a publisher. It came back over and over again, until at last a brave editor bought it for the *North American Review* and paid ninety dollars for it, more money than I thought the world contained. What a great party we had in celebration!

It takes only the tiniest pinch of encouragement to keep a writer going, and if he gets none, he sometimes learns to feed even on the acid of failure.

Tortilla Flat grew out of my study of the Arthurian cycle. I wanted to take the stories of my town of Monterey and cast them into a kind of folklore. The result was *Tortilla Flat*. It followed the usual pattern. Publisher after publisher rejected it, until finally Pascal Covici published it. But it did have one distinction the others had not: it was not ignored. Indeed, the Chamber of Commerce of Monterey, fearing for its tourist business, issued a statement that the book was a lie and that certainly no such disreputable people lived in that neighborhood. But perhaps the Chamber of Commerce did me a good service, for the book sold two editions, and this was almost more encouragement than I could stand. I was afraid that I might get used to such profligacy on the part of the public, and I knew it couldn't last. A moving-picture company bought *Tortilla Flat* and paid four thousand dollars for it. Thirty-six hundred came to me. It was a fortune. And when, a few years later, the same company fired its editor, one of the reasons was that he had bought *Tortilla Flat*. So he bought it from the company for the original four thousand dollars and several years later sold it to M-G-M for ninety thousand dollars. A kind of justification for me, and a triumph for the editor.

Of Mice and Men was an attempt to write a novel in three acts to be played from the lines. I had nearly finished it when my setter pup ate it one night, literally made confetti of it! I don't know how close the first and second versions would prove to be. This book had some success, but as usual it found its enemies. With rewriting, however, it did become a play and had some success.

There were long books between these little novels. I think

the little ones were exercises for the long ones. The war came on, and I wrote *The Moon Is Down* as a kind of celebration of the durability of democracy. I couldn't conceive that the book would be denounced. I had written of Germans as men, not supermen, and this was considered a very weak attitude to take. I couldn't make much sense out of this, and it seems absurd now that we know the Germans were men, and thus fallible, even defeatable. It was said that I didn't know anything about war, and this was perfectly true, though how Park Avenue commandos found me out I can't conceive.

Subsequently I saw a piece of war as a correspondent, and following that wrote *Cannery Row*. This was a kind of nostalgic thing, written for a group of soldiers who had said to me, "Write something funny that isn't about the war. Write something for us to read—we're sick of war." When *Cannery Row* came out, it got the usual critical treatment. I was wasting my time in flippancy when I should be writing about the war. But half a million copies were distributed to troops, and they didn't complain. We had some very warlike critics then, much more bellicose than the soldiers.

In Mexico I heard a story and made a long jump back to the *Tortilla Flat* time. I tried to write it as folklore, to give it that set-aside, raised-up feeling that all folk stories have. I called it *The Pearl*. It didn't do so well at first either, but it seems to be gathering some friends, or at least acquaintances. And that's the list in this volume. It is strange to me that I have lived so many lives. Thinking back, it seems an endless time and yet only a moment.

John Steinbeck's Authentic Characters

Joseph Warren Beach

Joseph Warren Beach claims that John Steinbeck has unusual talent and imagination capable of creating characters with souls. Though his characters live in economically poor conditions, and some of them function with marginal ethical standards, they are individuals with rich and diverse inner natures and people who commit themselves in humorous and compassionate relationships. Beach provides extensive evidence for his claim from such stories as "The Chrysanthemums," "The Red Pony," *Tortilla Flat*, and *Of Mice and Men.*

The first thing we should take note of in Steinbeck is the sheer literary genius with which he is endowed. . . . This was an unusually versatile talent, capable of being turned to themes of various sorts, and suiting itself to the theme like hand in glove. . . .

There is the opening story of the volume entitled *The Long Valley* (1938). It is called "Chrysanthemums." It gives us the picture of a wholesome and attractive woman of thirty-five, wife of a rancher in that enchanting Salinas Valley where Steinbeck lived as a boy. This woman has what are called planter's hands, so that whatever she touches grows and flourishes. She is shown on a soft winter morning working in her garden, cutting down the old year's chrysanthemum stalks, while her husband stands by the tractor shed talking with two men in business suits. Nothing is said about the relationship of this married pair, but everything shows that it is one of confidence and mutual respect. He refers with simple pleasure to the size of her chrysanthemums. She applauds his success in selling his three-year-old steers at nearly his own price. And she welcomes his suggestion that, since it is

Excerpted from "John Steinbeck: Journeyman Artist," in *American Fiction, 1920–1940* by Joseph Warren Beach, as revised by the author for inclusion in *Steinbeck and His Critics*, edited by E.W. Tedlock Jr. and C.V. Wicker (Albuquerque: Univ. of New Mexico Press, 1957); © Joseph Warren Beach. Reprinted by permission of Christopher Beach, executor of the author's estate.

Saturday afternoon, they go into town for dinner and then to a picture show. But she wouldn't care to go to the fights. The feminine note is sounded in the unaffected shrinking of the refined woman from the brutality of a sport which men enjoy. "Oh, no," she said breathlessly, "I wouldn't like fights." And he hastens to assure her he was just fooling; they'll go to a movie. It is not the author who tells us that he is making a sacrifice, and that he is glad to do so, for he likes his wife better thus than if she wanted to go to the fights. The beauty of this kind of storytelling is that the author does not waste words and insult his reader with that sort of explanation. He gets his effects with an elegant economy of words, and leaves some scope for the reader's imagination.

And now is introduced a third character, picturesque and individual, and a new balance of forces in human relations. The new character is an itinerant tinker who comes driving up in his queer covered wagon from the country road that runs along the bank of the river. He is a big stubble-bearded man, in a greasy black suit, graying but not old-looking, with dark eyes "full of the brooding that gets in the eyes of teamsters arid of sailors." He is a shrewd, dynamic personality. And there ensues between him and Eliza Allen a combat of wits in which she shows herself a person of right feeling, one who doesn't let her charitable instincts run away with her, but who has at the same time a soft side where you can get round her. That is her love of flowers, and the pride she takes in her way with chrysanthemums. The author says nothing of this tug-of-war, nor of the shrewdness of the tinker, nor of the quality in Eliza Allen that makes her a victim. All these things he *shows* us in the brief dialogue—again with a richness of reference which makes us feel the whole quality of these two by no means commonplace lives. Among other things he makes us feel how, beneath her brisk and contented exterior, this woman harbors an unsatisfied longing for some way of life less settled than that of the rancher's wife, something typified by the shabby tinker camping nightly in his wagon underneath the stars.

Eliza Allen has nothing that needs mending, but the tinker does not want to leave without something to feed his hungry frame. He has the inspiration to take an interest in her chrysanthemums; he begs her for some of the shoots to take to a lady down the road who has asked him to bring her some. The upshot of it is that she finds some old pans for him to mend and he goes away with fifty cents in his pocket and a pot of chrysanthemum shoots. She watches him go down the road by the river, and is filled, as the author manages to make us know, with a kind of troubled joy at the thought of him on his vagabond trail.

And now she turns to the bustle of washing up and dressing for the trip to town. I wish I knew how the author manages here to convey the sense he does of the energy and well-being of this rancher's wife moved by thoughts unnamed and perhaps not brought above the level of consciousness. Her husband observes how "strong" she seems, but has no notion of the special occasion for it.

But Eliza Allen has a grief in store, and we have still the pleasure of seeing how mad and hurt she can be when she realizes that she has been outwitted by the man who means so much to her in the obscure places of her imagination. As she drives along to town with her husband she discovers a dark spot on the pavement where the tinker had thrown her chrysanthemums the moment he was out of sight of the ranch. The pot he kept. The thing remains a secret with her. She says nothing of it to her husband. We know it only by the tone she takes in asking him again about the fights. She asks him if the fighters do not hurt each other very much. "I've read how they break noses, and blood runs down their chests. I've read how the fighting gloves get heavy and soggy with blood." He is surprised and rather shocked that she should ever have thought of things like that; but he is willing to take her to the fights if she really wants it. "She relaxed limply in the seat. 'Oh, no. No. I don't want to go. I'm sure I don't.' Her face was turned away from him. 'It will be enough if we can have wine. It will be plenty.' She turned up her coat collar so that he could not see that she was crying weakly—like an old woman."

This is no tragic grief. But it does assure us that Eliza Allen is very much of a woman, and of the same flesh and blood with ourselves—that she shares with us our sensitive pride, our reluctance to let someone get the best of us, and more than that, our secret romantic longing for something more than "human nature's daily food." She is one of the most delicious characters ever transferred from life to the pages of a book. There is no doubt that she has a "soul." And she is much less simple than she seems.

"THE RED PONY"

The most famous story in *The Long Valley* is "The Red Pony." This is dedicated to a boy's passion for animal pets, and is quite in a class with [American writer Marjorie Kinnan] Rawlings' *Yearling*. It represents a more privileged level of human living than that, and aspects of nature more benign and lovely. It has its own splendor and pathos. I mention it here as another case of human types and relationships as fine and subtle as any in [Russian writer Anton] Chekhov. There is the opening enchantment of a boy's world in touch with the primitive joys of wild life. And there is the boy's shyness and secretiveness—the sternness of responsibilities laid on him as a member of a serious farming community—the ticklish balance of his relation to a stern but just and loving father—and the suffering inflicted on him by the indifferent cruelties of nature. The finest thing of all is the relation between the boy Jody and Billy the hired man, whose pride of skill as well as his affection for the boy is involved in his effort to save the lives, first of the red pony, and then of the mare who is chosen to be the mother of Jody's colt. . . .

But it is time we were coming to what will be our special subject, which is Steinbeck's dealing with children of the earth. By this I mean human beings more lowly than prosperous ranchers—I mean those helpless children of earth who can never raise themselves more than a few feet from its surface, and for whom the question of the next meal remains a major obsession.

But here again I must distinguish types and dwell once more on the versatility of this author, who has a different manner for each class of subject matter which he treats. Before the publication of *The Grapes of Wrath* (1939) Steinbeck had already produced two books which were widely read and hailed by critics as masterpieces. The first of these was *Tortilla Flat* (1935) and the second was *Of Mice and Men* (1937). . . .

Tortilla Flat

Steinbeck's subject in *Tortilla Flat* is the paisano of Monterey. The paisano is, as he tells us, "a mixture of Spanish, Indian, Mexican, and assorted Caucasian bloods. His ancestors have lived in California for a hundred or two years. He speaks English with a paisano accent and Spanish with a paisano accent. When questioned concerning his race, he indignantly claims pure Spanish blood and rolls up his sleeve to show that the soft inside of his arm is nearly white." The paisano lives in a special district in Monterey where town and pine forest intermingle. He has little property and is little subject to the civic and financial worries of other citizens. Steinbeck's particular subject is one Danny and his friends Pilon and Pablo and Portagee Jo, Jesus Maria Corcoran, and a certain ragamuffin called the Pirate. For the most part these men have no occupation, but work occasionally on ranches or cutting squids in a canning factory. Most of them were enlisted in the war with Germany. On his return from the army, Danny, who had preferred as a boy to sleep in the woods, finds that his grandfather, a man of exceptional wealth in this community, has died and left him two small unpainted houses in Tortilla Flat. So for the first time in his life he is a man with a roof over his head and burdened with the cares of property. Unable to support this condition alone, he invites his friends to join him. They rent his second house, but never pay him any rent except an occasional purloined chicken or gallon jug of red wine. When the Virgin Mary gently admonishes them for their careless life by burning down their rented house, they move in with Danny, who welcomes them to his small room on condition that no one occupy his bed but himself. When the Pirate is added to the group with his five mangy dogs, a special corner is assigned to the dogs, and they all live happily together.

They lead an eventful life. These are true stories, Steinbeck assures us, though sometimes elaborated by the people of Tortilla Flat in oral narration. "It is well," he says, "that this cycle be put down on paper so that in future time scholars, hearing the legends, may not say as they say of Arthur and of Roland and of Robin Hood—'There was no Danny nor any group of Danny's friends, nor any house. Danny is a nature god and his friends primitive symbols of the wind, the sky, the sun.' This history is designed now and ever to keep the sneers from the lips of sour scholars."

The first reviewers of the book perceived that these people were curious or quaint, dispossessed or underdoggish. Steinbeck's feelings were hurt, so he tells us. He had never thought that they were anything of the sort. They were friends of his, people whom he liked, and if he had thought they were quaint he would never have written of them. This disclaimer it is impossible to take at its face value. He liked these people and they were his friends. Well and good. That we can heartily believe. It is clear throughout his writing that Steinbeck is fond of the underdog; and that for good and sufficient reasons. Because he *is* the underdog, and because of his many virtues. And then, because in him the primary human impulses are less overlaid with disguise, and stand out in stark simplicity. But this last, observe, is an artistic reason, a literary reason.

The likings of an artist are always open to suspicion; and we have to distinguish between his liking for people themselves and his liking for his *subject*. The paisanos are doubtless likable in themselves; but they are still more likable as subject for the literary artist. And they are all the more likable, it may be, for traits of which the artist could not well approve. Danny and his friends were frank and courtly in manner, fond of wine and women, full of charity, piety and good nature, ingenious and enterprising in odd ways of securing food and drink; and these may well be regarded as virtues as well as subjects for artistic representation. But they were also shiftless and lazy; they were inveterate if petty thieves; they were ignorant and superstitious; they were something very like drunkards; and these are hardly traits which their author could regard as moral virtues.

He likes them, he says, because they are people who merge successfully with their habitat. Well, that may be argued. On his showing they do make shift to live with satisfaction according to their notions; perhaps they have adapted themselves instinctively to the conditions imposed on them by race and the social set-up. But I doubt whether any jury of sociologists would rate them high as members of the body politic, or would give a clean bill of health to the social set-up which calls for this sort of adjustment.

The fact is, of course, that Steinbeck is not thinking primarily in sociological terms. The blending of these people with their background is an artistic circumstance, like that of [French painter Jean François] Millet's peasants in the Angelus and the Man with the Hoe. We'll not call it quaint if that hurts his feelings, but he can hardly stop us from calling it picturesque. And the proof that he himself regards these people as at least curious is that he has written an essentially comic history of them. If he doesn't know that this is funny, then he doesn't know what he has done; and that is quite obviously contrary to fact.

It is certainly funny when Danny, in pursuit of amorous designs on Sweets Ramirez, presents her with a vacuum cleaner though it is well known that there is no electrical power in Tortilla Flat to run it. It is funnier still that she should daily pass this vacuum cleaner over the floor "on the theory that of course it would clean better with electricity, but one could not have everything"; that her stock should rise so much in her community because of the possession of a machine that would not work; so that she grew puffed up with pride and dragged her sweeping-machine into the conversation on every occasion. It was funniest of all when, Danny growing tired of this lady, his loving friends took back the vacuum cleaner by stealth and sold it to Torelli the bootlegger for two gallons of wine, and when on their departure Torelli looked into the machine and found it had no motor—it had never had a motor.

ELISA ALLEN'S ANGER AND HURT

John Steinbeck creates a moment of anger and hurt in "The Chrysanthemums" when Elisa Allen sees her flowers dumped out onto the road. Her feelings illustrate the deep and authentic nature of her soul.

The little roadster bounced along on the dirt road by the river, raising the birds and driving the rabbits into the brush. Two cranes flapped heavily over the willow-line and dropped into the river-bed.

Far ahead on the road Elisa saw a dark speck in the dust. She suddenly felt empty. She did not hear Henry's talk. She tried not to look; she did not want to see the little heap of sand and green shoots, but she could not help herself. The chrysanthemums lay in the road close to the wagon tracks. But not the pot; he had kept that. As the car passed them, she remembered the good bitter smell, and a little shudder went through her. She felt ashamed of her strong planter's hands, that were no use, lying palms up in her lap.

The roadster turned a bend and she saw the caravan ahead. She swung full round toward her husband so that she could not see the little covered wagon and the mismatched team as the car passed.

In a moment they had left behind them the man who had not known or needed to know what she said, the bargainer. She did not look back.

John Steinbeck, "The Chrysanthemums." In *American Poetry and Prose*, edited by Norman Foerster. 3rd ed. Boston: Houghton Mifflin, 1947.

The story of the Pirate is funny too in a way—this ragamuffin who lives in a chicken house with his five dogs, and every day in a secret place buries the quarter of a dollar he earns from the sale of firewood. Danny's friends conclude by some process of paisano logic that he must have a buried treasure; and with a view to making it theirs, they treat him with a friendliness that he has never known. They bring him to their house and install him there with his five mangy dogs. They use on him every wile they know to worm out of him his secret. What is their surprise when he finally brings to them his treasure of two hundred dollars and puts it under their special protection! He has dedicated this treasure to the Virgin, promising her a gold candlestick for the favor she had done him in saving the life of a sick dog. These scalawags have their honor and piety, and much as they crave this money for their own uses, they guard it sacredly for the Virgin Mary.

On the day when the candlestick was dedicated, the dogs were admonished not to enter the church. They did break into the church in their enthusiasm and interrupted the sermon on Saint Francis of Assisi and his love for dumb beasts. But Father Ramon was indulgent. He could not help laughing. "Take the dogs outside," he said, "let them wait until we are through." The Pirate took them out and gave them a good scolding. "He left them stricken with grief and repentance and went back into the church. The people, still laughing, turned and looked at him, until he sank into his seat and tried to efface himself. 'Do not be ashamed,' Father Ramon said. 'It is no sin to be loved by your dogs, and no sin to love them. See how Saint Francis loved the beasts.' Then he told more stories of that good saint."

This anecdote ends with the Pirate's taking the dogs out into the woods, ranging them as an audience, and telling them the story of Saint Francis. And then a miracle occurred.

> The dogs sat patiently, their eyes on the Pirate's lips. He told everything the priest had told, all the stories, all the observations. Hardly a word was out of its place.
>
> When he was done, he regarded the dogs solemnly. "Saint Francis did all that," he said.
>
> The trees hushed their whispering. The forest was silent and enchanted.
>
> Suddenly there was a tiny sound behind the Pirate. All the dogs looked up. The Pirate was afraid to turn his head. A long moment passed.
>
> And then the moment was over. The dogs lowered their eyes. The tree-tops stirred to life again and the sunlight patterns moved bewilderingly.
>
> The Pirate was so happy that his heart pained him. "Did you see him?" he cried. "Was it San Francisco? Oh! What good dogs you must be to see a vision."
>
> The dogs leaped up at his tone. Their mouths opened and their tails threshed joyfully.

There is much more than humor here, and the book shows throughout a genuine love for the charm and virtue of these childlike paisanos. I will not quarrel with Mr. Steinbeck over terms to characterize his people. Let them not be quaint or dispossessed. The point I wish to make is that his artistic sensibility has led him to choose for his subject here a manner of living and feeling which is not much in evidence in contemporary America, which reminds us more of rural Mexico today or of Italy of the Middle Ages. He has invested his tale with the tender pathos of distance that attaches to Saint Francis and Robin Hood. . . .

OF MICE AND MEN

Steinbeck's next major literary venture was in a very different vein, as far as possible from the gentle comedy of *Tortilla Flat. Of Mice and Men* is a tragic story of friendship among migratory laborers. And it is told with the directness and severe economy of a tale of [Guy de] Maupassant. The economy is that of drama as well as short story. We are told that Steinbeck's aim was to see how near he could come in narrative to the form of a stage play. And the story was no sooner written than it was turned into a successful drama.

It is the tale of two men whose custom it is to move from ranch to ranch, spending their little stake in town as soon as they have made it and passing on to another place where work may be had. But as with the Okies in *The Grapes of Wrath*, the secret dream of these two men is to save up enough money to buy a little farm and live in peaceful and settled independence. One of them is the mentally defective Lennie, a huge man of colossal strength, but simple as a child and helplessly dependent on the care of his friend George. George had taken him after the death of Lennie's aunt. Lennie is a millstone round his neck, standing between him and everything he would like to do. But George is deeply attached to his backward friend, knowing that without him he would lapse himself into the dreary state of a friendless wanderer. The huge Lennie has a child's passion for small animals, which he loves to hold in his hands and stroke; but the strength of his hands is so great that the frail creatures are likely to be broken and killed without his meaning any harm. He wishes earnestly to keep from doing anything bad, so as not to incur the wrath of George, but with the best of intentions he is forever getting them into trouble. And when it is a woman and not a puppy who becomes the victim of his ill-directed force, there is nothing left for his friend but to put an end to Lennie. That is the only way to save him from lynching.

One who has not read the book can hardly be made to

appreciate the tone of humanity and beauty with which Steinbeck invests this tragic episode. The almost paternal affection of George for his blundering witless pal, and the sore grief he suffers over the necessity of putting him away—all this you are made to feel without the use of sentimental phrase or direct statement. Back of this lies the life of the bunkhouse— the essential decency and pathos of these rough homeless men whom circumstance has condemned to a life of physical and moral squalor. There is no touching on the industrial and social problems involved, as in *The Grapes of Wrath*, though the tale may have its bearing on the treatment of certain types of mental defectives. In this as in the earlier books, Steinbeck was content with the imaginative, the basically human, factors in the drama.

John Steinbeck's Naturalism

Charles Child Walcutt

Charles Child Walcutt analyzes John Steinbeck's form of naturalism and finds that a pattern exists in nearly all of Steinbeck's novels. Steinbeck, Walcutt says, explores two elements of American naturalism: the spirit, or the demands of the heart, and fact, or the demands of the mind. While Steinbeck explores these polarized elements, his sympathy varies from novel to novel. As a naturalistic writer, Steinbeck tries to describe human life precisely, but, unlike many naturalistic writers, he uses conventional forms to explore these elements. Walcutt identifies Steinbeck's use of mock epic, dramatic conflict, cinema script, epic, farce, parable, and fable in presenting his characters' lives as they naturally are.

The two great elements of American naturalism [literature that describes precisely the actual circumstances of human life]—spirit and fact, the demands of the heart and the demands of the mind—are Steinbeck's constant preoccupation; they form the poles of his thought in almost every one of his novels. ... In Steinbeck's work these principles exist in tension, appearing to pull in opposite directions, and the writer deals with them as if he were confused and doubtful and somewhat surprised to see them emerging from a single phase of experience, as they repeatedly do. It is a surprise and a climax when a blundering Okie like Tom Joad perceives that his spirit is one with all Spirit; it is matter for interest that "the boys" in *Cannery Row* live at an opposite extreme from the scientist, with his music and his research, and at the same time find themselves temperamentally closer to him than to anyone else they know; it is likewise remarkable that the communist and the doctor in *In Dubious Battle* have compa-

Excerpted from *American Literary Naturalism: A Divided Stream* by Charles Child Walcutt. Minneapolis: University of Minnesota Press, 1954.

rable aims and are able to talk with each other about the plight of man. These oppositions show that Steinbeck is everywhere seeking, if not to re-unite, at least to reconcile the divided stream of transcendentalism [the notion that ideal spiritual reality exists, a reality that transcends factual matter and science]—but that he sees its parts in dramatic conflict. The forms of his novels depend, however, not alone upon these dramatic oppositions (although these are indeed crucial in the structure of his books) but also upon the conscious imitation of a number of well-established traditional forms. Steinbeck's naturalism is neither mechanistic, nor clinical, nor descriptive; rather it is dramatic and exploratory. The forms of his novels are patterned, as I shall show, on conventional types; his naturalism figures as a set of conflicting ideas in them. It is not a new way, for him, of arranging reality or of dealing with causation or personality.

Thus we see in novel after novel a belief in science, a firm belief in material causation, a belief in the spontaneous goodness of simple men, and a radical distrust of commerce, industry, the business outlook, and conventional piety and morality. The latter he finds either fraudulent or irrelevant to the fundamental problems of men—except insofar as they interfere. These ideas seem to pull Steinbeck in various directions: toward science, toward brotherhood, and less clearly toward transcendentalism and revolution. His ideals draw him to naturalistic primitivism [the belief that simple living in a natural environment is good] and toward mysticism [the belief in a reality beyond that which can be seen or thought]; his despair at the inhumanities of commercialism pulls him toward the opposing extremes of retreat and revolution. His forms do not embody these forces; rather they are conventional genre-forms that permit his characters to express and to move about among these ideas.

TORTILLA FLAT—A MOCK EPIC

In *Tortilla Flat* (1935) we turn to a mock epic. Danny and the other *paisanos* [an ethnic mix of poor natives] of Monterey live a wild life of irresponsible gaiety, as happy as they are poor, until they find treasure. Then come greed and fear and drink and finally a mock-epical disaster in which the hero is destroyed in a general debacle. The rollicking independence of these *paisanos*, their poverty, their touching poetic enthusiasms are calls of a spirit free from the drudging materialism of conventional American life. But, alas, Danny and his friends are not finally proof against the demands of the devil of materialism, for although they will not work for money they will gladly take and use it when it comes to them free; and since their use of it is not disciplined by puritanical thrift and responsibility, or by a typical businessman acquisitiveness, they cannot use it without being destroyed by it. Here again there is double counterpoint: the unspoiled *paisanos* are ignorant and miserable even while they are gay—for the demands of spirit are not fully met within the limitations imposed on them by their ignorance and consequent poverty. And when the money comes they have the source of power without the means to control it, and they run wild. Steinbeck is thus in effect lamenting the division of the American transcendental ideal into a condition where knowledge and spirit (power and love) are nowhere properly joined. Because it is not exactly feasible to defy the whole massed array of American materialism with a handful of barefoot *paisanos*, Steinbeck draws the action in mock-epic tone—but the grim idea is not far under the rowdy surface, and Steinbeck's sympathy is clearly with the simple, goodhearted people who are not equipped to cope with evil.

IN DUBIOUS BATTLE—A DRAMA OF CONFLICT

The form of *In Dubious Battle* (1936) is sharply dramatic, building a conflict between the communist organizer who is dominated by an idea so completely that he has lost his sense of the value of the individual and the simple, pathetic goodness of the fruit pickers whom he "organizes" into strikes, starvation, bloodshed, and defeat. The fruit growers, with their deputies and their guns, are set in dramatic opposition to the pickers, who are loyal and generous. And in a sort of counterpoint there stands opposed to the heartless (or misguided) communist a doctor who tends the sick and injured and comments wisely and tenderly upon the dubious battle as he observes it. The intellectual pattern here is too rich to be simply formulated, but we can identify the issues of love (or sharing) versus greed where the true and false attitudes toward matter appear, and of dispassionate benevolence (the doctor) versus misguided idealism (the organizer) where the true and false expressions of spirit appear. In this book Steinbeck obviously believes in the tender wisdom of the scientist and the warm hearts of the people. The people are good but weak; the doctor is wise but a condition of his wisdom is nonparticipation. The conflict is not satisfactorily resolved because the battle is dubious. That is, it does not appear in 1936 that love and intelligence are winning over greed and bigotry; whereas the violent force of communism that has undertaken to act in the interests of the people becomes as destructive as the rapacity of the fruit growers. The dialectic of the situation does not work into a new synthesis but remains in tension, for the antithesis of communism is not valid for America, and the antitheses of love and wisdom are not yet powerful enough to prevail.

NATURALISM

Naturalism in American literature is a movement that began at the end of the nineteenth century. Though naturalistic writers try to portray life precisely, according to modern scientific and economic theories, none ever achieves a pure form of naturalism. Norman Foerster et al. elaborate on the definition of naturalism in American Poetry and Prose.

Literary naturalism in America had its origins in European theory, in scientific thought, and in the movement of social protest at home. . . . The function of the novelist for [French novelist Emile] Zola was like that of the scientist, to study the phenomena of man's social life and to observe and report impartially on his findings. . . . Zola maintained the pose of the detached recorder and, like his fellow naturalist [French writer Gustave] Flaubert, believed that the author should entirely efface himself from his material and simply report without sentiment or moralizing. Zola and Flaubert became the advance guard of Continental naturalism. They were pessimistic and deterministic, and they chose materials from the sordid, ugly side of life: sex, hunger, poverty, disease. . . .

The American naturalists of the 1890's absorbed these assumptions and adapted them to the conditions of social unrest and the special variety of social Darwinism identified with the cultural climate of that decade. Stephen Crane, Frank Norris, and Theodore Dreiser became the leading spokesmen of the fiction of naturalism, each with a style distinctly his own, but all three sharing the fundamental premises of a literary creed which included: (1) a biological determinism in which man was conceived of as controlled by his primitive, animal instincts; (2) a sociological determinism whereby the weak were destroyed and the strong survived in a world of struggle and chance; (3) a scientific detachment and the impartial role of the newspaperman toward the author's material; and (4) the search for reality, not in the average, but in the violent and the sensational, in war, murder, disaster, poverty and strife, and among the lower orders of mankind.

Norman Foerster et al., eds., *American Poetry and Prose.* 5th ed. Boston: Houghton Mifflin, 1970.

In Dubious Battle evolves in a closely knit action as the strike mounts in stubbornness and the reprisals of the owners mount in violence. The strike fails because the force of the owners is superior to the force of the strikers, but, as I have suggested, the issue is not pointed in favor of the stronger order and discipline which the communist would impose upon the workers. The communist's values receive their *dramatic* evaluation in the scene where the old communist, Mac, uses the body of his young friend and convert to arouse the spirit of the strikers. He appears to have no feeling for the humanity of his dead friend. Such impersonality, one feels, outrages the sense of brotherhood, the transcendental dream of the dignity of man, without which social reform becomes meaningless. This idea (penetrating indeed for a radical in 1936!) finds significant expression in the note of inconclusiveness which closes the book. The dramatic form has enabled Steinbeck to present an issue, to elaborate some of its ideological implications, and to pass in the end a judgment. He demonstrates that the battle is fruitless because neither side is right. The love and brotherhood of the workers must be implemented by something closer to the American grain than communism if it is to come into its own and unify the American Dream of a full life for all.

The doctor in the story regards all forms of human warfare as "diseases" of society that periodically destroy its effectiveness. He thinks that mankind would preserve itself if it could eliminate these terrible plagues of violence. But his speculations do not lead him to moral zeal or commitment to action, so that he lacks the power without which his thought is ineffective. This constant separation of power and wisdom seems to be the great puzzle to Steinbeck. It is a version of the flaw in creation that philosophers call the Problem of Evil. It is to be solved by some sort of rational idealism which grasps the *meaning* of the physical universe. Here is a transcendental-naturalistic outlook which does not control the form of Steinbeck's novel so much as appear in it. The form is a conventional dramatic opposition of groups of people, and the action seems controlled by intention and choice rather than by forces superior to the wills of the individuals involved. All modern writing with any degree of sophistication of course acknowledges the forces that limit individual freedom. In this area Steinbeck is not unusual. Beyond mechanism and determinism structurally, he discusses as it were in dramatic form the problems that arise from the divided stream of transcendentalism.

OF MICE AND MEN—A CINEMA SCRIPT

Of Mice and Men (1937) is a script for a cinema, a scenario of a little well-made drama. The title suggests that the best laid plans of mice and men gang aft agley [often go awry, a reference to Robert Burns's poem "To a Mouse"], and the idea is quite explicitly naturalistic. The leading characters of this story, George and Lennie, are little better than mice in the maze of modern life. Loyal, foolish, weak, yet possessed of physical power to destroy themselves, they are the People. They are spirit and power inchoate, mixed in chaos rather than fused in form. Lennie's feeblemindedness symbolizes the helplessness of the folk in a commercial society; perhaps in a larger frame it symbolizes the bewilderment of man in a mindless cosmos. The bond between him and George is not strong enough to let them succeed in the modern world.

THE GRAPES OF WRATH—AN EPIC

The Grapes of Wrath (1939) presents the same issues in the form of epic. The great movement of the Okies across the dustbowl and into the Promised Land of California suggests the biblical analogy of the Chosen People fleeing into Israel. The story is shaped in heroic dimensions, and like the great epics of the past it is laid out over the face of the nation whose struggle it depicts. America struggling with the Depression, struggling for very life, is epic. The Joads are heroes specified among a whole people at war, hurling themselves against the armies of finance and fear. The conflict is not personal but national—which is the essence of the epic spirit. The crossplay of the major themes of Steinbeck's naturalism appears as before: in the people are love, brotherhood, integrity; in the exploiting classes fear, power, suspicion, violence. And in counterpoint speak the ideal forms of these elements: although the people are inadequately equipped to triumph through love, Casy, the Okie preacher, utters thoroughly transcendental statements of the perfection and universality of spirit, and Tom Joad toward the end of the story speaks the same language; whereas the interchapters constitute the author's running commentary on science and material power misused. These chapters say again and again that the fruits of invention and industry need not be human waste and social desolation. The epic search of the Joads overland, a symbol of quest, may indicate the proportions of the effort that will have to be made before any solution to the problem of abundance and desolation is reached. No solution is reached in the book: the climactic incident of Rose of Sharon, having lost her own baby, suckling a starving stranger, indicates that Steinbeck finds his answer in love rather than in revolution. The need for the interchapters, however, reveals that the author's acceptance of a transcendental idea has not carried over into significant form: the themes of quest and struggle and the exposition of the capitalist dilemma of scarcity and "overproduction" are not structurally unified. . . .

CANNERY ROW—A FARCE

Cannery Row (1945) resembles in tone and spirit *Tortilla Flat*, but whereas I have called the latter a mock epic I should call the former a farce. It is the story of a group of self-determined social outcasts—"the boys," they are called—who loaf by their wits on the outskirts of a California town, inhabiting a deserted house which serves as office and binder of their fellowship. Their irresponsible doings are presented farcically and with gusto. What these doings seem to mean is that formal society is a mechanical stupidity, an outrage to the free spirit, an absurd waste of life which must be defied by the cunning "misfits" and resourceful loafers who make a glory of having neither goal nor purpose in their lives.

This genial irresponsibility is balanced by the wholly admirable figure of a scientist who, although equally independent of formal society, does have a purpose. "Doc," a marine biologist, lives in the same town a life of utter unconventionality and devotion to science. The "boys" discover that he is like them, that he can understand and help them, and that his life embraces values which they can wholly admire if not emulate. Thus emerge, more or less fused, the two great strands of Steinbeck's transcendental naturalism: the belief in the unfettered human spirit, and the belief that exact scientific knowledge will bring us to inmost truths. Both strands appear with noteworthy differences from what they were a generation earlier. The unfettered human spirit of the boys is not socially active, whereas the liberating value of Doc's science consists in its being a way of life rather than a key or an answer to the riddle of the universe. Doc's life has form because it is controlled in devotion to an ideal. The boys are admirable because they are spontaneous and because they take joy in the simple physical pleasures of life.

The story, which I have called a farce, comes to a climax when these boys invade Doc's house and in a night of wild irresponsible drunkenness reduce it to a shambles. What does this mean? I believe it shows that Steinbeck is not as irresponsible himself as he has often been considered. He has been blamed for presenting his boys as if they were exemplary citizens; reviewers of *Cannery Row* wanted to know what would happen to America if the boys were taken as examples. But the way they destroy the possessions of their good friend who trusts them shows that mere defiance of accepted standards and values does not make a way of life. The boys represent only half the answer. Doc's quiet expeditions to the seaside to collect specimens illustrate the devoted rather than the irresponsible escape from society. . . .

THE PEARL—A SERIOUS PARABLE

Tortilla Flat and *Cannery Row* are comic (i.e., mock epic and farce) presentations of the conflict between the demands of matter and the demands of spirit. Whereas *Tortilla Flat* makes a mock epic of the destruction of the corrupted *paisanos*, *Cannery Row* brings in an early flash of Steinbeck's solution, namely, science. His scientist is neither footless like "the boys" nor sordidly materialistic like those whose major goal is money. He is a local outcast with larger affiliations to the worlds of knowledge and spirit. Steinbeck's third use of the same sort of situation in *The Pearl* (1947) is a serious parable. Wealth brings misery to the poor Indian pearl diver. The misery indeed precedes the wealth, for Kino is beleaguered by thieves and murderers who would wrest his enormous pearl from him. The only actual prosperity he knows is the feverish generosity of those who seek to dupe him. After terrible hardship and the loss of his baby, Kino and his wife return to the simple life by the sea, but they have been brayed in the crucible of the world and burned black by its evil. They are bewildered and sad but hardly wiser. Kino does hurl the great pearl back into the sea, as his wife had tried to do earlier, but this is an act of desperate withdrawal from the world that has hurt them. The parable seems to suggest both that Kino is better off as a primitive and that he is defeated because he does not have the knowledge of civilized men which enables them to trick and destroy him. It says that wealth is the root of all evil. But on the other hand it says that knowledge is power and power over the material world is good. And it says there is strength in simplicity. But Kino's strength fails through ignorance: the pure heart is not enough, just as it was not enough for the fruit pickers of *In Dubious Battle*. *The Pearl* has the quiet strength of its hero, Kino, and in this respect is impressive; but the simple symbolism of the parable cannot resolve the great contradictions of its themes. Once again we see that Steinbeck's naturalistic themes have not been finally welded, in significant form, into that marriage of spirit and matter by science that Steinbeck so obviously yearns for.

Steinbeck's use of traditional forms appears in the parables with which he sets forth the theme of more than one of his novels. In *The Grapes of Wrath* there is the parable of the tortoise crossing the highway. Knocked by a car, carried off by Tom Joad, beaten by sun and wind, he is the People; he struggles on indomitably, and he probably in the end reaches his destination. This is the story of *The Grapes of Wrath*. *Cannery Row* contains a charming chapter about a gopher who builds a beautiful home on a perfect site, where there are no cats and no traps and perfect drainage, but where, alas, he waits in vain for a mate to appear, and so finally has to leave his paradise and go seek a mate where there are traps and other dangers. This is the story of Cannery Row: you can't eat your cake and have it; you can't enjoy the luxuries of civilization without paying for them. . . .

ANIMAL FABLES

I assemble these animal fables [stories with animals that have human qualities, acting and speaking to illustrate a moral] because they epitomize Steinbeck's typical mixture of naturalistic idea with conventional form. The form merely illustrates the idea with a sort of analogy. It does not represent the successful embodiment and interaction of the forces from which the idea grows. This statement does not only describe Steinbeck; to a degree it describes the presence of naturalistic ideas in a great deal of contemporary fiction: naturalistic ideas and attitudes are everywhere now, but they rarely control the form as the early naturalists attempted to make them do. In many contemporary novels naturalistic ideas have prevented the use of ethical-dramatic motivation and structure and have left the novelist with nothing in the way of form but a loose chronological stringing-together of experience. This has gone on to the point where the line between the novel and the journalistic autobiography has nearly disappeared. A truly significant form would solve symbolically the problem of the tension—at present unresolved—between the ideal and the material, the demands of spirit and the cold force of matter, the dream of brotherhood and the instrument of science. It would, that is, if this were possible.

If the test of a philosophy is whether it can be imaginatively incarnated in works of art, the formal looseness of so much contemporary fiction would seem to indicate that naturalism cannot achieve the coherence and integrity that go with a completely acceptable criticism of life. Or it may merely indicate that naturalism lost its grip before it took a real hold, that modern man has been baffled by the findings of science and by his inability to assimilate them and has therefore turned away from them toward either the growing religiosity or the defeated questing of existentialism which have dominated the period from 1930 to the present. . . .

Steinbeck has advanced beyond mechanistic naturalism to the point where he has recognized the two halves of the divided stream of American transcendentalism. His conventional forms have provided means for illustrating his ideas (which are for the most part questions) but they have not permitted him to embody the forces with which his ideas deal.

Escape and Commitment in John Steinbeck's Heroes

Peter Lisca

According to Peter Lisca, John Steinbeck's late-career statement that humans need to be individuals and also to fulfill a place in society is inconsistent with the heroes in several of his novels. In his early novels, Steinbeck sympathizes with the heroes who escape from the demands of society. He portrays heroes as committed martyrs in two later novels, *In Dubious Battle* and *The Grapes of Wrath.* Steinbeck takes yet another attitude in *The Pearl* and *The Wayward Bus,* presenting heroes that experience disillusioned escape, but no commitment. Although the heroes in Steinbeck's late novels display greater wisdom, Lisca suggests that the novels of youthful folly are the ones readers prefer.

In one of the little essays Steinbeck did for the *Saturday Review* in 1955, "Some Thoughts on Juvenile Delinquency," he writes as follows concerning the relationship of the individual to the society in which he lives: ". . . I believe that man is a double thing—a group animal and at the same time an individual. And it occurs to me that he cannot successfully be the second until he has fulfilled the first." The nice organic relationship which Steinbeck here postulates near the end of his writing career is seldom to be met in his fiction. Much more frequently we are presented with characters who choose one of two extremes—either to reject society's demands and escape into individualism, or to reject individualism and commit themselves to goals and values which can be realized only in terms of society.

In Steinbeck's very first novel, *Cup of Gold* (1929), in the

Excerpted from "Escape and Commitment: Two Poles of the Steinbeck Hero" by Peter Lisca, in *Steinbeck: The Man and His Work*, edited by Richard Astro and Tetsumaro Hayashi (Corvallis: Oregon State Univ. Press, 1971). Copyright © 1971 by Richard Astro and Tetsumaro Hayashi. Reprinted with permission.

figure of Merlin, is found not only an extreme example of escapism, but one of its most eloquent philosophers. As a young man, a greatly talented bard, he had taken up a hermit's life in a stone tower on a lonely mountain top. There he has grown old with his harp and his books of history and mythology, a legendary figure in his own lifetime. It is suggested that the cause of this self-imposed isolation may have been his losing a bardic contest through political influence. The consequent disillusionment is reflected in his remarks to the young Henry Morgan, who has come to consult him before going off into the world to make his fortune: "'I think I understand,' he said softly. 'You are a little boy. You want the moon to drink from as a golden cup; and so, it is very likely that you will become a great man—if only you remain a little child. All the world's great have been little boys who wanted the moon; running and climbing, they sometimes caught a firefly. But if one grows to a man's mind, that mind must see that it cannot have the moon and would not want it if it could—and so it catches no fireflies.'" Merlin goes a step further, and adds as a compensation for this loss of worldly ambition the attainment of community with mankind ("He has the whole world with him . . . a bridge of contact with his own people. . . ."), whereas the worldly successful and therefore immature man "is doubly alone; he only can realize his true failure, can realize his meanness and fears and evasions.". . .

In Steinbeck's next book, *The Pastures of Heaven*, three years later, we find James Flower's [James Flower is also an escape character in *Cup of Gold*] same impracticality and indiscriminate bookishness in the character of Junius Maltby, who is treated at greater length and with more obvious sympathy. Again he is a man of "cultured family and good education." Also, his way into an escape from a worldly existence is an enforced one, a threat to his health, but is clearly congenial to him. Through his abstraction and impracticality the little farm which comes to him by marriage becomes unproductive; his wife's two children by former marriage die of influenza because they are undernourished while Maltby helplessly reads aloud *Treasure Island* and *Travels with a Donkey*. Finally his wife dies in childbirth, leaving him a son whom he names Robert Louis. Maltby makes an attempt at practicality by hiring an old German to work the farm, but within a week the two men become boon companions and spend their days sitting around together "discussing things which interested and puzzled them—how color comes to flowers—whether there is a symbology in nature—where Atlantis lay—how the Incas buried their dead. In the spring they planted potatoes, always too late, and without a covering of ashes to keep the bugs out. They sowed beans and corn and peas, watched them for a time and then forgot them. The weeds covered everything from sight." The three of them manage to survive, barefoot, ragged, ill-fed, but happy in their discussions of the battle of Trafalgar, the frieze on the Parthenon, the Spartan virtues, Carthaginian warfare, and other erudite topics. Steinbeck's description of their conversation reflects its impracticality in terms of their agricultural theories: "They didn't make conversation; rather they let a seedling of thought sprout by itself, and then watched with wonder while it sent out branching limbs. They were surprised at the strange fruit their conversation bore, for they didn't direct their thinking, nor trellis nor trim it the way so many people do.". . .

GROUP ESCAPE IN *TORTILLA FLAT*

Clearly, then, in his first two books of fiction Steinbeck demonstrates a serious interest and sympathy for what in today's slang might be called the "drop-out." . . . A more direct relationship [between escape and commitment] can be established with the novel that followed in two years—*Tortilla Flat*.

This novel introduces two important changes in Steinbeck's treatment of the "drop-out" (which is a better term than "escapee"). First, whereas the earlier characters of this type had deliberately rejected the clear advantages available to them, in the form of family and education, these Mexican-American *paisanos* [natives of Monterey] find themselves initially in a poor position to compete in modern society. Second, and more important, the "drop-out" is no longer a shy, retiring, solitary, but an active, gregarious member of a whole community of "drop-outs." They have in common with their prototypes in earlier novels, however, a disinclination toward industrious labor and a disrespect for material property, for through the loss of possessions comes sorrow—"It is much better never to have had them." They also share a love of the contemplative life. True, sometimes pure contemplation arrives at the practical result of procuring a jug of wine or a chicken in a highly imaginative manner, but the process is enjoyed as much as the result, and sometimes consoles them for material lack or loss. The morning after Danny's other house burns down, for example:

. . . Danny came out on his porch to sit in the sunshine and to muse warmly of certain happenings. He slipped off his shoes and wriggled his toes on the sunwarmed boards of the porch. He had walked down earlier in the morning and viewed the square black ashes and twisted plumbing which had been his other house. He had indulged in a little conventional anger against careless friends, had mourned for a moment over that transitory quality of earthly property which made spiritual property so much more valuable. He had thought over the ruin of his status as a man with a house to rent; and, all this clutter of necessary and decent emotion having been satisfied and swept away, he had finally slipped into his true emotion, one of relief that at least one of his burdens was removed.

. . . One evening the solitary contemplation of Pilon leads to a moment of mystic revelation and Franciscan prayer. "He raised his face into the sky and his soul arose out of him into the sun's afterglow. . . . Pilon went up to the sea gulls where they bathed on sensitive wings in the evening. . . . 'Our Father is in the evening,' he thought. 'These birds are flying across the forehead of the Father. Dear birds, dear sea gulls, how I love you all. . . . Dear birds, . . . fly to our Lady of Sweet Sorrows with my open heart.' And then he said the loveliest words he knew, '*Ave Maria, gratia plena—*'" [Hail Mary, full of grace].

Perhaps these examples create a suspicion that what is described here is not really the contemplative life but the lazy one. For Steinbeck, the distinction was not clear-cut. In *Sea of Cortez* (1941), he writes: "Only in laziness can one achieve a state of contemplation which is a balancing of values, a weighing of oneself against the world and the world against itself. A busy man cannot find time for such balancing." And laziness has other virtues as well: "We do not think a lazy man can commit murders, nor great thefts, nor lead a mob. . . . And a nation of lazy contemplative men would be incapable of fighting a war unless their very laziness were attacked. Wars are the activities of busy-ness." . . .

COMMITMENT AND SELF-SACRIFICE IN *IN DUBIOUS BATTLE*

All of this changes in 1936 with the publication of *In Dubious Battle*, which remains the best strike novel in the English language. Here Steinbeck demonstrates not only his detailed, quite professional knowledge of communist labor organization tactics in the field, but also presents us with central characters who are totally committed to bringing about substantial changes in American society. Prior to the strike novel, only "The Raid" had suggested this involvement by Steinbeck and had projected such commitment in the characters. In light of the importance which Judeo-Christian symbols and reference have in *The Grapes of Wrath*, it is interesting that this first treatment of proletarian [poorest working class] subject matter should also find such references necessary. There is the master-apostle relationship of the two organizers, the portrait of their anonymous precursor who inspires them by his example, their own sense of sacrifice for mankind, and certain allusions in the dialogue. Root tells the vigilantes, "We're all brothers," and "It's all for you. We're doing it for you. All of it. You don't know what you're doing." Later, in the hospital, Dick, the more experienced organizer, repeats his instruction to the neophyte [a beginner or novice]: "It wasn't them. It was the System. You don't want to hate them. They don't know no better" (which is the Christian concept of hating the sin and not the sinner). And the neophyte recalls that in the Bible ". . . it says something like 'Forgive them because they don't know what they're doing.'" The importance of these references is that they underscore the sacrificial nature of the action. The organizers had warning of the vigilantes' approach and could have escaped, but chose to stay. They were determined that what had been written by their precursor should be brought to pass—"The men of little spirit must have an example of steadfastness. The people at large must have an example of injustice."

This commitment and self-sacrifice is even more extreme in Jim Nolan of *In Dubious Battle*, and in them he finds his personal fulfillment. "I used to be lonely," he says, "and I'm not any more. If I go out now it won't matter. The thing won't stop. I'm just a little part of it. It will grow and grow." This commitment is accompanied by an even wider Christian reference. Whereas the neophyte in the short story had been merely *willing* to be used as "an example of injustice," Jim Nolan of the strike novel is so anxious as to have a martyr complex. Over and over he tells Mac, his mentor, "I want to get into it" and "I want you to use me." Only after he has gotten into it and has been wounded is he happy and sure of how strongly he is committed: "'Then I got hurt. . . . I got to know my power. I'm stronger than you, Mac. I'm stronger than anything in the world, because I'm going in a straight line. You and all the rest have to think of women and tobacco and liquor and keeping warm and fed.' His eyes were as cold as wet river stones." Not many Christian martyrs were so pure in spirit and had so few temptations. Perceiving this quality in another of Jim's statements, Doc Burton remarks, "Pure religious ecstasy. Partakers of the blood of the lamb." When he is killed, Jim does not have a chance to say "You don't know what you're doing"; he and Mac are ambushed and his head is blown off by a shotgun at close range, so that Mac finds him in a still kneeling posture and exclaims simply, "Oh, Christ!" Beginning with the book's title, epigraph, and numerous details taken from [British poet John Milton's] *Paradise Lost*, to the crowing of cocks and several allusions to the Holy Family (two of them pointed out by the characters themselves), clearly the committed hero is presented as an imitation of Christ.

Steinbeck's next published novel, *Of Mice and Men* (1937) offers a serious temptation and several pitfalls to anyone dealing with these two themes of escape and commitment. It could be used to illustrate the escape theme by pointing out the persistent dream of George and Lennie to get a place of their own; and even the mercy killing of Lennie by George could be seen as providing Lennie with permanent escape from a world with which he cannot cope. . . . But the escape theme in *Of Mice and Men* is essentially different from the "drop-out" kind of rebellion against society which concerns us here, and is clearly an illusion besides. . . .

SOCIAL COMMITMENT IN *THE GRAPES OF WRATH*

But in 1939, with *The Grapes of Wrath*, Steinbeck clearly returns to his theme of social commitment, utilizing, even more extensively than before, pertinent Judeo-Christian analogues and references. It is more than personal friendship that causes Jim Casy to give himself up to the deputies in place of Tom Joad and Floyd. It is an action consequent upon his turning from an individualistic, sin and hell-fire, Bible-belt evangelism to a revelation of the Holy Spirit, which he comes to identify with "all men and all women," the "human sperit— the whole shebang. Maybe all men got one big soul ever'body's a part of." And it occurs to him then that his commitment is not to Jesus but to the people; "An' sometimes I love 'em fit to bust. . . ." This love finally expresses itself in his activities as a labor organizer, devoted to a vision of the Holy Spirit's kingdom on earth, so that he dies saying, twice, "You don' know what you're doin'."

The movement from escape to commitment is even clearer in Tom Joad. He enters the novel determined to avoid all involvement: "I'm laying my dogs down one at a time" and "I climb fences when I got fences to climb." But through the experiences of the migration and through Casy's words and deeds he becomes converted and committed to a vision of social justice beyond hope of his personal experience. Even more than Jim of *In Dubious Battle*, he knows that although he may be killed, "I'll be ever'where—wherever you look. Wherever there's a fight so hungry people can eat, I'll be there. Wherever they's a cop beatin' up a guy, I'll be there. If Casy knowed, why, I'll be in the way guys yell when they're mad an'—I'll be in the way kids laugh when they're hungry an' they know supper's ready. An when our folks eat the stuff they raise an' live in the houses they build—why I'll be there." Beyond this mystic identification, no commitment can go. It is a commitment which gains strength and approval not only by means of its sacrificial Christ figures, but by a wealth of Judeo-Christian references extending from Exodus, Deuteronomy, Canticles and Prophets through John the Baptist, Gospels, and Revelation. *The Grapes of Wrath* is the high point in Steinbeck's theme of commitment. . . .

NEITHER ESCAPE NOR COMMITMENT IN *THE PEARL* AND *THE WAYWARD BUS*

Whatever the reasons, this mood [of sympathy for the "dropouts"] was strong enough to carry over into a variation on the theme in *The Pearl*, originally published in the same year. Strictly speaking, perhaps, this novelette, like *Of Mice and Men* and *The Moon Is Down*, enters only peripherally in this discussion. The pearl diver Kino does seek to physically escape an economically and socially repressive society, but only so that he may return to that same society at a higher level. He can be seen, in his struggle to escape, as what the author of *Cannery Row* called a "tiger with ulcers." And he arrives within reach of his goal with much worse than "a blown prostate and bifocals." He arrives with his house burned down, his wife physically beaten, his only son killed, and the lives of three men on his soul. And then Kino and his wife make their true "escape." They return to their village, throw the Pearl of Great Price back into the sea, and return to the edge of unconsciousness, an unthinking existence governed by the rhythms of sun and tide.

In its interesting variation on the theme of escape, *The Pearl* looks forward to Steinbeck's next novel, published two years later (1947). With this novel Steinbeck finally comes to a resolution of his two themes. Society as pictured in Steinbeck's previous novels is essentially an institutional entity from whose evils a character might decide to escape, or to whose improvement he might dedicate himself. In either case, the monolithic magnitude of the antagonist, society, lent dignity and possible tragedy to his course of action. In *The Wayward Bus,* however, we get very little notion of society as institution; we see it instead as an aggregation of human characters, from the hypocritical businessman, Elliot Pritchard, to Camille Oaks, the honest stripper. Juan Chicoy's decision to escape, therefore, is made in terms of disentanglement from certain people—his neurotic wife and his querulous bus passengers. This, of course, leaves him with no simple distinct notion of direction such as motivated the "drop-outs" and committed characters of Steinbeck's previous fiction. Thus, immediately after abandoning his allegorical bus and its passengers, Juan Chicoy (whose initials are J.C.) becomes merely confused by his escape. "It didn't seem as good or as pleasant or as free" as he had imagined it would. "His nerves itched and he felt mean. . . . Back in the bus he had felt, in anticipation, a bursting orgasmic delight of freedom. But it was not so. He felt miserable. . . . He wondered; 'Won't I ever be happy? Isn't there anything to do?'" So he returns to the bus, as Kino in *The Pearl* returns to his village; but not with a sense of escape or commitment, rather with a sense of involvement without either acceptance or resignation.

Although Steinbeck published five novels after *The Wayward Bus,* the two themes which concern us here play little part in them. . . .

What we have, then, in Steinbeck's last novels is neither the individual or communal escapes of his early work and the immediate post-war novels, nor the inspired, Christ-like, sacrificial commitment of his proletarian fiction. Instead, we have a further development of the adjustment made by Juan Chicoy in *The Wayward Bus.* Society continues to be corrupt, although the blame is not so easy to fix; but there is no need for escape or commitment to reform. Steinbeck finally seems to completely accept the observation he had made on marine ecology, in *Sea of Cortez:* "There would seem to be only one commandment for living things: Survive!" This is qualified in *East of Eden* only by a faith in every man's ability to choose between good and evil. This is an old man's wisdom. We continue to read Steinbeck for the folly of his youth.

John Steinbeck: A Successful Failure

R. W. B. Lewis

R. W. B. Lewis analyzes the past popularity of John Steinbeck and the decline of his reputation by the late 1950s. Steinbeck does the reading public a valuable service by making the realities and themes of his time visible, according to Lewis, but he fails to probe deeply enough into those elements with the techniques available to the artist. Instead, Steinbeck remains political, focused on the group; he stops short of portraying the tragic fate of the individual and the flaws of the human heart. According to Lewis, only in *The Red Pony* and *Of Mice and Men* does Steinbeck get close to exposing the nature of what brings misery and misfortune to human lives.

Steinbeck's literary reputation is not very high at the moment [in the late 1950s] and I see few reasons why it should grow greater in the future. It has declined a good deal since its peak during the war years. Following the publication of his most determined novel, *The Grapes of Wrath*, in 1939, it declined in America, where Steinbeck had for some years exerted a strong but as it were non-literary, and hence non-durable, appeal....

There is a sense of promise unfulfilled in Steinbeck's writing between 1943 and 1958. His career is something of a casualty, and a casualty I think in this particular case of an unlucky wedding between art and rebellion which developed into a fatal marital hostility between the poetic and the political impulse. His career to date has the shape of a suggestive, a representative, and a completely honourable failure.

If, as [American writer William] Faulkner has rather perversely contended, a writer is to be measured these days by the extent and quality of his failure, Steinbeck must inevitably be reckoned among our most sizeable novelists. Steinbeck's

Excerpted from "John Steinbeck: The Fitful Daemon" by R.W.B. Lewis, in *The Young Rebel in American Literature*, edited by Carl Bode; © 1959 by Carl Bode. Reprinted by permission of the author and the publishers, William Heinemann, Ltd.

failure is great, and it is incomparably more interesting and valuable than the successes of nine-tenths of his contemporaries. For where Steinbeck has failed is in an effort to engage, with the resources of fiction, the complex realities, the evolving motifs, the outlines and images of things, the very sense of life which make up the matter truly, if deeply and almost invisibly, available to an American novelist of his generation. I am not cheaply hinting that Steinbeck deserves, as the schoolboy saying goes, 'E' for effort. I am saying that because of his effort and even because of its failure he has made more visible for the rest of us the existence, indeed the precise character, of the realities and themes and images he has not finally succeeded in engaging. This is the kind of failure which is, in the end, almost indistinguishable from success, though we may not be sure where to catalogue it; whether, for example, under the heading of literature or of criticism, of art or of history. . . .

Steinbeck's editor, Pascal Covici, has accurately noted in Steinbeck "an expression of the joy of living." It should be remembered here that by communicating that joy Steinbeck has given very many people a great deal of pleasure, revived in them perhaps some lost sense of the sheer excitement of being alive. And I cannot resist adding personally that behind his stories I detect a figure who is to me altogether sympathetic; a person of zest and humour and nervous anger, and with an uncommonly large fund of humanity. The difficulty with Steinbeck's peculiar brand of joyfulness is not so much that it can easily turn fuzzy or mawkish (a kind of melting process observable in the development, or the decline, from *Tortilla Flat* to *Cannery Row* and *Sweet Thursday*). The difficulty is rather that it is constitutionally unequipped to deal with the more sombre reality a man must come up against, in these times or in any times, if he is honest and alert.

STEINBECK'S FAILURE TO PROBE DEEP

Steinbeck was up against a part of that reality during the years between 1936 and 1942 when he was writing *In Dubious Battle*, *The Grapes of Wrath* and *The Moon Is Down*, and when he was also writing the one work in which his trapped daemon did squirm out and get almost completely into the language—*Of Mice and Men*. With the important exception of the latter, the work of those years is characterised among other things by a seeming refusal, or perhaps an inability, to confront tragic truth. The result of having done so might have been a considerable enlargement of Steinbeck's art; the

STEINBECK'S TRACT

The fortune of America's poor who lived in the Southwest during the 1930s was indeed bad. The Grapes of Wrath successfully moves its readers to sympathize with the plight of these disadvantaged sharecroppers. However, as good a tract as the book is, it hardly warrants the exaggeration, "greatest single creative work," claimed by its publisher's marketers, according to Louis Kronenberger's 1939 review in the Nation.

The publishers refer to the book [*The Grapes of Wrath*] as "perhaps the greatest single creative work that this country has produced." This is a foolish and extravagant statement, but unlike most publishers' statements, it seems the result of honest enthusiasm, and one may hope that the common reader will respond to the book with an enthusiasm of the same sort. And perhaps he will, for *The Grapes of Wrath* has, overwhelmingly, those two qualities most vital to a work of social protest: great indignation and great compassion. Its theme is large and tragic and, on the whole, is largely and tragically felt. No novel of our day has been written out of a more genuine humanity, and none, I think, is better calculated to awaken the humanity of others.

Throughout the Southwest hundreds of thousands of small farmers and share-croppers have been driven, by the banks and the big landowners, from their farms—to move westward, with their families, in a dusty caravan of jalopies, to California. To California, because handbills lure them there with promises of work. But the real purpose of the handbills is to flood the California market with such a surplus of workers that the price of labor sinks to almost nothing. Hungry men, by accepting lower wages, oust ill-paid men from their jobs; then, in desperation, the ousted men snatch the jobs back at wages even lower. The result is a horde of the starving and homeless, living in filth in roadside camps, forever wandering, all thought of security ended. . . .

The Grapes of Wrath is a superb tract because it exposes something terrible and true with enormous vigor. It is a superb tract, moreover, by virtue of being thoroughly animated fiction, by virtue of living scenes and living characters (like Ma), not by virtue of discursive homilies and dead characters (like the socialistic preacher). One comes away moved, indignant, protesting, pitying. But one comes away dissatisfied, too, aware that *The Grapes of Wrath* is too unevenly weighted, too uneconomically proportioned, the work of a writer who is still self-indulgent, still undisciplined, still not altogether aware of the difference in value of various human emotions.

Louis Kronenberger, *The Nation*, April 15, 1939.

transformation, for instance, of the earlier earthy humour into what [nineteenth-century American writer Nathaniel] Hawthorne once called "the tragic power of laughter."

But the work of those years was characterised, too, by a relatively superficial analysis and a makeshift solution of the case, whether it be social injustice or Fascist invasion and oppression. To have looked more searchingly into those ugly phenomena would have been to have discovered their tragic implications for the nature of man—the proper concern, I venture, of the artist if not of the politician or the sociologist. *The Moon Is Down*, for example, is intended as a consoling image of heroism—that of a number of European villagers in a town occupied by the Nazi forces. But it is woefully limited by the absence of anything but the slightest hint that the fault, the guilt, the very Fascism, is a manifestation of the human heart, and so detectable on all sides of the conflict. Steinbeck typically permits a portion of goodness to modify the badness of some of the invaders—especially the commanding officer, the book's one interesting characterisation—but none of the invaders' badness is reflected in the hearts of the staunch and faithful villagers. Be good, sweet maids and men, Steinbeck seems to be telling them, and let who will be Fascist.

I am not now raising the somewhat tired issue of the artist's responsibility. I am sure that responsibility is a great one, but I am talking about the form it can most suitably and effectively take—and that is the prophetic form, penetrating to hidden realities and not combing up appearances. Neither *The Grapes of Wrath* nor *In Dubious Battle*, the novels where Steinbeck's rebellious sympathy for the wretched and the luckless is most evident, succeeds in arriving at that form; and in the absence of the prophetic we are left with the merely political. There are many fine, pungent and moving things in each of these books, and Steinbeck has given *The Grapes of Wrath* momentum, an inner drive, which in its generation only Faulkner—and he only a few times—has equalled. It also has a sweetness which never once goes sticky. Yet neither book quite touches bottom, quite manages to expose beneath the particular miseries and misfortunes the existence of what used to be called fate, what now is called the human condition—that twist or flaw in the very nature of things which Steinbeck has himself laid poetic hold of and expressed in the very similar phrases which conclude *The Red Pony* and *Of Mice and Men*, and which refer to two very similar acts of destruction: "I had to do it—had to" and "You hadda, George, I swear you hadda." *In Dubious Battle* and *The Grapes of Wrath* have, as it were, everything but that simple acknowledgment of the secret cause of our suffering and our violence. The secret cause is the ally of the poetic impulse, but these novels reach only as deep as the political cause, and politics in its usual meaning is the enemy of poetry, or anyhow of Steinbeck's poetry.

THE GRAPES OF WRATH: A POLITICAL BOOK

The Grapes of Wrath does not manage to transcend its political theme because the question "What is man?" was not really accepted by Steinbeck as the root question. He could not bring himself to believe that there was anything really wrong with the human heart, so that the causes of the wrongs observed must be other—practical, even mechanical; political, in short. The point here is that the application of Steinbeck's special and happy-natured poetry to his newly discovered and unhappy historical materials could only result in a defeat of the poetry. It would have taken a different brand of poetry, something with a more tragic thrust to it, to have survived. *The Grapes of Wrath* remains with the political answer, the same political theme—unity—of *In Dubious Battle*, but what it does is to expand on that theme.

To the story of Tom Joad and his family—their long, rickety journey westward, their exhausted efforts to make a living in California, and the bitter resistance they encounter among the rich, frightened, and greedy landowners—Steinbeck has added a large sky-blue vision of things which is not only like the vision of [American writer Ralph Waldo] Emerson, it is straight out of Emerson. It is his notion of the over-soul, the world-soul of which each individual has his modest and particular share. Jim Casy, the former preacher and future martyr, pronounces this idea: "Maybe all men got one big soul and everybody's a part of it." He had come to this vision during his retirement into the hills: "There was the hills, an' there was me, an' we wasn't separate no more. We was one big thing. An' that one thing was holy. That's the Holy Spirit—the human spirit—the whole shebang. An' it on'y got unholy when one mis'able little fella got the bit in his teeth, an' run off his own way. . . . Fella like that bust the holiness."

The doctrine of the whole shebang is the warrant for all the desperate organisational efforts, the violence and the heroism which follow later; they are all efforts to reconstruct the busted holiness, to mend once more the unity of the one soul of mankind. That doctrine also is the philosophical basis for the famous speech that Tom Joad makes to his mother after Casy has been killed—those words which rang bravely and beautifully in 1939 but which, if you will forgive me, seem to have lost a little of their glow since. Tom Joad is about to leave, to continue the whole struggle in hiding. His mother asks: "How'm I gonna know about you? They might kill ya an' I wouldn' know."

"Tom laughed uneasily. 'Well, maybe like Casy says, a fella ain't got a soul of his own, but on'y a piece of a big one—an then . . . then it don't matter. Then I'll be all aroun' in the dark. I'll be ever'where—wherever you look. Wherever they's a fight so hungry people can eat. I'll be there. Wherever they's a cop beatin' up a guy, I'll be there. If Casy knowed, why, I'll be in the way guys yell when they're mad an'—I'll be in the way kids laugh when they're hungry an' they know supper's ready. An' when our folks eat the stuff they raise an' live in the houses they build—why, I'll be there. See?'"

STEINBECK'S FAILURE TO FOCUS ON INDIVIDUALS

What does get lost amidst the genuinely lyrical flow of that passage and in its infectious hopefulness is the element on which not only the social struggle but the art of narrative depend—the image of the sharply outlined, resolutely differentiated, concrete individual personality. The political movements of the 1930s did tend to submerge the individual in the group, whether or not at the behest of the over-soul, but in reflecting that fact in his fiction Steinbeck has again yielded up his poetry to his politics. And his poetry is not saved by adding above that political tendency a metaphysical principle which (even if true, as most probably it is not) is totally unsuited for the craft of fiction. Fiction deals with individuals, however intimately related. The relationship, in turn, which both fiction and politics were seeking, and are seeking, must be composed of inviolable and separate persons. A modern philosopher has wisely said that relationship depends upon distance. What seems to be needed, both for society and for art, is not unity, which dissolves the individuals within it, but community, which is a sharing among distinct human persons. What is needed is not group-men but companions. Steinbeck has always had trouble focusing on individuals, and he has always known it. "You have never known a person," Joseph Wayne's sister-in-law says to him; and we feel it is Steinbeck admonishing himself. "You aren't aware of persons, Joseph; only people. You can't see units, Joseph, only the whole." Therefore it is heartening as well as a trifle surprising to come at last and in *East of Eden* upon the long awaited awareness, the long delayed perception; to arrive in Steinbeck's pages at the revelation withheld from Joseph Wayne and even from Doc Burton and Jim Casy. And this occurs in a passage not wholly justified by the immediate context, but erupting with a fierceness of feeling reminiscent of the explosive and superficially irrelevant ode to democracy which pops up in the early pages of *Moby-Dick.* "And this I believe," Steinbeck's voice suddenly announces to us: "And this I believe. That the free, exploring mind of the individual human is the most valuable thing in the world. And this I would fight for: the freedom of the mind to take any direction it wishes, undirected. And this I must fight against: an idea, religion or government which limits or destroys the individual. This is what I am and what I am about. I can understand why a system built on a pattern must try to destroy the free mind, for this is the one thing which can by inspection destroy such a system. Surely I can understand this, and I hate it and I will fight against it to preserve the one thing that separates us from the uncreative beasts. If the glory can be killed, we are lost."

It can no doubt be explained that such a belief and the passion behind it have been generated by revolt against the peculiar misbehaviours, the conformist pressures, of the 1950s, just as the emphasis on unity and the world-soul were stimulated by the ruggedly destructive individualism of the 1930s. But this time Steinbeck's rebellious impulse has produced a theme which goes beyond politics; which is, very simply and very greatly, human; which is the actual stuff of the art of narrative. *East of Eden* itself does not, as a novel, demonstrate this new and potentially happier wedding. But in the passage quoted Steinbeck's familiar daemon leapt out at us for an instant, and some day he will emerge to stay.

John Steinbeck's
Paisano Knights

Charles R. Metzger

Charles R. Metzger reports on John Steinbeck's
Mexican characters. Of the twenty volumes that make
up Steinbeck's work, half deal with Mexicans—
Mexicans in Mexico, Mexican immigrants in
California, and American descendants of Mexicans.
Throughout his work, Steinbeck presents them in a
variety of ways, but in *Tortilla Flat*, he focuses on one
kind of Mexican American—the *paisanos*. These men
from the poor class pride themselves in living by a
code of dignified, knightlike behavior similar to that of
Arthurian knights of legend. Metzger identifies them
in detail and shows how Steinbeck romanticizes them
in the novel and describes their actions with humor.

John Steinbeck completed twenty volumes of novels, short
stories, plays, motion picture books, and filmscripts during
the years 1929 to 1962. Half deal in part or altogether with
Mexicans of one sort or another. Of this half only three works
treat native-born Mexicans living *in* Mexico, i.e., *The Forgotten Village*, *The Pearl*, and *Viva Zapata!* Seven deal with
Mexican-Americans, i.e., with Mexican-born immigrants to
Upper California, or with California-born natives of Mexican
descent.

Steinbeck mentions by name nearly sixty Mexican-American
characters in the seven works: *The Pastures of Heaven*, *To a God
Unknown*, *Tortilla Flat*, *The Long Valley*, *Cannery Row*, *The
Wayward Bus*, and *Sweet Thursday.* . . .

Steinbeck's interest in all people, and in *paisanos* specifically, is in effect both scientific and in a sense romantic. As a
scientist, he identifies his characters, the *paisanos*, biological-
ly, in terms of structure and habitat, in terms of genetic origin
and range of distribution. To the question, What is a *paisano*?

Excerpted from "Steinbeck's Mexican-Americans" by Charles R. Metzger, in *Steinbeck:
The Man and His Work*, edited by Richard Astro and Tetsumaro Hayashi (Corvallis:
Oregon State Univ. Press, 1971). Copyright © 1971 by Richard Astro and Tetsumaro
Hayashi. Reprinted with permission.

Steinbeck answers:

> He is a mixture of Spanish, Indian, Mexican and assorted Caucasian bloods. His ancestors have lived in California for a hundred or two years. He speaks English with a *paisano* accent and Spanish with a *paisano* accent. When questioned concerning his race, he indignantly claims pure Spanish blood and rolls up his sleeve to show that the soft inside of his arm is really white. . . . He is a *paisano*, and he lives in that uphill district above the town of Monterey called Tortilla Flat, although it isn't flat at all.

Subsequently in the novel, and somewhat also after the manner of a biological scientist, Steinbeck describes his *paisanos* in their relations to local climate, food supply, and, since they are men, in relation to such modes of shelter, clothing, habits, and customs as are prevalent in the area over which they range. For example, the climate around Monterey is mild. Except for sea-formed fogs and overcasts, it is mostly sunny and arid. One can easily live in it, as the *paisanos* do when it pleases them, with a minimum of clothing and shelter. They can sleep, as for centuries before them their Indian ancestors did, in the woods or on the beach. They gain their food, as did their Indian ancestors, by a latter-day version of hunting, fishing, gathering, and barter, with minimum recourse to so-called gainful employment and the use of money. They eat what has been traditionally consumed in the area for centuries—beans, tortillas, some vegetables and fruit, some chicken and fish or other meat protein—and they drink the wine of California or anything else they can get hold of.

Historically, as I have suggested, the *paisanos*' mode of subsistence is a venerable and traditional one traceable back through the customs of their Mexican ancestors to the customs of their Indian ancestors, and modified, like all surviving traditional modes, to adjust to current conditions, namely those in and around Monterey just after the end of World War I. Steinbeck's view of the *paisanos* of Tortilla Flat is in effect scientific in a version of the way that [Steinbeck's friend] Ed Ricketts' view of the cephalopods [marine mollusks such as octopus and squid] of Monterey Bay was, that is, both taxonomical and ecological. But with men, even more noticeably than with octopi, ecological study pursued with even minimal industry quickly develops into sociological study of habits, customs, and traditions. And for men, certainly, these are just as much a part of environment as, say, temperature range. It is at this point, upon expanding the study of environment to include habits, customs, and traditions, that we come face to face with "the strong but different philosophic moral system" of Steinbeck's *paisanos.* This "different philosophical moral system" of the *paisanos* operates, Steinbeck suggests, in two ways: negatively or conservatively, by means of a Thoreau-like economy to protect the integrity of the organism as biological man; and positively or liberally, by way of promulgating and sanctioning a romantic image of a life-style for the man conceived as a conscious, self-regulating individual.

THE ABSENCE OF MATERIALISM AND WORK ETHIC

Somewhat after the manner of [American writer Henry David] Thoreau at Walden, the *paisanos* live economically, in terms of money and effort, at the subsistence level. They are, as Steinbeck says, "clean of commercialism [and therefore] free from the complicated systems of American business, and, having nothing that can be stolen, exploited or mortgaged, that system has not attacked them vigorously."

They live lives singularly devoid of the imperatives that dominate most of their non-*paisano* neighbors, devoid of the imperatives outlined by the so-called Protestant work-ethic. They do not work in order to avoid idleness or sin. They do not accept the concept of sin as a chastening and regulating instrument. Rather they look upon the sinful act (for example Big Joe's stealing four of the Pirate's "two-bitses") as an unfortunate human fact to be punished or forgiven as each act warrants. They do not work to gain or defend the status, the approval, the luxury, that derive from traditionally symbolized wealth. Yet they are not altogether opposed to work. Danny has a trade, he is a mule-skinner; the Pirate is a woodchopper, Tall Bob Smoke is a somewhat inept dog catcher. Tito Ralph spends most of his time in jail serving in the official capacity of jailer.

When there is a big party coming up, the *paisanos* are willing to work for as much as a whole day to get money for the party, when, of course, there is no other way to get it. Even the salvaging of lost articles of property to get money, articles such as a skiff, a water-soaked copy of Bowditch [a navigational guide], a gallon of wine, or a sack of dried beans for immediate use, requires some effort, particularly when, in the case of the wine or the beans, it is necessary to arrange for the article to get lost in the first place.

The *paisanos* have not, of course, taken even the initial step in the direction of arriving at the more sophisticated work-esthetic understood by such Steinbeck characters as Juan Chicoy [in *The Wayward Bus*], Joseph and Mary Rivas, and

STEINBECK'S EXPERIENCE WITH *PAISANOS*

John Steinbeck's knowledge of the characters in Tortilla Flat *has a long, deep history. He knew several of them in Monterey, and he listened to many stories told by citizens who had lived and worked among them for years. In* The True Adventures of John Steinbeck, Writer, *Jackson J. Benson describes the* paisanos *living in Steinbeck's area.*

Steinbeck himself was acquainted with several of the town characters, whom he brought together as Danny and his friends in the novel. Their adventures became, even while they were happening, a sort of living folklore that was passed around and became common knowledge. All the major characters in the novel had their real-life counterparts, although they were not all part of one group, as indicated in the novel, nor did they live in Tortilla Flat. They tended to drift here and there, sometimes living on the beach, sometimes in the canyons above the town. . . .

The most notorious of these men in life, Pilon (Eddie Ramirez), has left a legacy of legend that has made him a sort of folk hero (a backhanded fulfillment of Steinbeck's prophecy in the novel that Danny would become the subject of a myth). Part of the time, he and a friend, Eddy Martin, lived in a cave in Iris Canyon, twenty feet up the bank, which they called their summer home; Pilon called the county farm his "rest home" and went there regularly to dry out.

Although once in a while some of the *paisanos* worked in the sardine canneries, characters such as Pilon made it a point of honor never to do anything more than collect bottles or chop a little wood if wine could be obtained in no other way. Sometimes a chicken disappeared, but more often good things, although second-hand, were passed out the back door of a restaurant. Although Pilon did not, as Danny does in the novel, inherit a house, he did inherit $600, which, through prodigious effort, he managed to spend in one weekend, taking taxis everywhere and showering gifts on everyone he knew.

A couple of the *paisanos* came from good families, including one of the men who was probably the model for Danny, who had a habit of selling off everything from his former life of respectability, piece by piece, in order to get wine. Once he was apprehended walking down the center of the Salinas-Monterey highway at three in the morning, wearing little more than the jacket of a custom-made tuxedo. He had apparently been able to find a buyer for his shirt and his pants, but for some reason not his jacket.

Jackson J. Benson, *The True Adventures of John Steinbeck, Writer.* New York: The Viking Press, 1984.

their Anglo counterpart, Doc [in *Sweet Thursday*]. Their economy is the more exclusively negative, the more practically defensive economy of an ancient citizenry that has been invaded, surrounded, and outnumbered by newer neighbors subscribing to a foreign ethic. As Steinbeck suggests, "the old inhabitants of Monterey" have, like the "Ancient Britons . . . embattled in Wales" survived and indeed prevailed by refusing to change in crucial ways. They have refused to give up the less strenuous ways of living practiced by their Indian and Mexican campesino ancestors. They have refused to accept the gross forms of ambition, of materialism, of pride and guilt imported by their new and unsought neighbors—except, of course, on those rare occasions when to do so is consistent with their preexistent life style, as in the case of Peaches Ramirez's joining the Native Daughters of the Golden West.

Steinbeck's *paisanos* have refused to subscribe to those views of the world and of right conduct in it which would render them respectable and/or understandable to such neighbors or readers as have bought the White Anglo-Saxon Protestant ethic. They have refused essentially by way of defending their own positive, more liberal, more nearly aristocratic, because romantic in the old sense, image of an appropriate life style. It was not at all by accident or in the interest of irony that Steinbeck chose to describe his *paisanos* in Arthurian terms— after the manner of that great and wistful romantic Thomas Malory [British writer who collected tales of King Arthur] who celebrated the ancient, embattled, and romantic Britons, the knights of the round table, in his own prose.

Perhaps before discussing the knightly virtues ascribed to Danny and demonstrated by him and his *paisano* friends, I ought to say a few words about their romantic self-deceptions, i.e., their lying in order to justify, among other things, their thievery. In its own special way the lie, the romantic deception, is a necessary as well as a satisfactory instrument for making realistic adjustments to the romantic's idealistic image of exemplary conduct. I am suggesting in effect that every romantic, if he is to make his romanticism work, must of necessity operate on occasion after the realistic manner of the picaro [a rogue]. Thus, out of Big Joe's solicitous concern for the welfare of one of Mrs. Morales' chickens, develops a badly needed chicken dinner. Out of a shortage of chickens and a ready supply of sea gulls develop some of Mrs. Pastanos' memorable tamales. Without an instrument of rationalization, without romantic deception, these necessary practical adjustments to reality would have been impossible to achieve gracefully, while yet maintaining the romantic image of a properly mannered and adventurous life style. Possibly Steinbeck had the romantic's need for adjustment to some of the grimmer aspects of reality in mind when he said of the "Arthurian Cycle," what he could have said of his *paisano* cycle, that the stories contain "the stuff psychiatry is made of," the stuff, the rationale, of the psychology of adjustment. . . .

STEINBECK'S VIEW: *PAISANOS* AS KNIGHTS

Steinbeck does not specifically tell his Anglo readers what he knows, and what most Mexican-Americans know, about the very real and actively operating conceptions of the "dignidad de la persona," of being "muy hombre," of being "macho." These conceptions describe in Mexican terms some of the very real things that Steinbeck is talking about when he refers to the *paisanos'* "different philosophic moral system," when, indeed, he describes his *paisanos*, as seen through their own eyes, in aristocratic Arthurian terms. . . . He is [concerned] with celebrating the dignity of a superior sort of romantic hero, one more like Danny, one possessing in vernacular form a dignity akin to that of Chaucer's knight, the dignity of one who exhibits the "courtesy beyond politeness" of the *paisano*, the courtesy which Chaucer called *gentilesse*.

Indeed Steinbeck's *paisanos* are not soldiers any longer. . . . Although they respect a man, and measure him, in terms of his willingness to fight and his relative success at it, their concern is more with those branches of chivalric endeavor having to do with errant adventure and courtly love. In this respect they are again very much like [American writer Ernest] Hemingway's veterans in *The Sun Also Rises*, with this distinctive difference—they are more generous. They share their women, politely, without rancor, each graciously observing accustomed propriety, each courteously waiting his turn, or perhaps his chance. Teresina Cortez, accordingly, does not, frankly, know which of Danny's friends is responsible for her current conditions. As amorists the *paisanos* not only do not compete viciously, as Robert Cohn and Mike Campbell do for Lady Brett, they look after each other's interests. Pilon and Pablo are concerned that Danny might be lured into matrimony by Mrs. Morales. Danny and the others lend the Pirate the best items of their only clothing so that he can appear dressed properly at the dedication of his gold candlestick to San Francisco de Assisi in the Church of San Carlos in Monterey.

They manage to keep Mr. Torrelli from claiming ownership of Danny's remaining house. They share housing, food, and wine, as well as women. As amorists the *paisanos*, after the manner of courtly Arthurians, perform love service. Jesus Maria Corcoran plans to give Arabella Gross a pink rayon brassiere. Rebuffed by her and her soldier companions, he allows Danny to give it to Mrs. Morales. Danny gives a motorless "sweeping machine" to Sweets Ramirez. He, like his friends, grants favors to ladies upon request, or when they do not object too vigorously.

As befits their nobility, their courtesy beyond politeness, the *paisanos* perform genuinely good deeds on behalf of the Pirate, of the Caporal with the infant son, on behalf of Teresina Cortez and her many hungry children. They even, on occasion, round up dogs for Tall Bob Smoke by way of protecting him in his office of dog catcher, being careful to return borrowed pets to the neighborhoods of their masters after their capture has been recorded.

Like Galahad [the purest Knight in King Arthur's court, the one who succeeded in the quest for the Holy Grail], the *paisanos* seek, but do not quite find, a version of the Holy Grail. And they are at least religiously proper, when not truly devout. Much, for example, as Danny's friends are pained by their propriety, they refrain from attending his funeral mass because they can not be properly dressed. They respect the piety of others—of the Pirate, of Cornelia Ruiz, of Teresina's aged mother Angelica Cortez. They honor the memory of their heroic dead, of Arthur Morales "dead in France . . . for his country."

Danny, of course, is chief of the *paisano* heroes. After his passing, as after the passing of King Arthur, the group dissolves. The hero cannot be replaced. Of Danny deceased the group agrees in summary that "that Danny who had fought for lost causes, or any other kind; that Danny who could drink glass for glass with any man in the world; that Danny who responded to the look of love like an aroused tiger," that "*that* Danny was a man for you!"—that Danny was "muy hombre," exemplary in "his goodness, his courage, his piety."

TOO MUCH WINE AND TOO LITTLE FAMILY

One can argue with some justice that the knights of the round table were not so alcoholic as Danny and his friends, that Steinbeck has romanticized alcoholism and understated its degenerative and lethal effect. Yet the fact remains that Danny's heroic passing is occasioned by alcohol. And the reader must bear also in mind that Steinbeck is telling his story in "the manner of the *paisanos* themselves." And it turns out that the *paisanos* are relatively undeceived. They are aware that "there are plenty of people who die through abuse of wine." They are aware, or at least Steinbeck's readers are made aware, of the depressive, of the often violently manic, as well as the sociable effects of drink.

One also can argue with strong justification that Steinbeck's presentation of his *paisanos* does not do anything like justice in the way of presenting the very powerful family ties that dominate the lives of most Mexican-Americans. But not all persons classed in any type can be guaranteed, or even realistically expected, to fit into all the sub-categories of the type. Strong family ties, as a matter of fact, do not show up much in Malory either. Indeed, whether in literature or in real life, romantic-chivalric heroes tend in the main not to be family men, at least not while they are romantic and chivalrous.

It is necessary now, at last, to point out that Steinbeck's portrayal of *paisanos* in *Tortilla Flat* does not purport to do more than present one kind of Mexican-American, the *paisano* errant, in one place, Monterey, and at one time, just after World War I.

John Steinbeck's Myth of Manhood

Dan Vogel

Dan Vogel argues that John Steinbeck's short story "Flight" is more than an allegory; it has characteristics of myth and tragedy. "Flight" is the story of a boy who kills a man on an errand in town. As a result, he has to flee alone. Steinbeck treats the adventure as a rite of passage, a myth of a boy becoming a man. Ironically, just when Pepé can stand alone as a man, he becomes the target of a posse. Like many myths, this one also ends in violence.

In "Flight," a narrative of the Monterey country, John Steinbeck tells the story of Pepé, an immature 19-year-old who grows up in a moment when he kills a man. As a result of this murder, Pepé must flee to the desert and the hills, but he is chased relentlessly, fights thirst and gangrene [decay of body tissue, caused by insufficient blood supply], and finally is shot down. [In *The Wide World of John Steinbeck*,] Peter Lisca has called the tale an "uncomplicated plot" which veils the theme of man's "reduction to the state of a wild animal," and his retention nevertheless of "something more than an animal." In the plot, Mr. Lisca discerns "a thread of moral allegory—the growth of a boy to manhood and the meaning of that manhood."

More than a mere allegory, "Flight" reveals characteristics of myth and tragedy. A myth is a story that tries to explain some practice, belief, institution, or natural phenomenon, and is especially associated with religious rites and beliefs. The natural phenomenon, for Steinbeck, is not the facts of nature, with which historical myths deal; rather, it is, as Mr. Lisca points out, the development of innocent childhood into disillusioned manhood. The myth that Steinbeck wrought also contains another quality of myth, the rite. The plot of "Flight"

Dan Vogel, "Steinbeck's 'Flight': The Myth of Manhood," *College English*, December 1961.

narrates symbolically the ritual: the escape from the Mother, the divestiture of the Father, and the death and burial of Childhood. To discern these mythic symbols, it is necessary to review the narrative facts.

ONLY THE FACTS OF DEATH

As a naturalist, John Steinbeck records in dispassionate language Pepé's last actions as the posse overtakes him. Steinbeck's treatment of Pepé's fate leaves readers to elicit their own feelings of sympathy or justice.

He lifted his head to listen, for a familiar sound had come to him from the valley he had climbed out of; it was the crying yelp of hounds, excited and feverish, on a trail.

Pepé bowed his head quickly. He tried to speak rapid words but only a thick hiss came from his lips. He drew a shaky cross on his breast with his left hand. It was a long struggle to get to his feet. He crawled slowly and mechanically to the top of a big rock on the ridge peak. Once there, he arose slowly, swaying to his feet, and stood erect. Far below he could see the dark brush where he had slept. He braced his feet and stood there, black against the morning sky.

There came a ripping sound at his feet. A piece of stone flew up and a bullet droned off into the next gorge. The hollow crash echoed up from below. Pepé looked down for a moment and then pulled himself straight again.

His body jarred back. His left hand fluttered helplessly toward his breast. The second crash sounded from below. Pepé swung forward and toppled from the rock. His body struck and rolled over and over, starting a little avalanche. And when at last he stopped against a bush, the avalanche slid slowly down and covered up his head.

John Steinbeck, "Flight," in *American Poetry and Prose.* 5th ed. Edited by Norman Foerster et al. Boston: Houghton Mifflin, 1970.

At the beginning of the story, Pepé, though 19 years of age, has all the innocence of the "toy-baby" his mother calls him. He is called lazy, but "his mouth was as sweet as a girl's mouth"; he was perhaps lazy, but his most significant trait was a girlish purity. He has also the universal childish characteristic of eagerness to do things by himself, evident in the alacrity with which he goes on an errand alone into Monterey.

In these days of childish innocence, his most prized possession is his father's switchblade knife. It is an inheritance, with which he proudly plays at sticking the post, to the delight of his little brother and sister. When his rather domineering mother—

who constantly taunts him with his inability to be "a man"—asks him to go to Monterey, "a revolution took place in the relaxed figure of Pepé." He is asked, surprisingly, to go alone; he is permitted to wear his father's hat and his father's hatband and to ride in his father's saddle. In departing, Pepé says, "You may send me often alone. I am a man." To which his mother retorts, "Thou art a foolish chicken."

When Pepé returns, he has killed a man with his father's knife, left behind him at the scene of the crime. The look of innocence is gone; he has been shocked by a fact of life, an extreme independent act. His mother quickly understands and helps him outfit himself for the flight into the mountains. She gives him especially his father's black coat and rifle. Weighted down by the accoutrements of his father, Pepé separates himself from his mother. She recognizes the change. She tells the little boy, "Pepé is a man now. He has a man's thing to do." Logically, however, this is not necessarily so. A man might possibly have been expected to give himself up and pay for his crime. It seems to me, then, that Pepé's mother perceived that her son is entering manhood and must stand alone. This he must do.

FROM INNOCENCE TO EXPERIENCE

The ordeal of transformation from innocence to experience, from purity to defilement begins. There is the physical pain of the ordeal, symbolized by a cut hand that soon becomes gangrenous. There is the psychological pain—the recognition of a strangeness in this life that is omnipresent, silent, watchful and dark—the sense of Evil, or Tragedy, or Retribution. This realization is symbolized by the narratively gratuitous, unrealistic presence of the black figures, the "dark watchers" who are seen for a moment on the tops of ridges and then disappear. "No one knew who the watchers were," Steinbeck tells us, "nor where they lived, but it was better to ignore them and never to show interest in them. They did not bother one who stayed on the trail and minded his own business." They are not the posse, who are physical figures behind Pepé with horses and guns and dogs. These are the silent inscrutable watchers from above, the universal Nemesis [the goddess of retributive justice and vengeance], the recognition of which signals a further step into manhood.

Pepé meets wild animals face to face, but they are quiescent and harmless. They seem to recognize a fellow creature who also lives for a moment in a wilderness, they in the throes of an instinctive existence, he in the playing out of an inevitable phenomenon. He is no danger to them.

Clambering over rocks, staggering across sunbaked flats, fleeing before sounds and shapes, Pepé forgets his father's hat; his father's horse is shot out from under him and his father's saddle is now useless; he divests himself of his father's coat because it pains his swollen, gangrenous arm; and in his pain he leaves his father's rifle on the trail behind him.

Only now, having been separated from his mother and having cleansed himself of all the accoutrements and artifacts of his father, can the youth stand alone. But to Steinbeck this is far from a joyous or victorious occasion. It is sad and painful and tragic. Pepé rises to his feet, "black against the morning sky," astride a ridge. He is a perfect target and the narrative ends with the man against the sky shot down. The body rolls down the hillside, creating a little avalanche, which follows him in his descent and covers up his head. Thus innocence is killed and buried in the moment that Man stands alone.

Thus the myth ends, as so many myths do, with violence and melodrama. What the myth described is the natural miracle of entering manhood. When serenity of childhood is lost, there is pain and misery. Yet there is nevertheless a sense of gain and heroism which are more interesting and dramatic. It is a story that has fascinated many from [British poet William] Wordsworth to [American writer Ernest] Hemingway, and what Steinbeck has written is a myth that describes in symbols what has happened to each of us.

John Steinbeck's Mature Style in *The Red Pony*

Harry Thornton Moore

Harry Thornton Moore claims that John Steinbeck's early writing in *The Red Pony* is mature. In this partly autobiographical story, Steinbeck writes glowingly about ranch life in the Salinas Valley. This collection of four stories tells about the boy Jody's exposure to birth and death, hard experiences that initiate him into the realities of life. Steinbeck's style succeeds both in his creation of characters and his depiction of the ranch and the valley.

Between the publication dates of *To a God Unknown* [1933], which demarcated the end of Steinbeck's first period as a writer, and those of that very different first book of his next phase, *Tortilla Flat* [1935], there was a gap of more than a year and a half. During this interval (indeed, soon after the appearance of *To a God Unknown*) the first two parts of the short-story group later called *The Red Pony* were printed in the lone magazine which would accept Steinbeck's work at this time, the *North American Review*. Four years later, in 1937, the whole of *The Red Pony* was issued in book form in a limited edition; it was given to the wide public a year after that in the first collected volume of Steinbeck's short stories. The important point to remember is that *The Red Pony* is an early work, though it may seem otherwise because of its late appearance in book form and because its straightforward observation and its sense of control make its writing resemble the later books.

The Red Pony tells the story of "the boy Jody," obviously a partly autobiographical character, who is seen in relation to different phases of life at his father's ranch—the animals, the people, the surrounding country. The harshness of the world

Excerpted from *The Novels of John Steinbeck: A First Critical Study* by Harry Thornton Moore. Chicago: Normandie House, 1939.

STEINBECK'S LONG VALLEY

John Steinbeck grew up in the Salinas Valley, which lies near the Pacific coast in California. The valley is the setting for all of the stories in The Red Pony. *In* The Novels of John Steinbeck: A First Critical Study, *Harry Thornton Moore identifies the valley's location and explains its importance in Steinbeck's life and writing.*

Salinas is ten miles inland from the notch Monterey Bay makes in the California Coast. The town was settled about 1858, and since 1872 has been the seat of Monterey County, of which John Steinbeck's father was treasurer for many years. Salinas lies near the north end of the "long valley" whose checkerboard farms produce lettuce, cauliflower, beets, fruit and grain in one of America's richest agricultural regions. To the east of the valley the Gabilan Mountains rise, hill ranches on the slopes, black-green belts of pinewoods, and—just above Soledad—Vancouver's Pinnacles thrusting up their spirelike rock formations. On the west the Santa Lucia range cuts off the Salinas Valley from the coast: the flanks of these mountains carry the burden of sequoia forests, there are great passes of broken granite, and fogs from the sea are often tangled in the pine-crested heights. . . .

A friend has described Steinbeck's home-life as having been "definitely bourgeois" [middle class]. He must have been a somewhat solemn child, judging from the temperament of "the boy Jody" in *The Red Pony*, who seems to be a partly autobiographical character. Steinbeck has remarked that children are wise rather than gay.

There was much to make life interesting for a boy in that region: readers of *The Red Pony* will recall how impressed Jody was with the mountains that lifted above him—the Gabilans were "jolly," but the mountains on the coast side seemed to have a menace. It is evident from all his writing how the fertile bed of the valley attracted Steinbeck; it was full of living and growing things, cattle and the fruit and grain and vegetables being raised and produced there.

Harry Thornton Moore, *The Novels of John Steinbeck: A First Critical Study.* Chicago: Normandie House, 1939.

is always ready to make itself felt, but in the times between the descents of doom we again find the glow that seems to play over Steinbeck's work when he is writing of daily ranch-life. The story really comprises three stories: they concern the horrible death of a pony, the hard birth of a colt, and the return of an old *paisano* to the place where he had been born. This last-mentioned section is one of Steinbeck's finest stories, despite the too-obvious comparison of the weary old man with the spent old horse (a somewhat similar parallel was to be used with greater subtlety but no less trickery in *Of Mice and Men*). Yet the other parts of this story, "The Great Mountains," are effective. And there is something new: Steinbeck deals with the concept of private property in a way he had never dealt with it before. The old *paisano*'s home had once been on the site of the present ranch, and when he was a boy he had lived there with his father, even as Jody is now dwelling there with his own father. The old man is first seen by Jody, to whom he says simply, "I am Gitano, and I have come back." Jody's mother and father try to get rid of Gitano, but he is as implacable as [American writer Herman] Melville's [stubborn copyist] Bartleby. They think he is looking for work, but no, he is too old to work. "I will stay here until I die." But he is not permitted to stay, he is worth no more to Jody's father than the useless old horse. It was apparent that a new yeast was working in Steinbeck in his first story of the dispossessed.

The Red Pony contains some of the finest prose passages Steinbeck had yet written. There is for example this account of Jody rising early in the California morning and going out to see his new pony in the barn:

> In the grey quiet mornings when the land and the brush and the houses and the trees were silver-grey and black like a photograph negative, he stole toward the barn, past the sleeping stone and the sleeping cypress tree. The turkeys, roosting in the tree out of coyotes' reach, clicked drowsily. The fields glowed with a grey frost-like light and in the dew the tracks of rabbits and of field mice stood out sharply. The good dogs came stiffly out of their little houses, hackles up and deep growls in their throats. Then they caught Jody's scent and their stiff tails rose up and waved a greeting . . .

The pictures here are superb, and the passage is improved by the break in the prevailing style made by the word "good," which may seem faintly out of key, though it is essentially so right, giving a touch of informality and warmth in just the proper place. It is the kind of risk a man who is writing good prose can afford to take.

Oneness and Mysticism in *The Red Pony*

Arnold L. Goldsmith

Arnold L. Goldsmith analyzes the connecting themes and structural elements that integrate the parts of John Steinbeck's *The Red Pony*. The stories cover about two years of Jody's life on a ranch in the Salinas Valley. Even though *The Red Pony* consists of four stories, it has an underlying unity of time, place, and theme. The stories show Jody's maturing as he experiences the cycles of life and death, the life and death of horses and of men. The stories create a mystical connection that unifies humans, animals, and nature.

Underlying Steinbeck's four short stories which make up *The Red Pony* are thematic rhythms, structural balance, and a seasonal symbolism which skillfully integrate the whole work and relate it to his Emersonian mysticism [the idea that each individual soul is part of a greater soul, a greater whole, an idea expressed by Ralph Waldo Emerson] found in later books such as *The Grapes of Wrath* (1939) and *Sea of Cortez* (1941). "The Leader of the People," added by Steinbeck in 1938 to the three stories first published as *The Red Pony* in 1937, is an integral part of the whole work, but readers of college anthologies usually find one of the stories published separately or the first three as a unit, and thus miss a good opportunity to study Steinbeck's subtle extension of the themes expressed in "The Gift," "The Great Mountains," and "The Promise."

The central figure unifying all four stories is Jody Tiflin. Like [American writer Ernest] Hemingway's early hero Nick Adams, Jody is being initiated into a violent world where danger lurks everywhere, pain and death are imminent, and the best laid plans of mice and boys often go astray. In the first story Jody is ten, in the next apparently a year older, and in the third and fourth, probably twelve. The adventures of both

Excerpted from "Thematic Rhythm in *The Red Pony*" by Arnold L. Goldsmith, *College English*, February 1965. Copyright 1965 by the National Council of Teachers of English. Reprinted with permission.

youths are intended to teach them the need for stoic endurance in order to survive in an imperfect and cruel world. In this sense, Hemingway's stories and *The Red Pony* can be considered *bildungsromans* [a novel about the development of a young character], but there are some significant differences. Because of Jody's age, sex plays much less a part of his initiation than it does in Nick's, whose experiences are not just vicarious. And violence, which explodes all around Nick and finally wounds him in the war, destroys only the things Jody loves, not harming him physically. Where Nick's wounds are both physical and psychic, Jody's are only psychic, and we do not know whether they have a permanent effect on him. The third story ends with Jody's thrill at the birth of his new colt, but even this thrill is dampened by pain: "He ached from his throat to his stomach. His legs were stiff and heavy. He tried to be glad because of the colt, but the bloody face, and the haunted, tired eyes of Billy Buck hung in the air ahead of him." The last story substitutes the tired face of Jody's grandfather for that of Billy Buck, but the optimism implied in the title as well as Jody's kindness to the old man are adequate evidence of the kind of adjustments Jody will make in life.

UNITY OF PLACE AND TIME

More important than the above contrasts is the fact that Steinbeck composed *The Red Pony* as an integrated whole, while Hemingway wrote the Nick Adams stories sporadically at different times during his literary career. All four stories in *The Red Pony* take place in the Salinas Valley, where Steinbeck himself grew up as a boy. The stories are filled with realistic and lyric descriptions of the Valley's flora and fauna (*e.g.*, horned toads, newts, blue snakes, lizards, buzzards, rabbits, hoot-owls, turkeys, coyotes, muskmelons, oakwoods, and black cypresses) which Steinbeck knew as intimately as [American writer Henry David] Thoreau knew the woods, ponds, and fields around Concord.

The time sequence of the stories can be worked out as follows. "The Gift" begins in late summer and ends around Thanksgiving, the beginning of the winter with its rainy season in California. The reader of Hemingway's *A Farewell to Arms* is certainly familiar with the association of rain with disease, violence, and death, and such seasonal symbolism is most appropriate in the story about the death of Jody's pony suffering from pneumonia. "The Great Mountains" begins in the "heat of a midsummer afternoon," probably a year after the first story began. It spans less than twenty-four hours, ending the next morning. "The Promise" begins that spring and ends eleven months later, in a January rain, once again an appropriate setting for the death of the mare Nellie and the birth of her colt. "The Leader of the People" takes place a couple of months later, in March, probably the same year that the mare died. The same unity of time and place found in the second story is evident here also. As in "The Great Mountains," the story begins on an afternoon and ends the next morning.

This analysis of the time sequence helps illuminate the structural symmetry of the stories. Just as Hemingway in *A Farewell to Arms* alternates a book of war with a romantic interlude for dramatic contrast, Steinbeck follows the violence of the first story with the tragic quiet of the second, with this same pattern repeated in the third and fourth sections. Where the first and third stories are about the violent deaths of horses, the second and fourth are about the twilight years of two old men.

RHYTHMS AND CYCLES

The basic thematic rhythm unifying the four stories in *The Red Pony* is the life-death cycle. This organic theory of life ending in death which in turn produces new life is the major theme of Hemingway's "Indian Camp," where Nick Adams witnesses the Caesarean delivery of an Indian baby and the violent death of the father. It is the same cycle of life and death implicit in ["Out of the Cradle Endlessly Rocking," American poet Walt] Whitman's image of the "cradle endlessly rocking."

In *The Red Pony* we see this rhythm in the cycle of the seasons, the buzzards flying overhead, the life and death of Jody's pony Galiban, the death of the buzzard Jody kills with his bare hands, the approaching death of the paisano Gitano and the old horse Easter (his very name suggesting life in death), and the two opposing sets of mountains: Galiban (jolly, populated, suggesting life) and the Great Ones (ominous, mysterious, suggesting death, a place where we must all go eventually), the little bird Jody kills with his slingshot and then beheads and dissects, the death of Nellie and the birth of her colt, and the approaching death of Jody's old grandfather, the old leader of the people, with the implication that Jody is to be the new one. All of these objects and incidents represent the never-ending rhythm of life and death to which Jody is continually exposed. The subtle expression of this theme can even be found at the beginning of "The Leader of the People," when

Billy Buck rakes the last of the old year's haystack, an action which implies the end of one season and the beginning of the next. In terms of the story, life is ending for the grandfather, but it is just beginning for Jody.

The most obvious example of Steinbeck's conscious effort to present this theme in *The Red Pony* is the sharp contrast he develops in "The Promise" between the black cypress tree by the bunkhouse and the water tub. Where the cypress is associated with death, the never-ending spring water piped into the old green tub is the symbol of the continuity of life. The two paragraphs where Steinbeck explains the effect these things have on Jody should be given in full:

> Jody traveled often to the brush line behind the house. A rusty iron pipe ran a thin stream of water into an old green tub. Where the water spilled over and sank into the ground there was a patch of perpetually green grass. Even when the hills were brown and baked in the summer that little patch was green. The water whined softly into the trough all the year round. This place had grown to be a center-point for Jody. When he had been punished the cool green grass and the singing water soothed him. When he had been mean the biting acid of meanness left him at the brush line. When he sat in the grass and listened to the purling stream, the barriers set up in his mind by the stern day went down to ruin.

> On the other hand, the black cypress tree by the bunkhouse was as repulsive as the water-tub was dear; for to this tree all the pigs came, sooner or later, to be slaughtered. Pig killing was fascinating, with the screaming and the blood, but it made Jody's heart beat so fast that it hurt him. After the pigs were scalded in the big iron tripod kettle and their skins were scraped and white, Jody had to go to the water-tub to sit in the grass until his heart grew quiet. The water-tub and the black cypress were opposites and enemies.

As Jody daydreams about his colt, he finds himself under the black cypress and superstitiously moves over to the green grass near the trilling water. "As usual the water place eliminated time and distance."

MYSTICAL CONNECTIONS TO NATURE

Jody's communion with nature, a semi-mystical experience in which time and place are eliminated, is not very different from the withdrawal into the wilderness of Jim Casy in *The Grapes of Wrath*. Casy adds a religious dimension to the experience when he says, "There was the hills, an' there was me, an' we wasn't separate no more. We was one thing. An' that one thing was holy." The most explicit statement Steinbeck has made on this mystical feeling of oneness of the animate and inanimate is in *Sea of Cortez*, where he wrote:

> groups melt into ecological groups until the time when what we know as life meets and enters what we think of as non-life: barnacle and rock, rock and earth, earth and tree, tree and rain and air. And the units nestle into the whole and are inseparable from it. . . . And it is a strange thing that most of the feeling we call religious, most of the mystical outcrying which is one of the most prized and used and desired reactions of our species, is really the understanding and the attempt to say that man is related to the whole thing, related inextricably to all reality, known and unknowable. This is a simple thing to say, but the profound feeling of it made a Jesus, a St. Augustine [early Christian writer], a St. Francis [medieval Christian leader], a Roger Bacon [British scientist], a Charles Darwin [British biologist who wrote *Origin of the Species*], and an [Albert] Einstein [physicist who developed the theory of relativity]. Each of them in his own tempo and with his own voice discovered and reaffirmed with astonishment the knowledge that all things are one thing and that one thing is all things.

Throughout his literary career John Steinbeck has attempted to render dramatically his passionate belief in the oneness of all life, and *The Red Pony* is no exception, as the life-death cycle and Jody's romantic communion with nature will attest. But there is one final example which should be mentioned because of its effective fusion of character, theme, and setting. It occurs in "The Great Mountains." To Jody, these mountains represent the mystery of the unknown, unlived life, but to the old man they stand for the mystery of death. Beyond them lies the sea—eternity. As Gitano rides off into the mountains, he carries a long rapier with a golden basket hilt, a family heirloom passed down to him by his father. This rapier adds just the right touch of myth and folklore to the ancient legend of an old man returning to his birthplace to die. It echoes the classic tradition of such weapons as the magical sword of King Arthur and [epic warrior] Beowulf, the shield of Achilles [a warrior in the Greek epic *Iliad*], even the long rifle of Natty Bumppo [hero in James Fenimore Cooper's *Leatherstocking* series]. To Jody, Gitano is "mysterious like the mountains. There were ranges back as far as you could see, but behind the last range piled up against the sky there was a great unknown country. And Gitano was an old man, until you got to the dull dark eyes. And in behind them was some unknown thing." Thus the mountains are an extension of Gitano, and Gitano is an extension of the old horse with its ribs and hip-bones jutting out under its skin. All three objects blend into one as Jody watches them disappear in the distance, lying in the green grass near the water-tub, the symbol of timelessness:

> For a moment he thought he could see a black speck crawling up the farthest ridge. Jody thought of the rapier and Gitano. And he thought of the great mountains. A longing caressed him, and it was so sharp that he wanted to cry to get it out of his breast. He lay down in the green grass near the round tub at the brush line. He covered his eyes with his crossed arms and lay there a long time, and he was full of a nameless sorrow.

Jody's Growing Awareness in *The Red Pony*

Warren French

Warren French traces the maturing of the young Jody through the four stories of John Steinbeck's *The Red Pony*. At the beginning of the first story, Jody trusts and obeys adults implicitly. After the ranch hand fails to take care of his red pony, Jody learns step by step to realize the fallibility of both humans and nature. He is disappointed, angered, and saddened, but he emerges at the end of the fourth story as a compassionate, mature young man.

The Red Pony should be considered apart from the rest of *The Long Valley*, since it is more nearly a brief episodic novel than a group of stories. While each of its four parts can be read separately, together they tell a unified story of a child's growth from selfish ignorance to compassionate enlightenment as his own experiences teach him to see the world, not as he wishes it to be, but as it is. In the third episode, Billy Buck, the ranch hand, tells young Jody that the only way to learn a thing is by being in on it right from the start, since "nobody can tell you anything." The four stories tell what the boy learns by being in on things from the start.

"THE GIFT"

At the beginning of the first story, "The Gift," Jody is a child not only in the sense of being innocent of any knowledge of the world, but also in the sense of being completely controlled by others. The degree of his dependence is repeatedly stressed: "It didn't occur to him to disobey the harsh note" of the triangle calling him to breakfast; "Jody obeyed [his father] in everything without questions of any kind"; "Punishment

Reprinted with permission of Twayne Publishers, an imprint of Simon & Schuster Macmillan, from *John Steinbeck* by Warren French. Copyright ©1961 by Twayne Publishers, Inc.

would be prompt both at school and at home" if he had lied to get away from school. There are compensations, however, for this dependent status; Jody lives in a world of certainties and believes implicitly in the wisdom of those he obeys.

As the story opens, however, Jody feels "an uncertainty in the air, a feeling of change and of loss and of the gain of new

---

KINDNESS BEHIND A LEMONADE

Although neither the author John Steinbeck nor the character Jody speaks directly at the end of The Red Pony, *the action and dialogue say clearly that Jody has compassion for his grandfather, whose dream has died.*

"We carried life out here and set it down the way those ants carry eggs. And I was the leader. The westering was as big as God, and the slow steps that made the movement piled up and piled up until the continent was crossed.

"Then we came down to the sea, and it was done." He stopped and wiped his eyes until the rims were red. "That's what I should be telling instead of stories."

When Jody spoke, Grandfather started and looked down at him. "Maybe I could lead the people some day," Jody said.

The old man smiled. "There's no place to go. There's the ocean to stop you. There's a line of old men along the shore hating the ocean because it stopped them."

"In boats I might, sir."

"No place to go, Jody. Every place is taken. But that's not the worst—no, not the worst. Westering has died out of the people. Westering isn't a hunger any more. It's all done. Your father is right. It is finished." He laced his fingers on his knee and looked at them.

Jody felt very sad. "If you'd like a glass of lemonade I could make it for you."

Grandfather was about to refuse, and then he saw Jody's face. "That would be nice," he said. "Yes, it would be nice to drink a lemonade."

Jody ran into the kitchen where his mother was wiping the last of the breakfast dishes. "Can I have a lemon to make a lemonade for Grandfather?"

His mother mimicked—"And another lemon to make a lemonade for you."

"No, ma'am. I don't want one."

"Jody! You're sick!" Then she stopped suddenly. "Take a lemon out of the cooler," she said softly. "Here, I'll reach the squeezer down to you."

John Steinbeck, *The Long Valley.* New York: The Viking Press, 1938.

and unfamiliar things." The first gain is that of a red pony
Jody's father buys him; possession of and responsibility for the
pony is the first step toward Jody's becoming an adult, toward
his differentiation from the mass represented by the boys who
come to admire the pony: "Before today Jody had been a boy,
dressed in overalls and a blue shirt—quieter than most, even
suspected of being a little cowardly. And now he was different.
. . . [The other boys] knew that Jody had been miraculously
lifted out of equality with them, and had been placed over
them," because he has become a horseman.

With maturity comes disillusionment. The story is built
chiefly around the ranch hand Billy Buck's promises to Jody.
He promises first, when Jody is hesitant about leaving the
pony out in the corral on a sunny day during a rainy season,
that "it won't rain" and that, if it does, he will put the pony in.
"Billy Buck wasn't wrong about many things," Steinbeck comments, because if Jody's faith is to be preserved, "He couldn't
be." But this time he is; it does rain and Billy does not put the
pony in but seeks refuge for himself on a neighboring ranch.
"You said it wouldn't rain," Jody says accusingly to Billy, who
replies that it's hard to tell at this time of the year. Steinbeck
comments, "His excuse was lame. He had no right to be fallible, and he knew it."

The pony does catch cold, but Billy says that "he'll be all
right in the morning." But he isn't. He grows worse. When his
condition becomes serious, Jody asks about it. Billy does not
want to tell the truth, but does, realizing "he couldn't be wrong
three times." Later when Jody observes that the pony is very
sick, Billy thinks a long time about what to say. "He nearly
tossed off a careless assurance," the author explains, "but he
saved himself in time." He cannot save the pony, though; it
flees into a meadow at last and dies. When buzzards attack the
carcass, Jody manages to grab one of them that stares at him
"impersonal and unafraid and detached" even as he kills it.
Jody's father chides him and asks if he doesn't know that the
buzzard didn't kill the pony. Jody does, of course; he is simply
practicing displacement, as he has earlier when he threw a
clod at an unoffending but disgustingly healthy dog. He has
learned that man cannot always vent his feelings directly on
what has hurt him; he has also learned that nature is impersonal, no respecter of human wishes. The most important
thing he has learned, however, is that the human beings he
trusted implicitly are fallible and that even those who love us
sometimes have only the alternatives of telling us something

unpleasant or lying to us. He can never be a completely naive or dependent child again.

"The Great Mountains"

As the second story, "The Great Mountains," begins, we find that the once trusting Jody has become cruel and callous. He irrationally tortures a long-suffering dog and equally irrationally kills a thrush. Then he hides the bird's body to avoid telling the truth. "He didn't care about the bird, or its life," Steinbeck writes, "but he knew what the older people would say if they had seen him kill it; he was ashamed of their potential opinion." He is no longer respectful of adults, but he fears them. He has graduated to that intermediate state between childhood and manhood where one's principal guide to conduct is fear of public opinion, a state beyond which many, of course, never advance. Like fearful people, too, Jody has reached a state where he does not wish to accept responsibility. When an old man approaches him, he abruptly turns and runs to the house for help.

The old man is the central figure in this story. He has lived as a child on the land where the Tiflin ranch is, and he has come home to die now that he is too old to work. Jody's father unsympathetically refuses to let him stay; he compares him to an old horse "who ought to be shot." Only Jody talks to the old man and learns that he had once visited with his father the great mountains that Jody much admires, but that he remembers nothing of them except that it was "quiet and nice" there. Jody also learns that the old man's most prized possession is a rapier that he has inherited from his father. The next morning both the old man and the superannuated horse that Jody's father compared him to have disappeared; they have been seen heading towards the great mountains. Jody discovers that of his possessions the old man has taken only the rapier into this place that he remembers as "quiet and nice." As Jody thinks of the old man, he is full of "a nameless sorrow." This sorrow seems to be his recognition that adults, too, have their problems, that they become worn out, useless and unwanted, and frustrated by an indifferent nature. If youth, as he has learned earlier, has its tragedies, so does old age. His sympathies have been broadened.

"The Promise"

"The Promise," the third story, opens with Jody conscious of the hurt feelings of the adults he associates with, and he himself is treated in a more adult manner. His father promises him a colt to replace the red pony if he will take one of the mares to be bred, earn the stud fee, tend the mare until she is ready to deliver (nearly a year), and then train the colt. Jody promises and finds himself "reduced to peonage for the whole late spring and summer." His relationship with the adults has subtly changed. Billy Buck will do everything he can to deliver the colt safely, but "won't promise anything." Jody endures the long wait (a kind of knightly ordeal), but at the end tragedy strikes again. Something goes wrong with the delivery, and Billy must kill the mare to save the colt. During the tense moments of the tragic delivery, two other things happen: Jody, who used to obey automatically, refuses to obey until cursed, and Billy Buck for the first time in the stories loses his temper with the boy.

Jody is now irretrievably entered into the frustrating land of adult emotions and defeats. He has learned, furthermore, that just as man is fallible, so is nature. Although its operations continue indifferent to man's wishes, these operations are far from perfect. Nellie has delivered colts successfully before, but this time a hitch develops. Old life must sometimes be sacrificed not just because it has become useless (as in "The Great Mountains") but in order to make possible new. Nobody is at fault; the system is just not flawless. Jody has gotten what he wanted, but he has also learned what sacrifices men must sometimes make to achieve their ends.

"THE LEADER OF THE PEOPLE"

The last story, "The Leader of the People," although added later, serves to round out the history of Jody's maturing. The story is skillfully connected with "The Promise" by Jody's first use in the narrative of the profanity he has picked up from Billy at the end of the preceding story. When he says, "I hope it don't rain until after I kill them damn mice," he looks over his shoulder "to see whether Billy had noticed the mature profanity," but Billy makes no comment.

The story is built around a visit from Jody's maternal grandfather, who led a group of emigrants westward in pioneering days. Jody's father does not look forward to the visit because of the old man's unending talk about his great experience. "He just goes on and on, and he never changes a word in the things he tells," he complains. Mrs. Tiflin replies quietly, "That was the big thing in father's life. He led a wagon train clear across the plains to the coast, and when it was finished, his life was done. It was a big thing to do, but it didn't last long enough."

When the old man arrives, he begins talking again. Although Jody listens enthusiastically, there is tension in the air. The climax comes when Jody's father, thinking the old man cannot hear him, asks with irritation, "Why does he have to tell [the stories] over and over? He came across the plains. All right! Now it's finished. Nobody wants to hear about it over and over." This time the old man does overhear the remarks, and his spirit is broken. "Don't be sorry, Carl," he tells his son-in-law, "an old man doesn't see things sometimes. Maybe you're right. The crossing is finished. Maybe it should be forgotten, now it's done." Disconsolately he sits on the porch. Jody remains loyal to him, and in the course of their conversation, the old man's real tragedy comes out. He has not, it turns out, simply wished to reminisce about the old days to glorify himself. "I tell these old stories," he tells Jody, "but they're not what I want to tell. I only know how I want people to feel when I tell them.... It wasn't getting here that mattered, it was movement and westering.... Then we came down to the sea, and it was done. That's what I should be telling instead of stories."

The tragedy is not just that the old man's job was finished too soon—that "there's a line of old men along the shore hating the ocean because it stopped them"—but even more that he is unable to communicate the feelings that motivated his generation to the younger generation. From him Jody learns that just as nature is fallible, so it too, like man, has its limits, wears out, offers no new frontiers. Jody also learns something even more important; he learns that the reason why "nobody can tell you anything" is that experience is difficult to communicate. The intent may be there, but words fail to convey it, so that he who would inspire the young may seem just a long-winded old man.

Jody also shows that he has learned even more than these things. After hearing the old man, he offers to make him a lemonade. When his mother suggests that he wants to make one for the old man so that he can have one himself, he says, "No, ma'am, I don't want one." She supposes him sick; then recognizes that he wishes to do something genuinely altruistic. Small as this gesture is, it shows us that Jody has learned compassion—that he has truly emerged into adulthood since he has learned that the only way to deal with the fallibility and the limitations of both man and nature is to be compassionate.

The morals are not so obvious in the stories as in this explanation; Steinbeck has succeeded in this work in so fusing his form with his content that the complex "message" of the narrative is never forced nor obtrusive. Yet there is no wasted word in the chronicle. In his depiction of a young man's emergence into compassionate adulthood by his painful learning through four personal experiences of the fallibility of man, the wearing out of man, the unreliability of nature, and the exhaustion of nature, Steinbeck succeeds in doing what the old man failed to do—make the reader "feel" when he speaks.

The Allegory of *The Pearl*

Harry Morris

Harry Morris argues that John Steinbeck has been, for the most part, successful in adding realism to the allegory of *The Pearl*. The story portrays the allegorical journey of Kino, an ignorant, unsophisticated man, who confronts the injustices of a powerful society. Yet it also portrays a particular man of pride living in the real geographical places around La Paz, Mexico. As the allegory extends outward, *The Pearl* symbolizes all that is valuable and worth fighting for, as well as the plight of the poor and how they persevere.

When first published, [*The Pearl*] was reviewed by [critic] Maxwell Geismar, who wrote, ". . . the quality that has marked Steinbeck's work as a whole is . . . the sense of black and white things and good and bad things—that is to say, the sense of a fabulist [writer of fables] or a propagandist rather than the insight of an artist." The fabulist as Geismar describes him is neither more nor less than the allegorist [writer of allegories]. . . .

In reading *The Pearl*, we encounter the work of a professed parabolist [writer of parables], and we must assert, and so reject Geismar's explicit objections to *The Pearl*, that the fable is an art form and that the fabulist as artist has never lacked insight. We cannot evaluate Steinbeck's performance with the criteria employed for judgment of the realistic novel. We cannot condemn *The Pearl* because as Geismar says it is all black and white, all good and bad. Such was Steinbeck's intention:

> And because the story has been told so often, it has taken root in every man's mind. And as with all retold tales that are in people's hearts, there are only good and bad things and black and white things and good and evil things and no in-between anywhere.

Writing about its composition, Steinbeck said elsewhere, "I

Excerpted from "*The Pearl*: Realism and Allegory" by Harry Morris, *English Journal*, October 1963.

tried to write it as folklore, to give it that set-aside, raised-up feeling that all folk stories have." He was telling us again that *The Pearl* is not totally in the realistic tradition.

STEINBECK ADDS REALISM TO THE PARABLE

But Steinbeck knew that the modern fabulist could write neither a medieval *Pearl* [a poem by a British poet whose name is unknown] nor a classical Aesopian Fox and Grapes story [from Aesop's *Fables*]. It was essential to overlay his primary media of parable and folklore with a coat of realism, and this was one of his chief problems. Realism as a technique requires two basic elements: credible people and situations on the one hand and recognizable evocation of the world of nature and of things on the other. Steinbeck succeeds brilliantly in the second of these tasks but perhaps does not come off quite so well in the first. In supplying realistic detail, he is a master, trained by his long and productive journeyman days at work on the proletarian novels of the thirties and the war pieces of the early forties. His description of the natural world is so handled as to do double and treble duty in enrichment of both symbolism and allegory. Many critics have observed Steinbeck's use of animal imagery that pervades this novel with the realistic detail that is also one of its strengths:

> Kino awakened in the near dark. The stars shone and the day had drawn only a pale wash of light in the lower sky to the east. The roosters had been crowing for some time, and the early pigs were already beginning their ceaseless turning of twigs and bits of wood to see whether anything to eat had been overlooked. Outside the brush house in the tuna clump, a covey of little birds chittered and flurried their wings.

Kino is identified symbolically with low animal orders: he must rise early and he must root in the earth for sustenance; but the simple, pastoral life has the beauty of the stars, the dawn, and the singing, happy birds. Yet provided also is a realistic description of village life on the fringe of La Paz. Finally, we should observe that the allegory too has begun. The first sentence—"Kino awakened in the near dark"—is a statement of multiple allegorical significance. Kino is what modern sociologists are fond of calling a primitive. As such, he comes from a society that is in its infancy; or, to paraphrase Steinbeck, it is in the dark or the near-dark intellectually, politically, theologically, and sociologically. But the third sentence tells us that the roosters have been crowing for some time, and we are to understand that Kino has heard the cock of progress crow. He will begin to question the institutions that have kept him primitive: medicine, the church, the pearl industry, the government. The allegory operates then locally, dealing at first with one person, Kino, and then with his people, the Mexican peasants of Lower California. But the allegory works also universally, and Kino is Everyman [characteristic of all people, as in the medieval play *Everyman*, whose main character journeys toward death]. The darkness in which he awakes is one of the spirit. The cock crow is one of warning that the spirit must awake to its own dangers. The allegorical journey has often been called the way into the dark night of the soul, in which

---

A LEGENDARY STRUGGLE WITH EVIL

James Gray describes The Pearl *as a symbolic struggle of goodness and innocence against evil.*

In *Sea of Cortez* Steinbeck tells of hearing a story about a Mexican Indian pearl diver who found such a fine jewel that he knew "he need never work again." Possession of this rare object so poisoned the existence of the fisherman, however, that he cursed it and threw it back into the sea. . . .

The legend cried out for elaboration and interpretation. Showing a fine respect for the special quality of the material, he produced a touching story of good in desperate struggle with evil. An infant becomes his symbol of innocence betrayed. The baby, born to a pearl fisherman, Kino, and his wife, Juana, is bitten by a scorpion and the local doctor refuses treatment because he knows the family to be poor. The situation is reversed when it becomes known that Kino has found "the Pearl of the World." Everyone becomes eager to exploit his ignorance. The doctor tries to play on a father's fears for the child, hoping to get the pearl in payment for useless services. The dealer in pearls belittles the jewel thinking to get it for little. Thieves set upon Kino in the dark trying to rob him and beat him viciously in the attempt. His house is burned in the course of another invasion. Crises mount until Kino realizes that he must try to escape from a world that has turned into an implacable enemy. But there is no escape from the evil that has been loosed into this community. Kino is tracked into the mountains where he has taken wife and child to hide. Bullets from the gun of the trackers hit and kill the child. The irony is complete; the pearl which should have been the means of helping to fulfill Kino's ambitions for his son actually has been an agent of disaster, producing only suffering, despair, and finally death. Back it goes into the sea, flung by Kino's hand.

James Gray, *John Steinbeck*. University of Minnesota Pamphlets on American Writers, no. 94. Minneapolis: University of Minnesota Press, 1971.

the darkness stands for despair or hopelessness. We cannot describe Kino or his people as in despair, for they have never known any life other than the one they lead; neither are they in hopelessness, for they are not aware that there is anything for which to hope. In a social parable, then, the darkness is injustice and helplessness in the face of it; in the allegory of the spirit, darkness concerns the opacity of the moral substance in man.

The social element is developed rapidly through the episode of Coyotito's scorpion bite and the doctor's refusal to treat a child whose father cannot pay a substantial fee. Kino's helplessness is conveyed by the fist he crushes into a split and bleeding mass against the doctor's gate. This theme of helplessness reaches its peak in the pearl-selling attempt. When Kino says to his incredulous brother, Juan Thomás, that perhaps all three buyers set a price amongst themselves before Kino's arrival, Juan Thomás answers, "If that is so, then all of us have been cheated all of our lives." And of course they have been.

Kino is, then, in the near dark; and, as his misfortunes develop, he descends deeper and deeper into the dark night of the soul. The journey that the soul makes as well as the journey that the living Kino makes—in terms of the good and evil that invest the one and the oppression and freedom that come to the other—provides the allegorical statement of the novel. . . .

REALISTIC DETAIL EMBELLISHES THE ALLEGORY

Perhaps to add reality to a fable, Steinbeck has diminished realism. Narrative detail alone supplies this element. The opening of chapter three, like the beginning paragraph of the book, is descriptive:

> A town is a thing like a colonial animal. A town has a nervous system and a head and shoulders and feet. A town is a thing separate from all other towns, so that there are no two towns alike. And a town has a whole emotion.

Animal imagery again dominates the human scene, but this passage is only the first half of a statement that is concluded midway through the chapter:

> Out in the estuary a tight woven school of small fishes glittered and broke water to escape a school of great fishes that drove in to eat them. And in the houses the people could hear the swish of the small ones and the bouncing splash of the great ones as the slaughter went on. . . . And the night mice crept about on the ground and the little night hawks hunted them silently.

Symbol, allegory, and realistic detail are again woven satisfactorily together. The large fish and the hawks symbolize the doctor, the priest, the brokers, and the man behind the brokers, in fact all enemies of the village people from time prehistoric. Allegorically these predatory animals are all the snares that beset the journeying soul and the hungering body. Realistically these scenes can be observed in any coastal town where water, fowl, and animal ecology provide these specific denizens.

Somewhere in every chapter Steinbeck adds a similar touch: the tidepool description that opens chapter two, the pearl-buyer with his sleight-of-hand coin manipulation midway in chapter four, the great wind passages at the end of chapter five, and the wasteland imagery a third of the way into chapter six. All these passages operate symbolically as well as realistically, and some of them work even allegorically.

THE ALLEGORICAL JOURNEY

One of the major charges against allegory is obscurantism. Why does the author not say what he means outright? Is it not too easy to derive two or more entirely separate and frequently contradictory meanings from a single allegory? . . . *The Pearl* is most commonly understood as a rejection of materialism. Peter Lisca accepts the theme of anti-materialism but suggests a second layer of allegory which creates a "pattern of man's search for his soul." Others think *The Pearl*, like many another Steinbeck novel, to be a search for values, something like Odysseus' ten-year wanderings in the Homeric epic. . . .

Let us consider the general implications of any allegorical journey. Either it chronicles the transition of the soul from its captivity in the body and this mortality to liberation in Paradise and eternal life, or it records simply man's passing from a state of sin to one of grace. Quite often both these things happen at the same time. . . . But one thing always remains at the end of an allegorical journey. The traveler of the literal journey is still alive, still mortal, still in this world, and still to make the true journey from the corruption of this earth to the crystal bowers of heaven or sulphurous pits of hell that is undergone only after death.

KINO'S ALLEGORICAL JOURNEYS

Kino's flight may be seen as a double journey, with a third still to be made. The journey is one-half spiritual—the route to salvation of the soul—and one-half physical—the way to freedom from bodily want. The second half is obvious; it is the theme of most of the early Steinbeck works; it is delineated in the list of things Kino will buy with the pearl. The first half may not be obvious. . . .

One of Kino's journeys then is the search for salvation. The forces that necessitate the literal journey, the flight, are cloaked in mystery and darkness:

> "I was attacked in the dark," said Kino. "And in the fight I have killed a man."

> "Who?" asked Juan Thomás quickly.

> "I do not know. It is all darkness—all darkness and shape of darkness."

> "It is the pearl," said Juan Thomás. "There is a devil in this pearl. You should have sold it and passed on the devil."

We are reminded of the formlessness of [British poet John] Milton's allegorical Death. Juan Thomás, torn like Kino by desires for a better life but concerned for his brother's safety, both blesses the journey and argues against it:

> "Go with God," he said, and it was like a death.

> "You will not give up the pearl?"

> "This pearl has become my soul," said Kino.

> "If I give it up I shall lose my soul."

Already almost overburdened with multiple symbolic equivalences—it stands for greed, for beauty, for materialism, for freedom from want, for evil, for good, for effete society, degenerate religion, and unethical medicine, for the strength and virtue of primitive societies—the pearl, with these words of Kino, stands also for Kino's soul. . . .

The full significance of Kino's throwing the pearl back into the sea now becomes clear: the act represents his willingness to accept the third journey, the journey still to be made. . . . Kino, Dante [author of the *Divine Comedy*, whose characters descend into hell and ascend again], Everyman have been given nothing more than instruction. They must apply their new knowledge and win their way to eternal salvation, which can come only with their actual deaths.

KINO'S STRENGTH OUT OF SUFFERING

Kino is not defeated. He has in a sense triumphed over his enemy, over the chief of the pearl buyers, who neither gets the pearl nor kills Kino to keep him from talking. Kino has rid himself of his pursuers; he has a clear road to the cities of the north, to the capital, where indeed he may be cheated again, but where he has infinitely more opportunity to escape his destiny as a hut-dwelling peasant on the edge of La Paz. He has proved that he cannot be cheated nor destroyed. But his real triumph, his real gain, the heights to which he has risen rather than the depths to which he has slipped back is the immense knowledge that he has gained about good and evil. This knowledge is the tool that he needs to help him on the final journey, the inescapable journey that every man must take. . . .

Coyotito can, in several ways, be identified with Kino's "pearl of great value." The pearl from the sea is only a means by which Coyotito will be given an education. For the doctor, who at first refused to treat Coyotito, the child becomes his means to the pearl, i.e. the child is the pearl to him. But more important than these tenuous relationships is the fact that with the death of Coyotito the pearl no longer has any significance. The moment the pursuer with the rifle fires, Kino kills him. Kino then kills the two trackers who led the assassin to him and who were unshakable. This act gives Kino and his family unhindered passage to the cities of the north, where either the pearl might be sold or a new life begun. But the chance shot has killed Coyotito, and though Kino and Juana are now free, they return to the village near La Paz and throw the pearl back into the sea. Thus the sole act that has altered Kino's determination to keep the pearl which has become his soul is the death of his child; and, as I read the allegory, Kino and Juana turn from the waterside with new spiritual strength.

The Parable of *The Pearl*

Howard Levant

Howard Levant describes John Steinbeck's *The Pearl* as a carefully and artistically crafted parable. Levant shows how a specific family, which includes Kino, his wife, and his son, suffers because it lacks money, education, and power. Kino, a pearl diver, finds a large and valuable pearl, but trouble results when he tries to sell it. The pearl takes on multiple meanings throughout the narrative. As the story progresses, the small family becomes a microcosm of a wider and more complicated world filled with violence and injustice. Through symbol, irony, and character development, Steinbeck elevates *The Pearl* beyond a simple moral tale about good and evil.

Steinbeck's artistic aims in *The Pearl* tend to fuse the two main kinds of storytelling, the tightly controlled dramatic structure and the wider range of panoramic structure. The allegory is located in details that are realized beyond any doubt, and the allegory benefits in credibility. . . . Steinbeck conceived of *The Pearl* as a parable that is foremost an objective, credible narrative, a tight structure capable of expanded belief. . . .

STEINBECK'S PREFACE FRAMES THE PARABLE

There is no pretense of artlessness in his technique, no suggestion that truth is attained by accident. The short preface is a frame device, an announcement of the mythical purpose of the story, and a denial of the most overt species of allegory: "If this story is a parable, perhaps everyone takes his own meaning from it and reads his own life into it." This initial frame is a necessary entry into the story. *The Pastures of Heaven, Tortilla Flat,* and *Cannery Row* open with prefaces which invite an expansion of the physical events; the same invitation is realized more powerfully in *The Pearl* because the objective details support the parable structure and enlarge its reference, and the artful devices (framing, etc.) create the context and the narrative point of view. No one approach is so exaggerated as to exclude the others. A balanced harmony between structure and materials as well as an avoidance of the rigidity of outright allegory constitute the evident purpose of this beginning.

At once, in the story proper, Steinbeck uses the group-man concept to hold various characters and events within the submerged allegory without straining the credibility of the narrative. As in *The Moon Is Down*, there are two kinds of group-man, but here they are distinguished objectively so there is no need to load the distinction. The first group-man is conceived to be an organism, while the second is an artificial growth.

THE FAMILY AS GROUP-MAN: AN ORGANISM

The organism comprises the specific family—Kino, Juana, and Coyotito—and the entire fishing village. The family is the village in little, the microcosm, and the life of the village is represented in the common actions of the family's life in the literal and symbolic unity its Song implies:

> The Song of the Family came now from behind Kino. And the rhythm of the family song was the grinding stone where Juana worked the corn for the morning cakes. . . . Kino heard the creak of the rope when Juana took Coyotito out of his hanging box and cleaned him and hammocked him. . . . Kino could see these things without looking at them. Juana sang softly an ancient song that had only three notes and yet endless variety of interval. And this was part of the family song too. It was all part. Sometimes it rose to an aching chord that caught the throat, saying this is safety, this is warmth, this is the *Whole*.

As microcosm, the family provides a typical point of view, much like the family in *The Grapes of Wrath*. As metaphor, the Song suggests the quality of the family's actions in the specific fact; because the actions are rituals, not merely duties, their value lies in what they signify—"safety . . . warmth . . . the *Whole*"—as well as in what they are. There is no discontinuity between duty and ritual; each implies the other. So the unity of the family is rooted in the metaphor, which is itself a result of daily events. And the metaphor fuses the realistic level of objective fact with the allegorical level of meaningful action. The same fusion ritualizes the family's involvement in their village and in their communal past. Again, as metaphor, "the people" help to define the family, and in turn "the people" have a part in the family's special existence:

Now, Kino's people had sung of everything that happened or existed. They had made songs to the fishes, to the sea in anger and to the sea in calm, to the light and the dark and the sun and the moon, and the songs were all in Kino and in his people—every song that had ever been made, even the ones forgotten.

The consequence of this developed metaphor, and of its long, soothing clauses, is that we tend to accept the reality of a completely natural, unified life in terms of "our Father who art in nature." The device of the Song is a nuisance that can seem precious if we bring to it only our standards. But the objective narration and the close, functional view of the life of the family in the details of the Song establish a certain amount of narrative distance. We are outsiders, permitted to look for a time at a way of life that is altogether different from our own, not by reason of its quaintness (it is the natural life in its own context), but in its unity. To be sure, the family as metaphor and the use of such concepts as "the people" and group-man derive from explicit usages in *The Grapes of Wrath*; the narrative distance in considering a primitive folk in a remote place allows Steinbeck to omit the special explanations and the occasional detached essays that are necessary in *The Grapes of Wrath*. Indeed, the way of life in *The Pearl* is communicated far more by tone, by the limpid, uncurling sentences, than by overt statement. Certainly the linguistic experiment is as ambitious and as difficult as the corresponding experiment in *The Grapes of Wrath* and when the tone is pumped up too high (as it may be in "the *Whole*") conviction fails, as it does in several of the overly editorial interchapters in *The Grapes of Wrath*. Nevertheless, the metaphorical way of presenting the family is successful in the main, and it has an explicit narrative function. The family is so happy in its unity that it can be attacked only from "the world." That attack becomes inevitable in the development of the story.

THE TOWN AS GROUP-MAN: AN ARTIFICIAL GROWTH

The town is a microcosm of "the world," since it is an artificial formation of group-man. The town can *look* organic, as when Steinbeck describes it in biological terms and in his own voice:

> A town is a thing like a colonial animal. A town has a nervous system and a head and shoulders and feet. A town is a thing separate from all other towns, so that there are no two towns alike. And a town has a whole emotion.

The clue that the town is only an illusion of organic life is in the phrase, "a colonial animal," which means the animal must be somewhere. The truly organic unit is everywhere, but the town is "separate." It is "a thing" while the organic unit is "a song." The distinction suggests an inert object, a kind of "death," not the ancient, always changing song that is associated with "life." Literally, the artificial quality of the town lies in its basic purpose: it exists to feed on the fishermen. The pearl buyers are especially representative of this purpose and of "the world," which is involved in its artificial values, because they can seem to be "separate" and "competitive," although in reality they are a single, parasitic "thing" that cannot have any concern for dignity, justice, or life. Therefore, given its nature, the town is the obvious enemy of the natural man. This truth is concealed by custom and by the teachings of the Church (the priest is a townsman). It comes into sharp focus only when Kino refuses to be handled as "a thing" by the pearl buyers, when he insists on his manhood by demanding true value for the pearl that he has found. For then the town reveals itself by arranging to bring violence and murder to the family.

The corrupting power of the town is pervasive and more powerful than the organic life of the village, once it is stirred enough by Kino's find. Some of the fishermen simply fear that influence, and even Kino's supporters use a mercantile language: "From his courage we may all profit." Kino cannot trust anyone but his kinsmen after the fishermen have had time to imagine the money value of the pearl. Kino's practical but narrow insight in demanding a fair price in fact measures the extent to which "the world" immediately corrupts his values.

KINO'S IRONIC BLEND OF SELFISHNESS AND IDEALISM

Once these factors are established, Steinbeck takes the narrative time to subtilize Kino's motives: his fierce stubbornness has a somewhat idealistic basis in pride, in his determination to remain human. Steinbeck works out the implicit, ironic changes between a stubbornness that can involve greed and a self-respect that can presume idealism, always keeping the literal and the probable fused with the moral implications at the core of the story. Thus, on the first night, when he is sure the pearl is his, Kino imagines what he will do with it; he progresses from personal and rather selfish desires—a church marriage, new clothes, a harpoon, a rifle—to wholly selfless, idealistic thoughts of sending Coyotito to school:

> My son will read and open books, and my son will write and will know writing. And my son will make numbers, and these things will make us free because he will know—he will know and through him we will know.

Irony tenses the closely knit texture of this passage. It is the possessive "my son," and the knowledge is to be a revelation of the mystery the pearl buyers understand—words and numbers. So, indirectly and objectively, through the man's stumbling, rather mercantile thoughts, Steinbeck indicates the immediate, corrupting influence of "the world" on Kino's organic values.

THE LITERAL PEARL AND THE SYMBOLIC PEARL

This irony is deepened by the contrast between the literal pearl that Kino finds, and Coyotito, the symbolic pearl, the precious belonging of the family. Because Coyotito is stung by a scorpion, and the town doctor will not come to the Indian village unless he is paid, Kino is forced to hunt for something of value in the sea that normally provides fish. Or, on the allegorical level, Coyotito's need forces Kino to forgo the family's needs and values in nature and to obey the commands of "the world." Moreover, in keeping with the established ironic tension, Steinbeck suggests that Juana cures Coyotito with a traditional medicine, a poultice of "some brown seaweed . . . as good a remedy as any and probably better than the doctor could have done," before Kino sets out to hunt a pearl. The irony is maintained and widened in reference. The greed of the doctor parallels the values of the pearl buyers, and the doctor's mumbo jumbo when he does appear, having heard of Kino's pearl, rounds our perception of the thorough corruptness of "the world" by its echo of the faked competitive system of the pearl buyers. Clearly the doctor is "a thing" in denying Coyotito's humanity, and he foreshadows the violent, inhuman response of "the world" to Kino's good fortune when he gives Coyotito a medicine to make him sick in order to create an artificial need for his services, now they can be paid for. The ironic tension increases when the nameless men try to snatch the pearl on the first night (after the scuffle, Kino calls out to Juana: "I am all right. The thing has gone."), and it continues to increase as unidentified men hunt Kino, intending to kill him for the pearl. The reverse of the implicit contrast between the literal pearl and the family's pearl, Coyotito, is explored for its ironic possibilities: The scorpion that stings Coyotito is less inhuman than the doctor who makes the child sick in order to gain a fee. The scorpion is innocent of its evil function, like all nature in its various functions, but men act with reason and foreknowledge. The ultimate turn is that Kino is forced to kill in the end to keep the actual pearl, but, in the

THE WORKINGS OF A PARABLE

Stories that illustrate a truth or a moral have been told by all societies since humans first could imagine. In The Literary Guide to the Bible, *John Drury explains why such stories continue to engage readers.*

Narrative engages its readers by feeding them a mixture of the hidden and the open. We are told enough to get us interested because we understand it. Enough is kept back from us to keep us interested by the presence of things which we do not understand, but hope to understand by reading on or reading again more carefully. It happens horizontally, along the story line: how will it end? Or, how does this bit which I am reading connect with what is before and after it? It also happens vertically: what is the deep and mysterious ground or source of these events which I am reading about? . . . Parables clarify— but without blowing the narrator's cover or exhausting the underlying mystery of his subject matter. According to [French writer Gustave] Flaubert, a narrator should be submerged in his tale, but only up to the waist. He takes advantage of that position by looking about him and seeing much further than the submerged creatures in his story. He can look up and down into the sky and water which affect their little lives, around for anything that may be coming at them unawares.

John Drury, "Luke," in *The Literary Guide to the Bible.* Edited by Robert Alter and Frank Kermode. Cambridge, MA: The Belknap Press of Harvard University Press, 1987.

process, through an accident as casual as the scorpion's sting, Coyotito is killed by a stray bullet.

This rich development of irony demands an extensive list of paired terms, but the terms are associative, flowing out of the events in a natural sequence, not imposed on the events by the logic of an allegorical progression. Illusory needs dog real needs: the sick boy needs a doctor, doctors must be paid, pearls are worth money, Kino can buy a rifle with money, and so forth. The original "natural" need quickly involves the "artificial" cash nexus and the values of the town.

THE IRONIC OVERLAPPING OF NATURAL AND ARTIFICIAL ELEMENTS

This range of contrasted imagery extends into characterization, particularly Kino's, since he is the focus of attention, the man to whom things happen, and (unlike Lennie [a character in *Of Mice and Men*] in a similar crux) he is somewhat aware of the ambiguous consequences of his actions. His complex range of responses, his subtle growth of pride after Coyotito's "natural" recovery as he realizes that the pearl is his, a symbol of his daring and strength, to own and to sell, opposes his rising fear for the future. Late on the first night, Juana asks, "Who do you fear?" Kino replies, "Everyone." This admission of fear qualifies his brave announcements to the people and suggests his developing awareness of the threat within the real situation. The subsequent events might be eliminated simply by letting Kino throw away the pearl, as Juana wishes. Although her insistence on taking Coyotito to the doctor is the cause of Kino's discovery of the pearl, she draws back fearfully from protecting and exploiting the pearl. Kino's aroused anger and pride—his character—make the story happen. His possessive defense of the pearl is an ironic amalgam of a bullish pride in his strength, in his ability to feed and to protect his family, and his increasingly tragic sense of acting out an inescapable "fate" or "curse" that can destroy the family or enrich all of them. As a man, he demands justice; thereby he endangers his family. The ambiguity is balanced and total. Kino is right and wrong. He prevails, but at a price. His heroism is disastrous and admirable, an expression of the entire man.

A GROWING CONFLICT OF VALUES

Kino's character justly complicates the basically simple narrative. Pride, idealism, greed, strength, despair, and horror—all are contained in the precise focus of the man's actions.

The central image is expressed as a conflict of values—the Pearl of the World and the pearl of the family, the literal pearl and Coyotito. This conflict offers Steinbeck innumerable opportunities to range universals as objective, imagistic facts, and he can do this almost at will. The dramatic structure permits a great deal of specific resonance. In short, Steinbeck makes the most of the parable's potentialities. The exact object, however complex, not its allegorical sign, its simplicity, serves to locate the story in humanly potential experience. In this way, Steinbeck drives an apparently simple narrative into the darkest areas of human awareness, and he accomplishes his purpose with full credibility.

Imaged objects define values. The pearl connotes a false standard of value. Kino's real needs are the family and his canoe, both recalling "our Father who art in nature." The canoe is explicitly an aspect of the organic life of the family:

> It was at once property and the source of food, for a man with a boat can guarantee a woman that she will eat something.

And it is associated with a son, as when Kino finds his canoe broken by those who want to keep him from taking the pearl to a city:

> This was an evil beyond thinking. The killing of a man was not so evil as the killing of a boat. For a boat does not have sons, and a boat cannot protect itself, and a wounded boat does not heal.

The anthropomorphic thinking [attributing human characteristics to animals and inanimate objects] of a primitive man is a habit of mind which permits the association of canoe and son as a felt insight, a metaphorical depth of association in "the uncertain air that magnified some things and blotted out others." But the standards of "the world" produce evil. The canoe is misused for pearl diving; this use violates its proper function as a fishing boat. The entire family is the innocent cause of the evil. Coyotito's illness occasions the pearl hunt. Juana "prays out" the pearl in response to the doctor's demand for money:

> She had not prayed directly for the recovery of the baby—she had prayed that they might find a pearl with which to hire the doctor to cure the baby.

Kino finds the pearl by forcing the luck that is given "by God or the gods." Finally, since Coyotito recovers, there is no organic need for the pearl; but they do not escape the pearl's evil until Kino flings it back into the sea while Juana stands "beside him, still holding her dead bundle over her shoulder." This resolution does not imply a withdrawal. The differing values of organic and artificial life are set in balance again by the unconcerned sea. The act is an anthropomorphic form of penance, a ritual burial, an ejection of evil, a token of a return to the genuine life of the organism, shaded by the fact of death which no human act can alter.

AMBIGUOUS RESOLUTION GROUNDED IN EVENTS

The resolution is ambiguous, then, like the rest of the parable, for it echoes our flawed humanity. Yet it is firm enough to be pointed by an ironic association of the pearl and the baby. Coyotito recovers at the moment when Kino first sees the pearl, fresh from the sea, and thinks it lovelier than anything he has seen before. After the baby's death, the pearl becomes suggestive of death: "And the pearl was ugly; it was grey, like a malignant growth." The coincidences are not forced. Fresh pearls are lovely, and unpolished pearls do change color out of water. The recovered baby is lovely, but he is ugly when he is dead "with the top of his head shot away." Always the visible facts are the basis for any implicit expansion into symbolic or allegorical significance. Even possibly abstract terms, such as "the Pearl of the World," derive a basic validity from events; no term exists in a vacuum.

The fully rendered context, the developed characters, and a technique that eliminates overt statement in favor of objective, imagistic detail give *The Pearl* its narrative intensity and conviction. Steinbeck reproduces the form of the classic parable because he understands its secret in *The Pearl:* You must narrate objectively and let the reader discover whatever implications he can. No simple moralism is squeezed from the materials. The structural techniques serve only to embody a conception that is profound enough to reveal itself.

Symbolic Creatures in *The Pearl*

Martha Heasley Cox

Martha Heasley Cox shows how John Steinbeck expanded a true story of an Indian boy and a pearl into the novel *The Pearl*. Steinbeck's characters can be read as real people and as symbols, and he surrounded them with creatures from the animal kingdom. Some creatures are symbols, like the scorpion that stings Coyotito. More often Steinbeck describes actions and people using images of sea, air, and land creatures to form similes and metaphors. These images reinforce the message that Kino experiences moments when he lives an animal-like existence.

While Steinbeck has based his novella [*The Pearl*] on the "true story" he heard, he has expanded its meaning, ordered and controlled its action, and focused the reader's attention on the aspects of the story he wishes to stress. The seed story, as Steinbeck records it, is less than 350 words and fills about one page; the novella Steinbeck wrote contains six chapters and fills, in the Bantam edition, 118 pages.

The original story has no indication of time limitations; Steinbeck's version takes five days to lead its victims from happiness and hope to desolation and despair. It begins with daybreak and ends with sunset. . . .

The brief original story of the pearl contains several characters, all of whom Steinbeck uses in some form in his novella: an Indian boy, a number of girls, dead relatives, pearl brokers, a friend, attackers, and pursuers. The unnamed Indian boy is transformed into Kino, named, as the Priest tells him, for a great man and a great father of the church, who "tamed the desert and sweetened the minds of thy people." That man was the seventeenth-century Jesuit, Eusebius Kino, a missionary and explorer in the Gulf region. Kino, Steinbeck's pro-

Excerpted from "Steinbeck's *The Pearl* (1947)" by Martha Heasley Cox, in *A Study Guide to John Steinbeck: A Handbook to His Major Works*, edited by Tetsumaro Hayashi (Metuchen, NJ: Scarecrow Press, 1974). Reprinted with permission.

tagonist, is a young married man with a child, who is respected in the community. He has black hair; a thin, coarse moustache; and warm fierce eyes. Over his clean white clothes which have been washed a thousand times, he wears an ancient blanket and a large straw hat, properly tilted. A fisherman and pearl diver, he owns his own canoe, inherited from his father and grandfather before him, and his brush hut, but can offer the doctor what is seemingly his total wealth otherwise—eight ugly, misshapen, almost valueless seed pearls in payment for treating his son.

KINO

Kino is a quiet sensitive man, who has great strength and courage. His sigh of satisfaction is to him conversation, and his account of the future he sees in the pearl is the longest speech Juana has ever heard him make, causing her to wonder at his courage and imagination. He listens continually to an inner music, not knowing whether he alone or all of his people hear it. He speaks softly to his timid dog and always touches his canoe tenderly. When he leaves the cave to attack the pursuers, he lays his palm on Coyotito's head in farewell and touches Juana's cheek. But he fights fearlessly when his family is threatened, snarling and bearing his teeth when he destroys the scorpion; leaping, striking, and spitting at the dark thing in his house; and moving with the strength of a terrible machine as he kills the three pursuers. Yet when he encounters the brokers, his only defense is a slight slitting of the eyes, tightening of the lips, and a reticence. Angered at their collusion, he strides away, with blood pounding in his ears, and decides, though he has never been away from home and fears strangers and strange places, to go to the capital to sell his pearl. Beset by conflicting emotions of fear and anger when he approaches the doctor, his actions show the ambivalence he feels: his lips draw tight in anger as he knocks but he simultaneously raises his other hand to take off his hat. After his public shaming when the doctor refuses to see him, he, like [Herman Melville's character] Billy Budd, can only strike out. In the absence of his adversary, he strikes the gate such a crushing blow that the blood flows from his split knuckles.

Kino possesses a native shrewdness which serves him well: he instinctively knows his dramatic effect when bargaining with the broker; he hears the music of evil when the priest visits; he refuses to give the pearl to the doctor for safekeeping; he knows that the pearl is valuable because of the attempted thefts.

Kino changes after the discovery of the pearl. He feels trapped by his own ignorance and by the doctor's greed and duplicity. He becomes cautious and suspicious, fearing everyone, knowing that even the gods are hostile to his plans. His brain burns "even during his sleep." He is determined, however, to give his family a future, to see that his wishes for them, which are both modest and admirable, have a chance for fulfillment. He resists, therefore, Juana's pleadings that he throw the pearl—and the future he envisions—back into the water. When she defies him, and tries to throw the pearl away herself, he beats her brutally before he turns away in sick disgust. Later, however, he decides twice to sacrifice himself for his wife and son, once through surrender to the pursuers, once as a decoy to lead the trackers on while Juana hides with Coyotito. Only Juana's insistence that his surrender would be futile, since they would all be killed anyway and she wishes to stay with him, prevents either action. Finally, when Coyotito is dead, he returns to the city, as "dangerous as a rising storm."

JUANA

The number of girls the Indian boy wishes to marry or "to make . . . a little happy" coalesce in Juana, whose name means "woman" and who, in the novella, is Kino's only romantic interest. She has dark eyes which make "little reflected stars" and wears her black hair in two braids tied with ribbons. When the story opens she wears an old blue skirt and torn shawl, but changes to her wedding skirt and waist for the trip to the pearl brokers.

Juana is the idealized woman, obedient, respectful, cheerful, patient, and courageous. She is a good mother, caring for Coyotito and reassuring him with soft songs to make him feel warm and safe. When Coyotito is wounded, it is Juana who sucks the poison from his puncture, then insists that he be treated by the doctor. She keeps the baby quiet on the flight until, after many hours of silence, his murmuring cry alerts the pursuers to their presence. Then it is her "keening, moaning, rising, hysterical cry . . . of death" that reveals Coyotito's fate to Kino and to us.

A helpmate to Kino, she shows surprising strength and courage. In the canoe she rows like a strong man and withstands hunger and fatigue almost better than Kino himself. Her prayers in time of trouble are a mixture of ancient magic and a Hail Mary. It is she who first senses the evil in the pearl and twice pleads with Kino to destroy it. When he refuses, she tries to throw it back into the water herself. She tends Kino when he is wounded, rushes to help when he is attacked, and drags the body of the man he murdered into the bushes. It is Juana who then decides that they must flee. On their return "her wide eyes stared inward" and she was "as remote and removed as Heaven."

KINO AND JUANA

The relationship of Kino and Juana undergoes subtle changes as the story progresses, indicated, at least in part, by their relative standing or walking positions: when they go to see the doctor, Juana walks first, carrying Coyotito, with Kino following behind; on the way to and from the pearl brokers, Kino goes first and Juana follows; when they begin their flight, Kino again leads, while Juana, carrying the baby, trots after him. But in times of sorrow, shame, or renunciation, they stand or walk side by side: when they are humiliated by the doctor they stand side by side in rejection; when they return to La Paz, they walk not in single file but side by side; when Kino throws the pearl into the water, they stand side by side for a long time.

Whatever the specific and local cultural and ethnic patterns which at least help determine their relationship, they are also influenced by the man-woman syndrome, a pattern of behavior dictated by their, and perhaps Steinbeck's, attitudes toward their respective sexes. The narrator tells us that though Juana is puzzled by the differences between a man and a woman, she knows, accepts, and needs them. In reply to her repeated pleading that he destroy the pearl, Kino's face grows crafty and he refuses, saying twice, "I am a man"; and Juana is silenced, "for his voice was command." When, exercising her "quality of woman" for reason, caution, and preservation, she attempts the deed herself the next morning and receives a severe beating for her efforts, she neither resists nor tries to protect herself. When Kino said "I am a man," that "meant that he was half insane and half god"; and "Juana had need of a man; she could not live without a man." Though in her "woman's soul" she knew she would be destroyed, she would follow him without question, and sometimes her "quality of woman . . . could cut through Kino's manners and save them all." She does preserve the family unit twice on the flight; once, when she goads Kino out of surrender, and again, when he takes strength from her refusal to stay behind while he goes on alone. In the final scene, she softly refuses when he offers her the pearl; maintaining the man-woman roles, she leaves the gesture of renun-

THE ORIGINAL PEARL STORY FROM LA PAZ

John Steinbeck's record of his scientific expedition to the Gulf of California with Ed Ricketts, Sea of Cortez, *contains a story Steinbeck heard in the city of La Paz. The story, supposedly true, tells that an Indian boy found a great pearl, but threw it back into the sea because it caused him trouble. Steinbeck found it hard to believe the story because it sounded so much like a parable.*

An event which happened at La Paz in recent years is typical of such places. An Indian boy by accident found a pearl of great size, an unbelievable pearl. He knew its value was so great that he need never work again. In his one pearl he had the ability to be drunk as long as he wished, to marry any one of a number of girls, and to make many more a little happy too. In his great pearl lay salvation, for he could in advance purchase masses sufficient to pop him out of Purgatory like a squeezed watermelon seed. In addition he could shift a number of dead relatives a little nearer to Paradise. He went to La Paz with his pearl in his hand and his future clear into eternity in his heart. He took his pearl to a broker and was offered so little that he grew angry, for he knew he was cheated. Then he carried his pearl to another broker and was offered the same amount. After a few more visits he came to know that the brokers were only the many hands of one head and that he could not sell his pearl for more. He took it to the beach and hid it under a stone, and that night he was clubbed into unconsciousness and his clothing was searched. The next night he slept at the house of a friend and his friend and he were injured and bound and the whole house searched. Then he went inland to lose his pursuers and he was waylaid and tortured. But he was very angry now and he knew what he must do. Hurt as he was he crept back to La Paz in the night and he skulked like a hunted fox to the beach and took out his pearl from under the stone. Then he cursed it and threw it as far as he could into the channel. He was a free man again with his soul in danger and his food and shelter insecure. And he laughed a great deal about it.

Martha Heasley Cox, "Steinbeck's *The Pearl* (1947)," in *A Study Guide to Steinbeck: A Handbook to His Major Works.* Edited by Tetsumaro Hayashi. Metuchen, NJ: The Scarecrow Press, 1974.

ciation to him.

Hints of catharsis, on their emergence from the valley of the shadow of death after the sacrifice of their firstborn in the mountains, occur when the narrator tells us that as Kino and Juana return, walking side by side, they seem removed from human experience, as if they "had gone through pain and had come out on the other side" and "that there was almost a magical protection about them."

PEARL BUYERS, PURSUERS, AND A DOCTOR

Other characters mentioned in the seed story are the pearl brokers, the pursuers who were presumably also the attackers, a friend, and dead relatives. Four pearl buyers appear in Steinbeck's version, without names but with distinct personalities, all differentiated in some way from one another, but all alike in their desire to perform their duty to their common employer, conniving to convince Kino that the pearl is of little value and to buy it as cheaply as possible. In the novella, the attackers, even more ominous because they are without form or name, are assailants who creep in the night, identified as "the sound" or "the thing." The pursuers on the flight are three, the dark horseman carrying the rifle and the two inhuman trackers, who scutter, crawl, and whine "like excited dogs on a warming trail." The closest parallel to the friend of the seed story is Kino's brother, Juan Tomás, who offers counsel about selling the pearl and caution about defying the way of life of the fishermen. Like the Indian boy's friend, Juan Tomás shields Kino in his home after Kino has killed his unknown assailant. Although the dead relatives the Indian boy "could shift . . . a little nearer Paradise" do not appear in Steinbeck's version, the Masses of the seed story are mentioned in the sketch of the doctor, whose dead wife "if Masses willed and paid for out of her own estate could do it, was in Heaven."

The doctor; Coyotito; Juan Tomás's wife, Apolonia, and their four children; the doctor's servant; the priest; the neighboring fishermen; the four beggars; the shopkeepers; and the Chinese grocery store owners are not suggested in the seed story. Some are only supernumeraries; some more; but all add color and verisimilitude to the story.

The most fully developed is the doctor, a fat and lazy man, who is cruel and avaricious. A member of a race which has starved, robbed, frightened, and despised Kino's people for nearly four hundred years, he is the chief antagonist of the novella. His clothing, a Parisian dressing gown of red watered silk; his appearance, eyes which rest in puffy little hammocks of flesh, and mouth drooping with discontent; his breakfast, chocolate and other sweets served in silver and fine china—all delineate his position and character and differentiate between his life and Kino's. Though the doctor battens on the suspicion, fear, and ignorance of the fishermen, he tends their sick only when assured of ample recompense, feigning the need for his services when none exists, and practicing subterfuge rather than the healing art to attain his ill-gotten wealth.

Coyotito, the baby, serves chiefly as catalyst. His scorpion sting necessitates the visit to the doctor and, in turn, the search for the great pearl. Kino's desire to give his son an education is a major reason for retaining the pearl. Juana's concern for his welfare and safety help define her role as woman, even in defiance of her husband. His death is the ultimate pain, the death of hope, which leads to the return of his parents and the rejection of the pearl. His name, the diminutive of the Mexican-Spanish word for Coyote, derives from the Nahuatl word "coyotl." Steinbeck emphasizes the connection when he has one of the pursuers speculate that the baby's cry from the cave may be a coyote, for he has heard "a coyote pup cry like a baby.". . . When Kino and Juana return, he carries the rifle, the instrument of death for his son, across his arm; she carries the dead baby in her shawl crusted with dried blood. It is almost as if one has been exchanged for the other.

CREATURES OF THE SEA, AIR, AND LAND

Symbols less well integrated into the story, and obvious in their meaning, are the school of small fishes slaughtered by the great fishes and the little mice who creep about on the ground while the night hawk hunts them silently. In addition to fowls and fishes, Steinbeck uses insect and animal imagery throughout the novella, often for reasons other than symbolic. The skinny black puppy, for example, who appears three times, helps show the change in Kino, who speaks to it softly on the first morning but ignores it on subsequent appearances even though it "threshed itself in greeting like a wind-blown flag" or "nearly shook his hind quarters loose.". . .

These images frequently appear in similes and metaphors: when Kino strikes Juana, he hisses at her like a snake, and she stares at him "with wide unfrightened eyes, like a sheep before the butcher"; and later Kino edges "like a slow lizard down the smooth rock shoulder." Such images enforce the dehumanization process that occurs as the story progresses, as well as the animal-like existence the family leads while hunted and at bay in the mountains. After the destruction of the canoe, Kino became an animal "for hiding, for attacking"; when they left La Paz "some animal thing was moving in him"; and they run "for the high place, as nearly all animals do when they are pursued."

But this is man forced into an animal existence when he is pushed beyond the bounds of human endurance. In an earlier passage, the narrator is careful to distinguish between the two species and asserts the superiority of man: ". . . it is said that humans are never satisfied, that you give them one thing and they want something more. And this is said in disparagement, whereas it is one of the greatest talents the species has and one that has made it superior to animals that are satisfied with what they have."

Steinbeck has used animal and insect imagery frequently, and perhaps most effectively, to provide sound effects in the novella, and has indeed written a sound track into his story. Here is one of numerous examples: "The coyotes cried and laughed in the brush, and the owls screeched and hissed over their heads. And once some larger animal lumbered away, crackling the undergrowth as it went." Similar onomatopoeic passages sometimes contain visual, auditory, and olfactory imagery, as in this instance:

> He heard every little sound of the gathering night, the sleepy complaint of settling birds, the love agony of cats, the strike and withdrawal of little waves on the beach, and the simple hiss of distance. And he could smell the sharp odor of exposed kelp from the receding tide. The little flare of the twig fire made the design on his sleeping mat jump before his entranced eyes.

The most discussed and, initially, most obvious of the sound effects are the songs which accompany all action, warning, celebrating, comforting; roaring, soaring, intermingling, rising and falling until the symphony ends: the Song of the Family, the Song of Evil, the Song of the Enemy, the Song of the Undersea, the Song of the Pearl That Might Be. For Kino's people had been great makers of songs and "everything they saw or thought or did or heard" became a song; they made songs "to the fishes, to the sea in anger and to the sea in calm, to the light and the dark and the sun and the moon.". . .

Critics have interpreted *The Pearl* in a number of ways. It has been called a search for values, man's search for his soul, a study of the vanity of human wishes, the struggle of one man against a predatory community, a lesson showing that man must stay in his own niche and not encroach on others, and, most often, a rejection of materialism. Though the omniscient narrator guides the reader toward an interpretation or, at least, toward several thematic statements, Steinbeck, in the prefatory comment, invites every reader to take his own meaning from the story, to read his own life into it.

Attitudes Toward the Poor in *Of Mice and Men*

Edwin Berry Burgum

Edwin Berry Burgum explores John Steinbeck's attitude toward the poor, a class of people who had cap-
tured the attention of American novelists in the 1930s.
Burgum found that Steinbeck presents a wide range of
attitudes toward poor workers and vagabonds throughout his many novels. In the novel *Of Mice and Men*,
Steinbeck creates characters that evoke complex sociological attitudes—some defined, some ambiguous—
regarding the underprivileged. Burgum suggests that
Steinbeck leaves the reader pondering at the end of the
story, unclear about what attitude to take toward the
moral dilemma surrounding Lennie and George.

The novels of our most distinguished novelist of the thirties,
John Steinbeck, with one exception treat of farmers, impover-
ished workers or vagabonds, present life supposedly through
their eyes and create a sympathy for them. They are the most
conspicuous examples of a shift of attitude, general to the thirties, from the traditional absorption of American fiction with
the problems and personages of the middle classes to an
intense curiosity about the poor. . . .

The poor appeared at some times possessed of a mysterious
strength which should be admired and imitated, at others vic-
timized by circumstances and therefore to be wept for; but
most popularly they seemed caught in a common maelstrom
of disaster. . . . The novelist who presented the widest range of
these fluctuations was Steinbeck. . . .

Of Mice and Men, combining elements from all his previous novels, is his most characteristic work. George and
Lenny, his new heroes, are ignorant workers of native stock.
But their disorders of personality arouse Steinbeck's pity
rather than amusement, and they do not form his sole inter-

Excerpted from "The Sensibility of John Steinbeck" by Edwin Berry Burgum, *Science &
Society*, Spring 1946. Reprinted by permission of the author and Guilford Publications.

est in them. These men have modest aspirations for their welfare for which he also has respect and attention. Awareness of social issues, though it no longer forms the backbone of the novel as in *In Dubious Battle* [a novel about violence in a labor conflict], remains to condition both the motivation and the progress of the story. The psychological and the sociological combine (as they do normally in life) to afford a well-rounded characterization. But characterization does not become an end in itself. Achieved through the incisiveness of conversation, it becomes an integral part of the action. Though George and Lenny have their ambitions, they are scarcely in a position to attain them. They are caught between the dual pressures of their own limitations and those imposed by their station in society. The tone of the novel, therefore, is neither the extreme of tension between groups that characterized *In Dubious Battle* nor the opposite extreme of relaxing of tension found in *Tortilla Flat.* The sharpness of tension is dispersed by the fact that in this novel every relationship involves it in its own way. The tone of the novel is that precarious equilibrium where various minor tensions for the time being check one another off, where men are uneasy within themselves and in uneasy association with one another, but manage to maintain some sort of control until the storm breaks in the final crisis.

On the sociological side, *Of Mice and Men* assumes that these tensions are set up by the nature of capitalism. The cockiness of Curley, the son of the ranch owner, his willingness to fight at the drop of the hat, is not merely a trait of his individual personality. It is a trait that his position in society encourages; in fact, there is his real strength, it turns out, in his power to fire a worker, for as an individual he is a coward, beneath his braggadoccio. In a similar way the one skilled worker on the ranch, the mechanic Carlson, because he is difficult to replace, can assume an arrogance forbidden the others. He is the one employee who might dare to avail himself of the advances of Curley's wife, and the one who, free also to lord it over his more expendable fellow workers, orders Slim's dog to be put to death. The other workers are compliant either because they are old or afraid of losing their jobs. Only Lenny, whose intelligence is too limited to enable him to recognize these realities, among the common ranch hands, stands up against the boss's son, and, when challenged, crushes his hand in his iron grip.

Lenny has the strength to resist. But it is George who has the brains and the ambition. He is the most complex of the

STEINBECK'S PITY FOR THE PROLETARIAT

In the introduction to John Steinbeck's Of Mice and Men, *John T. Winterich cites a definition of proletarian literature; its aim is to portray the poor with sympathy and to expose the injustices and economic inequalities they endure. By this definition, he argues,* Of Mice and Men *barely qualifies.*

John Steinbeck's abounding sense of pity for his toiling fellow man, particularly for the hewer of wood and the drawer of water, rings loud and clear through much of his work, and it rings loudest and clearest in three successive novels: *In Dubious Battle* (1936), *Of Mice and Men* (1937), and *The Grapes of Wrath* (1939). All are superb examples of proletarian literature.

I have always liked William Rose Benét's definition of proletarian literature: "It has for its aim a sympathetic portrayal of the lives and sufferings of the proletariat [the poorest class of working people] and an exposure of injustices and economic inequalities seen by its writers in the society in which they lived, with a view to inducing amelioration."

Accepting this definition (as I hope he does), the reader of John Steinbeck's proletarian novels must admit that *Of Mice and Men* is the least proletarian of all his proletarian novels. George Milton and Lennie Small do not complain about their lot, or turn up their noses at their quarters, or beef about the beef; the only amelioration they are interested in is a piece of land that they can call home. The double tragedy that tears them apart has no slightest concern with time-and-a-half for overtime, or Social Security, or fringe benefits.

John T. Winterich, Introduction to *Of Mice and Men* by John Steinbeck. Norwalk, CT: The Heritage Press, 1970.

characters because he has not accepted his position, but carries around with him the longing to save money, buy a small farm, work as his own boss in an air of freedom. His ideal has infected his friend Lenny, and, breaking through the barrier of race prejudice because of the need for allies, it is taken over by the old Negro, who has lived alone in ostracism from the ranch hands. But three such as these form an alliance that is pathetically inadequate, and we foresee, implicit in the constellation, its eventual doom.

THE RELATIONSHIP BETWEEN LENNY AND GEORGE

But the pathos of ineffectual struggle towards an ideal is overshadowed by the reader's interest in the difficult relationship between George and Lenny. Their friendship is an obligation imposed upon George by Lenny's aunt, and it frequently irritates George since Lenny has always got them both into trouble in the past. George has no obscure desire to be ruined. The psychology of the friendship is presented with deft sufficient outline by Steinbeck. George's generosity of spirit responds to Lenny's need for him, and his self-esteem is increased by the knowledge that Lenny will obey him without question, provided he is around to give the command. What leaves George under constant tension is the knowledge that he cannot always be around, and Lenny is always destroying what he loves, hysterically overexerting his great strength to ward off what he fears, or what George has taught him to fear. The mouse he pets in his pocket (as though the world, even George, would not sanction so much affection if they knew about it), he stifles to death. Under George's injunction to behave himself and not ruin their chances to save money for the farm where he can have unlimited small animals to play with, Lenny's fear of his own clumsiness mounts to a new pitch. And it is not lessened when he senses that all the ranch hands resent the advances the new wife of Curley appears to be making them. When, with that zest for the sexually abnormal which is an irresistible undercurrent of Steinbeck's personality, Curley's wife is especially attracted to Lenny because he seems so grossly masculine, Lenny loses control of himself. He has not been affected by her sexual attraction, merely by the fact that George has told him he must keep from involvement with her. When she asks him to stroke her hair, he finds it as soft as the mouse's head. She draws back in fear at so unusual an interest, and he strangles her out of a strange melange of urges in which desire to possess utterly so soft an object is intensified by his sense of guilt at doing what he has been told not to do. After such an accident, all plans for a farm become impossible. Knowing that the law of the frontier must overtake Lenny and will destroy him, seeing the lynch mob of his own fellow workers gather under the boss's direction, George's last act of friendship is to kill Lenny to save him from the more cruel death at the hands of the mob and to pretend to the mob that he has been one of them in his action. Thus abjectly the forces of destiny in the novel reduce the struggling manhood of George to impotence. The generosity of his action must parade as a prevarication, and he must appear reduced to the level of brutality from which he had sought escape into the freedom of economic independence. . . .

Our acceptance of the story will depend upon our attitude

towards the two heroes as personalities, and in particular upon our reaction to Lenny. To some readers his strangeness is fascinating. Steinbeck leaves his motivation obscure; he does not make it explicit like that of George. He apparently desires to hold us by the very mysteriousness of Lenny's motives, to arouse a kind of awe for him as we witness this uncanny union of brute strength and childlike affection. But other readers may feel that in Lenny, Steinbeck's tendency towards the sentimental reaches its artistic culmination. And though they recognize the deftness with which he achieves his end, the precision that can create clarity or ambiguity of effect at will, they will nevertheless dislike the end. But at least it must be admitted that no character in Steinbeck is more characteristic of his peculiar talent. And the novel becomes a testimonial to the transformation of the picaresque tradition when it comes into contact with the American sensitiveness to the plight of the underprivileged. In more religious countries such a character would take on mystic proportions, such as [Italian novelist Ignazio] Silone gives to his imbecile in *The Blood Beneath the Snow.* It is precisely here, in his capacity to arouse awe without mysticism, that Steinbeck proves how essentially American is his talent. He leaves Lenny somehow entirely natural and human, and yet essentially a mystery, the mystery of the unfit in a practical world. The hopelessness of the petty bourgeoisie and its confusion before the problems of the depression era are truly symbolized in Steinbeck's attitude of sympathy for Lenny. And we are all to a certain extent Georges in the spontaneity of our protective reaction.

Patterns That Make Meaning in *Of Mice and Men*

Peter Lisca

John Steinbeck intended to create a microcosm in *Of Mice and Men*, a world which portrays the yearnings of common people. Peter Lisca points out that a microcosm is difficult to identify when the main characters act in such a small setting. But, Lisca argues, the microcosm is discernible by observing the motifs of symbol, action, and language. Recurring events establish a pattern—George's retelling the story about a little farm with rabbits and Lennie's repeated destruction of soft things. This pattern raises hope and destroys it again, giving the reader an opportunity to reflect on the elements that prevent success. In spite of their slim chance of ever arriving at their safe place, George and Lennie continue on, strengthened by their need for one another.

Concerning the book's theme, Steinbeck wrote his agents, "I'm sorry that you do not find the new book [*Of Mice and Men*] as large in subject as it should be. I probably did not make my subjects and my symbols clear. The microcosm is rather difficult to handle and apparently I did not get it over—the earth longings of a Lennie who was not to represent insanity at all but the inarticulate and powerful yearning of all men. Well, if it isn't there it isn't there." To Ben Abramson [a Chicago bookseller who admired Steinbeck's work], he wrote a similar comment on the book's theme: ". . . it's a study of the dreams and pleasures of everyone in the world."

Such words as "microcosm," "of all men," and "everyone in the world" indicate that the problem he set himself in *Of Mice and Men* was similar to that he had solved in his previous novel, *In Dubious Battle.* But whereas in the earlier work the de-personalized protagonists were easily absorbed into a greater pattern because that pattern was physically present in the novel, in *Of Mice and Men* the protagonists are projected against a very thin background and must suggest or create this larger pattern through their own particularity. To achieve this, Steinbeck makes use of language, action, and symbol as recurring motifs. All three of these motifs are presented in the opening scene, are contrapuntally [with contrasting but parallel elements] developed through the story, and come together again at the end.

A SYMBOLIC PLACE

The first symbol in the novel, and the primary one, is the little spot by the river where the story begins and ends. The book opens with a description of this place by the river, and we first see George and Lennie as they enter this place from the highway to an outside world. It is significant that they prefer spending the night here rather than going on to the bunkhouse at the ranch.

Steinbeck's novels and stories often contain groves, willow thickets by a river, and caves which figure prominently in the action. There are, for example, the grove in *To a God Unknown,* the place by the river in the Junius Maltby story, the two caves and a willow thicket in *The Grapes of Wrath,* the cave under the bridge in *In Dubious Battle,* the caves in *The Wayward Bus,* and the thicket and cave in *The Pearl.* For George and Lennie, as for other Steinbeck heroes, coming to a cave or thicket by the river symbolizes a retreat from the world to a primeval innocence. Sometimes, as in *The Grapes of Wrath,* this retreat has explicit overtones of a return to the womb and rebirth. In the opening scene of *Of Mice and Men* Lennie twice mentions the possibility of hiding out in a cave, and George impresses on him that he must return to this thicket by the river when there is trouble.

While the cave or the river thicket is a "safe place," it is physically impossible to remain there, and this symbol of primeval innocence becomes translated into terms possible in the real world. For George and Lennie it becomes "a little house an' a couple of acres." Out of this translation grows a second symbol, the rabbits, and this symbol serves several purposes. Through synechdoche [a figure of speech in which the part represents the whole] it comes to stand for the "safe place" itself, making a much more easily manipulated symbol than the "house an' a couple of acres." Also, through Lennie's love for the rabbits Steinbeck is able not only to dramatize Lennie's desire for the "safe place," but to define the basis of that desire on a very low level of consciousness—the attraction to soft, warm fur, which is for Lennie the most important aspect of their plans.

LENNIE'S RECURRING ACTION

This transference of symbolic value from the farm to the rabbits is important also because it makes possible the motif of action. This is introduced in the first scene by the dead mouse which Lennie is carrying in his pocket (much as Tom carries the turtle in *The Grapes of Wrath*). As George talks about Lennie's attraction to mice, it becomes evident that the symbolic rabbits will come to the same end—crushed by Lennie's simple, blundering strength. Thus Lennie's killing of mice and later his killing of the puppy set up a pattern which the reader expects to be carried out again. George's story about Lennie and the little girl with the red dress, which he tells twice, contributes to this expectancy of pattern, as do the shooting of Candy's dog, the crushing of Curley's hand, and the frequent appearances of Curley's wife. All these incidents are patterns of the action motif and predict the fate of the rabbits and thus the fate of the dream of a "safe place."

GEORGE'S REPEATED STORY

The third motif, that of language, is also present in the opening scene. Lennie asks George, "Tell me—like you done before," and George's words are obviously in the nature of a ritual. "George's voice became deeper. He repeated his words rhythmically, as though he had said them many times before." The element of ritual is stressed by the fact that even Lennie has heard it often enough to remember its precise language: "*An' live off the fatta the lan'.* . . . An' have *rabbits.* Go on George! Tell about what we're gonna have in the garden and about the rabbits in the cages and about . . ." This ritual is performed often in the story, whenever Lennie feels insecure. And of course it is while Lennie is caught up in this dream vision that George shoots him, so that on one level the vision is accomplished—the dream never interrupted, the rabbits never crushed.

The highly patterned effect achieved by these incremental motifs of symbol, action, and language is the knife edge on which criticism of *Of Mice and Men* divides. For although Steinbeck's success in creating a pattern has been acknowl-

"MY DOG ATE IT"

At a time when John Steinbeck was poor and busy trying to get work completed, his setter puppy Toby destroyed about half of the only copy of the manuscript for Of Mice and Men. *Steinbeck spared the puppy and tried to reconstruct the lost words.*

An amusing sequence of anecdotes, involving the various dogs that frequented the Steinbeck household from time to time, serves to measure the rapidly changing circumstances he experienced during the mid-1930s. . . . By 1933, dogs offered an audience, rather than a theme. Steinbeck was more determined than ever to support himself as a writer, but his books had been such financial disappointments that he could no longer afford a pet. Drawing on the only resource available, he outfitted himself in the same dream of success with a dog and an audience: "Even a little money would be better than a bundle of paper. We are very happy. I need a dog pretty badly. I dreamed of great numbers of dogs last night. They sat in a circle and looked at me and I wanted all of them.". . .

The final incident, to be taken no more facetiously than its predecessors, was a disaster that befell the initial manuscript of *Of Mice and Men.* Steinbeck now wrote his publisher about the dog-as-critic because, with the mixed reactions stirred by *In Dubious Battle,* hostile reviews, rather than indifferent sales, were his current preoccupation: "Minor tragedy stalked. My setter pup, left alone one night, made confetti of about half of my manuscript book. Two months' work to do over again. It sets me back. There was no other draft. I was pretty mad, but the poor little fellow may have been acting critically. I didn't want to ruin a good dog for a manuscript I'm not sure is good at all. He only got an ordinary spanking.". . . Steinbeck still felt that Toby might have been right. "I'm not sure Toby didn't know what he was doing when he ate the first draft," he wrote. "I have promoted Toby-dog to be lieutenant-colonel in charge of literature. But as for the unpredictable literary enthusiasms of this country, I have little faith in them."

John F. Slater, "Steinbeck's *Of Mice and Men* (Novel) (1937)," in *A Study Guide to Steinbeck: A Handbook to His Major Works.* Edited by Tetsumaro Hayashi. Metuchen, NJ: The Scarecrow Press, 1974.

edged, criticism has been divided as to the effect of this achievement. On one side, it is claimed that this strong patterning creates a sense of contrivance and mechanical action, and on the other, that the patterning actually gives a meaningful design to the story, a tone of classic fate. What is obviously needed here is some objective critical tool for determining under what conditions a sense of inevitability (to use a

neutral word) should be experienced as mechanical contrivance, and when it should be experienced as catharsis [a
release of emotional tension] effected by a sense of fate. Such
a tool cannot be forged within the limits of this study; but it is
possible to examine the particular circumstances of *Of Mice
and Men* more closely before passing judgment.

A BREAK IN THE PATTERN

Although the three motifs of symbol, action, and language
build up a strong pattern of inevitability, the movement is not
unbroken. About midway in the novel (chapters 3 and 4) there
is set up a countermovement which seems to threaten the pattern. Up to this point the dream of "a house an' a couple of
acres" seemed impossible of realization. Now it develops that
George has an actual farm in mind (ten acres), knows the
owners and why they want to sell it: "The ol' people that owns
it is flat bust an' the ol' lady needs an operation." He even
knows the price—"six hundred dollars." Also, the old workman, Candy, is willing to buy a share in the dream with the
three hundred dollars he has saved up. It appears that at the
end of the month George and Lennie will have another hundred dollars and that quite possibly they "could swing her for
that." In the following chapter this dream and its possibilities
are further explored through Lennie's visit with Crooks, the
power of the dream manifesting itself in Crooks's conversion
from cynicism to optimism. But at the very height of his conversion the mice symbol reappears in the form of Curley's
wife, who threatens the dream by bringing with her the harsh
realities of the outside world and by arousing Lennie's interest.

The function of Candy's and Crooks's interest and the sudden bringing of the dream within reasonable possibility is to
interrupt, momentarily, the pattern of inevitability. But, and
this is very important, Steinbeck handles this interruption so
that it does not actually reverse the situation. Rather, it insin-
uates a possibility. Thus, though working against the pattern,
this countermovement makes that pattern more credible by
creating the necessary ingredient of free will. The story
achieves power through a delicate balance of the protagonists'
free will and the force of circumstance.

LEVELS OF MEANING

In addition to imposing a sense of inevitability, this strong patterning of events performs the important function of extending
the story's range of meanings. This can best be understood by

reference to Hemingway's "fourth dimension," which has been defined by [critic] Joseph Warren Beach as an "aesthetic factor" achieved by the protagonists' repeated participation in some traditional "ritual or strategy," and by [critic] Malcolm Cowley as "the almost continual performance of rites and ceremonies" suggesting recurrent patterns of human experience. The incremental motifs of symbol, action, and language which inform *Of Mice and Men* have precisely these effects. The simple story of two migrant workers' dream of a safe retreat, a "clean well-lighted place," becomes itself a pattern or archetype which exists on three levels.

There is the obvious story level on a realistic plane, with its shocking climax. There is also the level of social protest, Steinbeck the reformer crying out against the exploitation of migrant workers. The third level is an allegorical one, its interpretation limited only by the ingenuity of the audience. It could be, as [critic] Carlos Baker suggests, "an allegory of Mind and Body." Using the same kind of dichotomy, the story could also be about the dumb, clumsy, but strong mass of humanity and its shrewd manipulators. This would make the book a more abstract treatment of the two forces of *In Dubious Battle*—the mob and its leaders. The dichotomy could also be that of the unconscious and the conscious, the id and the ego, or any other forces or qualities which have the same structural relationship to each other that do Lennie and George. It is interesting in this connection that the name Leonard means "strong or brave as a lion," and that the name George means "husbandman."

The title itself, however, relates the whole story to still another level which is implicit in the context of [Scottish poet Robert] Burns's poem.

> But, Mousie, thou art no thy lane,
> In proving foresight may be vain:
> The best laid schemes o' mice an' men
>   Gang aft a-gley
> An' lea'e us nought but grief an' pain
>   For promis'd joy.

In the poem, Burns extends the mouse's experience to include that of mankind; in *Of Mice and Men*, Steinbeck extends the experience of two migrant workers to the human condition. "This is the way things are," both writers are saying. On this level, perhaps the most important, Steinbeck is dramatizing the non-teleological [not determined by nature] philosophy which had such a great part in shaping *In Dubious Battle* and which would be fully discussed in *Sea of Cortez*. This level of mean-

ing is indicated by the title originally intended for the book—
"Something That Happened." In this light, the ending of the
story is, like the ploughman's disrupting of the mouse's nest [in
Robert Burns's poem], neither tragic nor brutal, but simply a
part of the pattern of events. It is amusing in this regard that a
Hollywood director suggested to Steinbeck that someone else
kill the girl, so that sympathy could be kept with Lennie.

A DEFINING SUBPLOT

In addition to these meanings which grow out of the book's
"pattern," there is what might be termed a subplot which
defines George's concern with Lennie. It is easily perceived
that George, the "husbandman," is necessary to Lennie; but it
has not been pointed out that Lennie is just as necessary to
George. Without an explanation of this latter relationship, any
allegory posited on the pattern created in *Of Mice and Men*
must remain incomplete. Repeatedly, George tells Lennie,
"God, you're a lot of trouble. I could get along so easy and so
nice if I didn't have you on my tail." But this getting along so
easy never means getting a farm of his own. With one important exception, George never mentions the dream except for
Lennie's benefit. That his own "dream" is quite different from
Lennie's is established early in the novel and often repeated:
"God a'mighty, if I was alone I could live so easy. I could go get
a job an' work, an' no trouble. No mess at all, and when the end
of the month come I could take my fifty bucks and go into town
and get whatever I want. Why, I could stay in a cat house all
night. I could eat any place I want, hotel or anyplace, and order
any damn thing I could think of. An' I could do all that every
damn month. Get a gallon whiskey, or set in a pool room and
play cards or shoot pool." Lennie has heard this from George
so often that in the last scene, when he realizes that he has
"done another bad thing," he asks, "Ain't you gonna give me
hell? . . . Like, 'If I didn't have you I'd take my fifty bucks—'."
    Almost every character in the story asks George why he goes
around with Lennie—the foreman, Curley, Slim, and Candy.
Crooks, the lonely Negro, doesn't ask George, but he does speculate about it, and shrewdly—"a guy talkin' to another guy and
it don't make no difference if he don't hear or understand. The
thing is, they're talkin'. . . ." George's explanations vary from
outright lies to a simple statement of "We travel together." It is
only to Slim, the superior workman with "God-like eyes," that
he tells a great part of the truth. Among several reasons, such
as his feeling of responsibility for Lennie in return for the lat-

ter's unfailing loyalty, and their having grown up together, there is revealed another: "He's dumb as hell, but he ain't crazy. An' I ain't so bright neither, or I wouldn't be buckin' barley for my fifty and found. If I was even a little bit smart, I'd have my own little place, an' I'd be bringin' in my own crops, 'stead of doin' all the work and not getting what comes up outa the ground."

This statement, together with George's repeatedly expressed desire to take his fifty bucks to a cat house and his continual playing of solitaire, reveals that to some extent George needs Lennie as a rationalization for his failure. This is one of the reasons why, after the body of Curley's wife is discovered, George refuses Candy's offer of a partnership which would make the dream a reality and says to him, "I'll work my month an' I'll take my fifty bucks an' I'll stay all night in some lousy cat house. Or I'll set in some poolroom till ever'body goes home. An' then I'll come back an' work another month an' I'll have fifty bucks more." The dream of the farm originates with Lennie and it is only through Lennie, who also makes the dream impossible, that the dream has any meaning for George. An understanding of this dual relationship will do much to mitigate the frequent charge that Steinbeck's depiction of George's attachment is concocted of pure sentimentality. At the end of the novel, George's going off with Slim to "do the town" is more than an escape from grief. It is an ironic and symbolic twist to his dream.

The "real" meaning of the book is neither in the realistic action nor in the levels of allegory. Nor is it in some middle course. Rather, it is in the pattern which informs the story both on the realistic and the allegorical levels, a pattern which Steinbeck took pains to prevent from becoming either trite or mechanical.

But whether because of its realism, its allegory, or its pattern, *Of Mice and Men* was an immediate popular success. It appeared on best-seller lists, was a Book-of-the-Month Club selection, and was sold to Hollywood. This financial success made it possible for Steinbeck to do some traveling.

Of Mice and Men: A Knight Dismounted and a Dream Ended

Warren French

Warren French analyzes *Of Mice and Men* as a novel in the tradition of Arthurian legends, the last of John Steinbeck's works in that tradition. Like the legendary knights, George is loyal and pure. But romance falters in the world of a ranch and a bunkhouse. With Lennie's death, George gives up his quest for a farm of his own and faces his own shortcomings and mediocrity. George is no longer a knight on a quest for an ideal, but, French says, he is nonetheless a hero simply because he survives.

Of Mice and Men marks the end of the first period in Steinbeck's literary career in several ways. First, this was the work that brought him at last really impressive national recognition and substantial reward and thus brought him face to face with the problems of a man in the limelight. Like Danny in *Tortilla Flat*, Steinbeck had achieved a position from which there was no turning back. Secondly, *Of Mice and Men* is the book in which Steinbeck found at last the form he had been struggling for—the method of objective storytelling which is really a fictionalized play. All of Steinbeck's novels had contained extraneous material (like the "Caporal" episode in *Tortilla Flat*, in which the *paisanos* expressed out-of-character views). The short stories to be collected into *The Red Pony* perfectly blended form and content, but it was not until *Of Mice and Men* that Steinbeck achieved the same structural soundness in a complex narrative.

Thirdly, in this novel Steinbeck at last discovered how to present the point underlying *Cup of Gold* in a convincing, contemporary setting. Behind the piratical trappings of the first novel stalked the ironic perception that maturity means the destruction of dreams. Other dreamers had learned this lesson in Steinbeck's novels; but Henry Morgan had been the only Steinbeck hero to survive his disillusionment. George in *Of Mice and Men* is the first contemporary figure in a Steinbeck novel to "split" before the onslaught of civilization rather than go under. Steinbeck had at last found the figure that could disentangle the grail quest from the mists of legend and make its futility explicit in down-to-earth terms.

INFLUENCE OF THE ARTHURIAN LEGEND

Of Mice and Men is Steinbeck's last novel to be directly influenced by Arthurian legend. In *The Grapes of Wrath*, the writer turns to Biblical-traditions for his analogues. This change makes his allegories more generally comprehensible because of the wide familiarity with Biblical imagery. There is an "ivory tower" quality about even Steinbeck's most realistic novels before *The Grapes of Wrath*; and it was probably his months of living among the migrants that enabled him to shake off the lingering effects of the—to American eyes—somewhat remote myths that had long provided the framework for his novels.

Although other critics have not noted to what extent *Of Mice and Men* is an Arthurian story, the fundamental parallels—the knightly loyalty, the pursuit of the vision, the creation of a bond (shared briefly by Candy and Crooks), and its destruction by an at least potentially adulterous relationship—are there. They are, however, so concealed by the surface realism of the work that one unfamiliar with Steinbeck's previous Arthurian experiments would be hardly likely to notice them. The one obvious Arthurian hangover is George, who is not only remarkably loyal to his charge—the feeble-minded Lennie—but also remarkably pure.

George not only warns Lennie against the blandishments of Curley's wife, but is himself obviously impervious to her charms. While the other ranch hands are excited by her presence, George says only, "Jesus, what a tramp!" When invited to join the boys in a Saturday night trip to a neighboring town's "nice" whorehouse, George says that he "might go in an' set and have a shot," but "ain't puttin' out no two and a half." He excuses himself on the ground that he is saving money to buy a farm, but not even Galahad might have found it politic to profess chastity in a bunkhouse. George seems to have stepped, in fact, not out of [British writer Sir Thomas] Malory's

Arthurian stories but [British writer Alfred Lord] Tennyson's. When he is told that Curley boasts of having his glove full of Vaseline in order to keep his hand soft for his wife, George says, "That's a dirty thing to tell around."

George is noticeably more critical of Curley's wife than Steinbeck is. *Of Mice and Men* is not so completely objective as *In Dubious Battle*; Steinbeck editorializes occasionally, for example, after the girl has been killed:

> ... the meanness and the plannings and the discontent and the ache for attention were all gone from her face. She was very pretty and simple, and her face was sweet and young.

George shows no such sympathy, and it is important to notice that the author is more flexible than his character, because it is a sign that he is not being carried away by his vision as are the characters sometimes assumed to represent his viewpoint. The Arthurian flavor here is faint, but unmistakable. Like Jim Nolan [in *In Dubious Battle*], George is a last Galahad, dismounted, armed only with a fading dream, a long way from Camelot. Steinbeck is his historian, not his alter ego.

One does not need to justify a search for an allegory in *Of Mice and Men* since the author has spoken of the book as symbolic and microcosmic. Just what the universal drama enacted against a Salinas Valley backdrop may be is not, however, so obvious as first appears. Unquestionably it concerns a knight of low estate and a protégé who share a dream, a dream that cannot come true because the protégé lacks the mental capacity to be conscious enough to know his own strength or to protect himself from temptation.

At first glance, it appears that nature is the culprit and that this is an ironic, deterministic fable like Stephen Crane's "The Open Boat." It is an indifferent nature that makes men physically strong but mentally deficient; dreaming is man's only defense against a world he never made. "The best-laid schemes o' mice an' men gang aft a-gley," [Scottish poet Robert] Burns said, providing Steinbeck with a title, because man is at the mercy of forces he cannot control which ruthlessly but indifferently destroy the illusions he has manufactured. The book may be read in this naturalistic manner, and those who speak of it as sentimental must think of it as an expression of Steinbeck's outraged compassion for the victims of chaotic forces.

GEORGE'S WILL AND MOTIVES

Such a reading, however, does not do the story justice. If George stood helplessly by and saw Lennie destroyed, the novel might be called deterministic; but he doesn't. George has a will, and he exercises it to make two critical decisions at the end of the novel—to kill Lennie and to lie about it.

THE SUCCESS OF *OF MICE AND MEN*

Both the novel and the play versions of Of Mice and Men *were published in 1937. Both were highly successful. In spite of success, however, John Steinbeck experienced a difficult time in 1938. The year included a family death, discouragement over the continued plight of migrant workers, and his own self-doubts. Robert DeMott comments on the success and the doubt in the introduction to Steinbeck's* Working Days: The Journals of The Grapes of Wrath, 1938–1941.

The winter of 1938 was a period of intense activity and vexation for Steinbeck. . . .

Privately, Steinbeck was contending with the ironic fruits of his public success. Deeper yet, he struggled with the paralyzing fear that his talent was inadequate for the writing task at hand. His success had been honorably earned, but Steinbeck, ever his own harshest critic, remained unconvinced. In fact, self-denunciation became a repeated theme throughout the entire journal. His brilliant novella, *Of Mice and Men*, published by Covici-Friede a year earlier, had sold well over 120,000 copies, thanks in part to its being a Book-of-the-Month Club selection. More immediately, the play version (directed by George S. Kaufman, and starring Wallace Ford, Broderick Crawford, and Clare Luce), which had opened at New York's Music Box Theatre on November 23, 1937, was still packing the house three months later. It eventually ran for 207 performances and won, that April, the prestigious New York Drama Circle Critics' Award.

Robert DeMott, ed., Commentary to John Steinbeck, *Working Days: The Journals of The Grapes of Wrath, 1938–1941.* New York: Viking Penguin Inc., 1989.

George could, of course, have killed Lennie simply to protect the giant brute from the mob; but, since Lennie doesn't know what is going on anyway, it is easy to oversentimentalize George's motives. Actually he has reasons of his own for pulling the trigger. Steinbeck makes it clear that George had tremendous difficulty bringing himself to destroy Lennie, although Lennie will not even know what has happened. What George is actually trying to kill is not Lennie, who is only a shell and a doomed one at that, but something in himself.

Peter Lisca points out that Lennie's need for George is obvious, but that George's need for Lennie, though less obvious, is as great. In his most candid appraisal of himself, George says, "I ain't so bright neither, or I wouldn't be buckin' barley for my fifty and found. If I was even a little bit smart, I'd have my own little place...." He needs him, however, as more than just a rationalization for his own failure; for George not only protects but *directs* Lennie. Lennie doesn't speak unless George permits him to; and, in the fight in which Curley's hand is broken, Lennie refuses even to defend himself until George tells him to. George, of course, directs Lennie partly to protect him from committing acts he could not mentally be responsible for, but George is not a wholly altruistic shepherd. Another aspect of the relationship becomes apparent when George tells Slim that Lennie, "Can't think of nothing to do himself, but he sure can take orders." Since George gives the orders, Lennie gives him a sense of power.

One aspect of the dream that George repeatedly describes to Lennie also needs scrutiny. The ritual ("George's voice became deeper. He repeated his words rhythmically.") begins "Guys like us, that work on ranches, are the loneliest guys in the world.... They ain't got nothing to look ahead to" and continues "with us it ain't like that ... because [here Lennie takes over from George] I got you to look after me, and you got me to look after you, and that's why." The dream not only gives a direction to their lives, but also makes them feel different from other people. Since this sense of difference can mean little to Lennie, it is part of the consolation George receives from the dream. George wants to be superior. With Lennie gone, his claim to distinction will be gone. Thus when George shoots Lennie, he is not destroying only the shared dream. He is also destroying the thing that makes him different and reducing himself to the status of an ordinary guy. He is obliged to acknowledge what Willy Loman in Arthur Miller's *Death of a Salesman*, for example, could never acknowledge but what Henry Morgan accepted when he turned respectable in *Cup of Gold*—his own mediocrity. George is much like Willy Loman; for he is forced to recognize the same self-deflating realization Biff Loman vainly tries to impress upon his father: he is a "dime a dozen." Because of their relationship, George has actually been able to remain as much a "kid" as Lennie; shooting him matures George in more than one way.

GEORGE'S ACCEPTANCE OF REALITY

It is equally important that George lies to the posse after the shooting. If the experience had not matured him, he had here his opportunity for a grand gesture. He could either destroy himself along with Lennie and the dream or, by an impassioned confession, force his enemies to destroy him. George, who by Romantic standards has little left to live for, chooses to go on living and to say that he had to shoot Lennie in self-defense. Actually the maturing effect of the experience upon George has been apparent from the moment when, in reply to Candy's offer to help him carry out the dream, he says: "—I think I knowed from the very first. I think I know'd we'd never do her. He usta like to hear about it so much I got to thinking maybe we would." With Lennie gone George will not try to keep the dream alive. When Slim leads George up toward the highway at the end of the novel, the wonder is not that George is badly shaken by his experience, but that he is alive at all.

Despite the grim events it chronicles *Of Mice and Men* is not a tragedy, but a comedy—which, if it were Shakespearean, we would call a "dark comedy"—about the triumph of the indomitable will to survive. This is a story not of man's defeat at the hands of an implacable nature, but of man's painful conquest of this nature and of his difficult, conscious rejection of his dreams of greatness and acceptance of his own mediocrity. Unfortunately, the allegory is less clear in the play version than in the novel, since Steinbeck, probably to provide a more effective curtain, eliminates George's last conversation with Slim and ends with the shooting of Lennie. The original ending would also probably have been too involved for playgoers to follow after experiencing the emotions engendered by the climactic episodes.

Lennie has been viewed sometimes as an example of Steinbeck's preoccupation with subhuman types; actually Lennie is not a character in the story at all, but rather a device like a golden coin in *Moby Dick* to which the other characters may react in a way that allows the reader to perceive their attitudes. So intensely focused upon the relationship between George and Lennie is the novel that the other characters are likely to be overlooked; yet each makes an important contribution to the narrative and provides a clue to Steinbeck's conception of the human condition.

THE CONTRIBUTIONS OF THE MINOR CHARACTERS

The protest against racial discrimination and the treatment of the aged through the characters of Crooks and Candy needs no elaboration. The symbolism of Curley and his ill-fated bride is perhaps summed up in her statement that they married after she "met him out to Riverside Dance Palace that same night." There is a sordid echo of [writer F. Scott] Fitzgerald and the "lost generation" here; for, like the Buchanans in *The Great Gatsby*, these are "careless people" who smash up things and "let other people clean up the mess." It is true that the girl is smashed up herself, but, unlike Curley, she did have dreams and disappointments. He simply, like the Buchanans, retreats into his "vast carelessness." The wife, not George, is the one in the novel who is destroyed when, instead of controlling her dreams, she allows them to control her; and Curley, not Lennie, is actually the willfully animalistic type.

The most interesting characters—except for George and Lennie are Carlson and Slim, two other ranch hands, who have the last words in the novel. They are complements, symbolizing, on one hand, the insensitive and brutal; on the other, the kindly and perceptive. "Now what the hell ya suppose is eatin' them two guys?" are Carlson's words—the last in the book—as Slim and George sadly walk off for a drink. Undoubtedly this sums up Steinbeck's concept of an unperceptive world's reaction to the drama just enacted. The uncomprehending responses to his books had given Steinbeck sufficient grounds for being aware of this "practical" attitude and through Carlson he strikes back at the men to whom Doctor Burton in *In Dubious Battle* attributes the world's "wild-eyed confusion." But Steinbeck also suggests that such men have the last word.

This bitterly ironic view is expressed through the major incident involving Carlson: the shooting of Candy's old dog. All Carlson can see about the dog is that "he don't have no fun . . . and he stinks to beat hell." He has no feelings about the animal, and, because his reactions are entirely physical, no concept that anyone else might have feelings about it. He is the same kind of man as the agitators Steinbeck condemned in *In Dubious Battle*—insensitive, violent, fanatical. This "practical" man's only contributions to the group are destructive.

To balance this destructive force, Steinbeck introduces and awards the next-to-last word to the jerkline skinner, Slim, the man who alone understands and tries to comfort George at the end of the novel. Steinbeck breaks his editorial silence, as he does in speaking of Curley's wife, to make it absolutely clear to the reader how Slim is to be regarded. "His ear heard more than was said to him," the author writes, "and his slow speech had overtones not of thought, but of understanding beyond thought." "His authority," the reader is told, "was so great that his word was taken on any subject, be it politics or love." What matters most, however, is the professional standing of this paragon:

> He moved with a majesty only achieved by royalty and master craftsmen. He was a jerkline skinner, capable of driving ten, sixteen, even twenty mules with a single line to the leaders. He was capable of killing a fly on the wheeler's butt with a bull whip without touching the mule.

The important thing about this passage is the emphasis placed upon skill and craftsmanship; here is the really "practical" man—not the callous boor, but the man who is able to do his job exceedingly well. We are to meet him again in *Cannery Row* and *The Wayward Bus*. It is notable that he is not a dreamer, but a doer. In another editorial aside that sets the tone for the whole book, Steinbeck points out that among other things with which the shelves where the ranch hands kept their personal belongings were loaded were "those Western magazines ranch men love to read and scoff at and secretly believe." Underneath the surface most men are not only dreamers, but unsuccessful dreamers; the real heroes are not these dreamers, but the doers. The heroic "doers," however, are not those who act only for personal aggrandizement, but those who try to do their best out of an affection for their craft and who feel compassionate rather than scornful toward the dreamers. With *Of Mice and Men*, Steinbeck himself unmistakably joins this class of craftsmen, for he not only shows compassion for the plight of the dreamer, but he accomplishes in the manner of a master craftsman his intention to sort out and evaluate the categories of men. Having mastered his craft, he was ready to execute his masterpiece.

Christian Symbolism in *The Grapes of Wrath*

Martin Shockley

Martin Shockley disagrees with two prominent
Christians and builds a case for the presence of
Christian symbols in John Steinbeck's *The Grapes of
Wrath*. Shockley argues that the novel contains lan-
guage, events, and characters that relate closely with
Christian theology and literature. Specifically, he con-
tends that the words and actions of Jim Casy parallel
in many ways the words and actions of Jesus Christ.
Moreover, he says that Tom Joad, Casy's follower, acts
like one of Jesus' twelve disciples. The novel's
Christian philosophy, according to Shockley, is, however, less like church doctrine and more like a direct
illustration of Jesus' words and acts. It is more like
Unitarianism and the transcendentalist philosophy of
Ralph Waldo Emerson and Walt Whitman than it is
like strict Protestantism.

In their recent study (*Saturday Review*, 1954) of the Christ-
symbol in modern fiction, novelist Alan Paton and theologian
Liston Pope dismiss Jim Casy because their reaction to him
"is essentially one of pathos rather than of awe." I hesitate to
disagree with two such eminent Christians, but I do disagree.
I propose an interpretation of *The Grapes of Wrath* in which
Casy represents a contemporary adaptation of the Christ
image, and in which the meaning of the book is revealed
through a sequence of Christian symbols.

STEINBECK'S USE OF CHRISTIAN IDEAS AND LANGUAGE

Before and after *The Grapes of Wrath* Steinbeck has used symbolism and allegory; throughout his work he has considered a
wide range of Christian or neo-Christian ideas; in relation to
the context of his fiction as a whole, Christian symbolism is

Martin Shockley, "Christian Symbolism in *The Grapes of Wrath*," *College English*,
November 1956.

common. His use of Biblical names, for instance, is an inviting topic yet to be investigated. *The Pearl* is an obvious allegory on the evil of worldly treasure. The Pirate in *Tortilla Flat* exemplifies a Steinbeck character type, pure in heart, simple in mind, rejected of men, clearly of the kingdom of heaven. More pertinent perhaps, the title of *The Grapes of Wrath* is itself a direct Christian allusion, suggesting the glory of the coming of the Lord, revealing that the story exists in Christian context, indicating that we should expect to find some Christian meaning.

It has, indeed, been found before. [In *College English*, 1941,] Frederic I. Carpenter has pointed out the relationship of the Joad philosophy to the Unitarian, transcendental pantheism of [American writers Ralph Waldo] Emerson and [Walt] Whitman. I would not deny that Casy preaches the gospel according to Saint Walt; but I find further, stronger, more direct relations to the Bible.

Consider first the language of the novel. Major characters speak a language that has been associated with debased Piedmont culture. It is, I suggest, easy to find in vocabulary, rhythm, imagery, and tone pronounced similarities to the language of the King James Bible. These similarities, to be seen in qualities of simplicity, purity, strength, vigor, earnestness, are easy to illustrate. The novel contains passages of moving tenderness and prophetic power, not alone in dialogue, but even in descriptive and expository passages.

Like the Israelites, the Joads are a homeless and persecuted people. They too flee from oppression, wander through a wilderness of hardships, seeking their own Promised Land. Unlike the Israelites, however, the Joads never find it.

JIM CASY AS A SYMBOL OF JESUS CHRIST

More specifically, let us examine the Christ-Casy relationship. Jesus began his mission after a period of withdrawal into the wilderness for meditation and consecration; Preacher Casy comes into the book after a similar retreat. He tells Tom "I went off alone, an' I sat and figured." Later when Casy and Tom meet in the strikers' tent, Casy says he has "been a-goin' into the wilderness like Jesus to try to find out sumpin." Certainly Steinbeck is conscious of the parallel.

Much has been made of Jim Conklin's name as a key to his identification in the symbolism of *The Red Badge of Courage*. Whether Steinbeck copied [Stephen] Crane is immaterial; Jim Casy is by the same initials identified with Jesus Christ. Like Jesus, Jim has rejected an old religion and is in process of replacing it with a new gospel. In the introductory scene with Tom Joad, Tom and Jim recall the old days when Casy

---

JOHN STEINBECK'S NEW VERSION OF AN OLD IDEAL

The ideal of the individual developed with America and has been expressed both in the Protestant tradition and in transcendentalism. In American Literature and the Dream, *Frederic I. Carpenter explains how John Steinbeck modified the old ideal from "I" to "we" in* The Grapes of Wrath.

So Ma Joad counsels the discouraged Tom: "Why, Tom, we're the people that live. They ain't gonna wipe us out. Why, we're the people—we go on." And so Steinbeck himself affirms a final faith in progress: "When theories change and crash, when schools, philosophies . . . grow and disintegrate, man reaches, stumbles forward. . . . Having stepped forward, he may slip back, but only half a step, never the full step back." Whether this be democratic faith, or mere transcendental optimism, it has always been the motive force of our American life and finds reaffirmation in this novel.

Upon the foundation of this old American idealism Steinbeck has built. But the Emersonian oversoul had seemed very vague and very ineffective—only the individual had been real, and he had been concerned more with his private soul than with other people. *The Grapes of Wrath* develops the old idea in new ways. It traces the transformation of the Protestant individual into the member of a social group—the old "I" becomes "we." And it traces the transformation of the passive individual into the active participant—the idealist becomes pragmatist. The first development continues the poetic thought of Walt Whitman; the second continues the philosophy of [American writers] William James and John Dewey.

"One's-self I sing, a simple separate person," [American poet Walt] Whitman had proclaimed. "Yet utter the word Democratic, the word En-Masse." Other American writers had emphasized the individual above the group. Even Whitman celebrated his "comrades and lovers" in an essentially personal relationship. But Steinbeck now emphasizes the group above the individual and from an impersonal point of view. Where formerly American and Protestant thought has been separatist, Steinbeck now faces the problem of social integration. In his novel the "mutually repellent particles" of individualism begin to cohere.

"This is the beginning," he writes, "from 'I' to 'we.'" This is the beginning, that is, of reconstruction.

Frederic I. Carpenter, *American Literature and the Dream.* New York: Philosophical Library, 1955.

---

preached the old religion, expounded the old concept of sin and guilt. Now, however, Casy explains his rejection of a religion through which he saw himself as wicked and depraved because of the satisfaction of natural human desires. The old Adam of the fall is about to be exorcised through the new dispensation.

It should not be necessary to point out that Jim Casy's religion is innocent of Paulism [the religion of the apostle Paul of the New Testament], of Catholicism, of Puritanism. He is identified simply and directly with Christ, and his words paraphrase the words of Jesus, who said, "God is love," and "A new commandment give I unto you: that ye love one another." Casy says, "What's this call, this sperit? . . . It's love. I love people so much I'm fit to bust sometimes." This is the truth Casy has found in his wilderness, the gospel he brings back to the people he loves.

Beyond this simple, central doctrine, identical and cardinal to Jesus and to Jim, there is the Emerson-Whitman-Unitarian-pantheism which Professor Carpenter notes. Jim elaborates: "There ain't no sin and there ain't no virtue. There's just stuff people do. It's all part of the same thing." I would avoid theological subtleties; I see Jim Casy as a simple and direct copy of Jesus Christ. Yet Casy's doctrine, "all that lives is holy," comes close to the doctrine of one of the most distinguished Christian theologians of our time, [the Frenchman] Albert Schweitzer, whose famous and familiar phrasing of the same concept is known to us as "reverence for life."

The third article of Casy's faith is a related one: " 'Maybe,' I figgered, 'Maybe it's all men and women we love; maybe that's the Holy Sperit—the human sperit—the whole shebang. Maybe all men got one big soul ever'body's a part of.' Now I sat there thinking it, an' all of a suddent—I knew it. I knew it so deep down that it was true and I still know it." Casy's knowledge of the oversoul is derived from the same source as Emerson's and Whitman's—from within himself, or if you prefer, from God speaking within him.

Jim realizes, as did Jesus, that organized religion will reject his new teaching. Tom points this out: "You can't hold no church with idears like that," he said. "People would drive you out of the country with idears like that." In both cases, people make the rejection.

I should like to go on from this formulation of a creed to the expression of doctrine through deeds, to the unfolding of the incidents of the plot in which Jim Casy reveals himself through significant, symbolic acts.

JIM CASY'S CHRISTIAN ACTS

First, he feels a compulsion to minister, to serve, to offer himself. When the Joads are preparing to leave for California, he tells them: "I got to go . . . I can't stay here no more. I got to go where the folks is goin'." Not long afterward, Casy offers himself as the sacrifice to save his people. When Tom is about to be arrested, Casy tells the police that he is the guilty one. "'It was me, all right . . . I'll go 'thout no trouble.'" So the Joads escape the consequences of their transgressions. "Between his guards Casy sat proudly, his head up and the stringy muscles of his neck prominent. On his lips there was a faint smile and on his face a curious look of conquest." Jim Casy had taken upon himself the sins of others.

Casy's death symbolically occurs in the middle of a stream to represent the "crossing over Jordan" Christian motif. Particularly significant, however, are Casy's last words directed to the man who murders him, "Listen," he said, "You fellas don' know what you're doin'." And again, just before the heavy man swings the pick handle Casy repeats, "You don' know what you're a-doin'." Jesus said, as they crucified Him, "Father forgive them; they know not what they do."

TOM THE DISCIPLE

One of the major emotional climaxes of the novel is the scene in which Tom tells Ma goodbye and explains why he must leave. He has told Ma about Casy, who "Spouted out some Scripture once, an' it didn' soun' like no hellfire Scripture." He goes on to repeat what Casy told him about two being better than one. He rehearses Casy's teaching about the individual and the collective soul [based on Ralph Waldo Emerson's essay "The Oversoul"], recalling that Casy went into the wilderness to find his soul, then found, "His little piece of a soul wasn't no good 'less it was with the rest, an' was whole." He explains to Ma Casy's theory of Christian Socialism. "'Tom,' Ma repeated, 'What you gonna do?' 'What Casy done,' he said." At this point Tom becomes Casy's disciple. He has learned from his master, and now he takes up his master's work. Two of Jesus' disciples were named Thomas. Most of those chosen by Him to found the religion we profess were called from among people like the Joads.

Tom's answer to Ma's worry lest he lose his life is the answer he has learned from Casy.

Then it don' matter. Then I'll be all aroun' in the dark. I'll be ever'where—wherever you look. Wherever they's a fight so hungry people can eat, I'll be there. Wherever they's a cop beatin' up a guy, I'll be there. If Casy knowed, why, I'll be in the way kids laugh when they're hungry an' they know supper's ready. An' when our folks eat the stuff they raise an' live in the houses they build—why I'll be there. See? God, I'm talkin' like Casy.

The One that Casy talked like said, "Lo, I am with you always."

These evidences of a Christ-Casy relationship mean more to me than they do to Mr. Paton and Dean Pope. I would not argue that Steinbeck's interpretation of the relationship of pathos and awe in the Christian tradition is identical with the interpretation of Paton and Pope, nor that his interpretation is more or less correct than theirs. Nevertheless, I find in the novel what seems to me to be adequate evidence to establish the author's intention of creating in Jim Casy a character who would be understood in terms of the Christ symbol.

DEATH AND RESURRECTION IN ROSASHARN

Beyond this personal identification, I find further use of Christian symbols. The conclusion of *The Grapes of Wrath* has been said to be extreme, sensational, overwrought. The Joads have reached at last a condition of utter desolation. Rosasharn, her baby born dead, is rain-drenched, weak, her breasts heavy with milk. In the barn they come upon a boy and a starving old man, too weak to eat the bread his son had stolen for him. Ma knows what must be done, but the decision is Rosasharn's: "Ma's eyes passed Rose of Sharon's eyes, and then came back to them. And the two women looked deep into each other. The girl's breath came short and gasping.

"She said, 'Yes.'"

In this, her Gethsemane, Rosasharn says, in effect: "Not my will, but Thine be done."

The meaning of this incident, Steinbeck's final paragraph, is clear in terms of Christian symbolism. And this is the supreme symbol of the Christian religion, commemorated by Protestants in the Communion, by Catholics in the Mass. Rosasharn gives what Christ gave, what we receive in memory of Him. The ultimate mystery of the Christian religion is realized as Rosasharn "Looked up and across the barn, and her lips came together and smiled mysteriously." She smiles mysteriously because what has been mystery is now knowledge. *This is my body*, says Rosasharn, and becomes the Resurrection and the Life. Rose of Sharon, the life-giver, symbolizes the resurrective aspect of Christ, common in Christian tradition and literature, used by [poet T.S.] Eliot in his "multifoliate rose" image. In her, death and life are one, and through her, life triumphs over death.

Cited incidents occur at points of major importance in plot and action, accompany major emotional crises, and relate to the major and most familiar examples of Christian symbolism. Other less obvious examples might be brought in, such as the incident at the roadside cafe where the waitress lets the migrant have a loaf of bread and is immediately rewarded by large and unexpected tips from the two truck drivers: she had cast her bread upon the waters. In a recent issue of the *Colorado Quarterly* (1954) Bernard Bowron notes Noah's wandering off down the stream as possibly "a biblical association." I would not, however, try to press my point further; major examples are enough.

Certain of these symbols may be identified as pre-Christian. The motif of crossing water in death is, of course, widespread in folklore; and the Freudian, totemistic interpretation of the miracle of transubstantiation lies in the background. It is not within the scope of this paper to explore these labyrinthine shadows. Suffice it to say that we recognize in Christianity elements of older religions. Further, it is easy to identify elements of Steinbeck's ideology with other religions. For example, the principle of reverence for life, or "all that lives is holy," has been believed and practiced for centuries by Buddhists.

Such, however, I regard as incidental. In *The Grapes of Wrath* the major intended meaning is neither Buddhist nor Freudian nor Marxist; it is, I believe, essentially and thoroughly Christian. In my interpretation, Jim Casy unmistakably and significantly is equated with Jesus Christ. [In the April 1954 issue of *The Annotator*, mimeographed house-organ of Purdue's English Department, "H.B." (Professor Howard Burton, I assume) lists "Biblical Analogies in *The Grapes of Wrath*" taken from term papers submitted by Barbara Hyland and John Hallett. Together they cite seven "Biblical Analogies," including "stylistic parallels," "attitude toward the rich," "Casy and Christ," "the wanderings of the children of Israel [and] . . . the migrants seeking California as a promised land," "Tom's return from McAlester [as] . . . the Prodigal Son." The most interesting analogy in relation to my purpose in this paper is the suggestion of a halo for Casy: "As Casy and Tom approach Uncle John's house, the morning sun lights Casy's brow—but not Tom's. And just before Casy is killed, an attacker says, 'That's him. Its that shiny one.'" Professor Burton's note was called to my attention after this paper was accepted for publication.]

Artistic and Thematic Structure in *The Grapes of Wrath*

J. P. Hunter

John Steinbeck came under heavy criticism after World War II; critics doubted the literary quality of *The Grapes of Wrath*, claiming it had been overrated when it was first published. J. P. Hunter disagrees and argues that *The Grapes of Wrath* has an artistic and thematic structure of merit. He shows how Steinbeck parallels a wide sweep of Judeo-Christian history with the journey of a single family, the Joads. The family transforms from a self-centered collection of individuals into a solidified and devoted group. Jim Casy, whose initials are the same as Jesus Christ's, leads the family to their changed attitudes. By the end of the book, after a dismal journey, the grapes have ripened into regenerated hope.

It has been about twenty-five years since John Steinbeck won the Drama Critics' Circle Award (1937) and the Pulitzer Prize (1939), and many of the critics who liked his work then have recently [in 1963] found little to praise. Since World War II, Steinbeck's new novels have received increasingly harsh reviews, and his critical reputation has declined steadily. Many of his most ardent admirers are now no longer confident that he will achieve the eminence once predicted for him, and some of them despair that he will ever do important work again. Now Steinbeck's decreasing stature seems to be reflected in another way—a growing tendency to find his later failures anticipated in his earlier work.

A few years ago it was popular to speculate on "what had happened" to Steinbeck. . . . An increasing number of critics seem to be turning to an answer given long ago by Steinbeck's

Excerpted from "Steinbeck's Wine of Affirmation in *The Grapes of Wrath*" by J.P. Hunter, in *Essays in Modern American Literature*, edited by Richard E. Langford, Guy Owen, and William E. Taylor; © 1963 by Stetson University Press. Reprinted by permission of the Provost of Stetson University.

detractors: that no decline in fact exists, that Steinbeck's talents, in his earlier period, were simply overrated by those who believed in the causes Steinbeck championed.... Again (as when it first appeared) Steinbeck's work needs to be defended as art rather than sociology.

CRITICS CITE FAULTS IN *THE GRAPES OF WRATH*

Almost everyone agrees that *The Grapes of Wrath* is Steinbeck's most important early work, and it may well be that his critical reputation will ultimately stand or fall on that one book. Those who do not like the novel contend that it exemplifies Steinbeck's most blatant artistic weaknesses: lack of character development, imperfect conception of structure, careless working out of theme, and sentimentality. The last two chapters of the novel have been considered especially illustrative of these weaknesses, for they are said to demonstrate the final inability of Steinbeck to come to grips, except in a superficial way, with the ideological and artistic problems posed in the novel. The final scene has drawn the sharpest criticism of all, for here Steinbeck is charged with a sensational, shocking, and therefore commercial substitute for an artistic solution. The charges are not new ones, but they have a peculiar urgency at a time when the reputation of Steinbeck's early work is in danger of eclipse. And they constitute a basal attack on Steinbeck as artist, for if it is true that his most important book is inadequately conceived and imperfectly worked out, Steinbeck's claim to a place among significant novelists is seriously impaired.

The inadequacy of the ending of *The Grapes of Wrath*, is, however, more apparent than real. When the events of the last two chapters (and particularly the final scene in the barn) are examined in relation to the novel's total structure, they demonstrate a careful working out of theme in fictional terms. At the end, the Joads who remain (only six of the original twelve) seem to have a grim physical future; as they hover in a dry barn while the deluge continues and the waters rise, they face the prospect of a workless winter in a hostile world. But even though their promised land has turned out to be "no lan' of milk and honey" but instead a battleground stained with the blood of Jim Casy, the Joads are at last able to come to grips with their world. Instead of idealists who dream of white houses and clusters of plenty they have become people of action who translate the prophecy of Jim Casy into the realities of wrath.

THE EARLY DELUDED JOADS

Under the old order in Oklahoma, the Joads were a proud people, individualists who asked nothing from anyone and who were content with their family-size world as long as they had a home surrounded by land which they could caress into fertility. Like the early Tom, they believed in "Just puttin' one foot in front a the other," and their thoughts did not stray beyond the limits of their families and their land. When the change comes, when early find themselves in captivity on land they have known as their own, and finally when the captor banks insult their dignity by driving them like nomads away from their homes, they do not understand the change, and they are helpless to oppose it. A few, like Muley Graves, may try, pitifully, to fight back with a sniper's bullet or a harassing laugh from parched fields, but the majority only know that the old is gone, and that they are powerless to fight against the new. As the dust covers the land and the burrowing machines cut their swath of progress through fields and houses, the men stand figuring in the dust, unbroken by events, but powerless to change them.

In their powerlessness, the Joads and their neighbors first choose the road of illusion, and they pursue their particular Western version of the American dream across Route 66. In their heads dance visions of plenty in California—their Canaan of the Golden West—but their map is an orange handbill, and soon their luxurious dreams of ripe fruit and white houses are changed to nightmares of hunger and Hoovervilles. Even in California, the Joads are merely individuals driven by forces they do not understand until, in wrath, they learn their lesson.

The lesson they learn forms the thematic base of *The Grapes of Wrath*, and although the Joads do not accept it fully until the end of the novel, the solution has been suggested quite early in the narrative. This theme—that strength can be achieved through a selfless unity of the entire community of Dispossessed—is first suggested when Tom and Jim Casy meet Muley Graves, a kind of mad prophet, on the old Joad place, and Muley is asked whether he will share his food. "I ain't got no choice in the matter," Muley says, then explains:

> "That ain't like I mean it. That ain't. I mean"—he stumbled— "what I mean, if a fella's got somepin to eat an' another fella's hungry—why, the first fella ain't got no choice. I mean, s'pose I pick up my rabbits an' go off somewheres an' eat 'em. See?"

> "I see," said Casy. "I can see that. Muley sees somepin there, Tom. Muley's got a-holt of somepin and it's too big for him, an' it's too big for me."

Though he still doesn't understand the concept fully, Casy has already incorporated Muley's prophetic wisdom into his own wilderness philosophy when, during his breakfast "grace" (two chapters later), he tells of his insights:

> I got thinkin' how . . . mankin' was holy when it was one thing. An' it on'y got unholy when one mis'able little fella got the bit in his teeth an' run off his own way, kickin' an' draggin' and fightin'. Fella like that bust the holiness. But when they're all workin' together, not one fella for another fella, but one fella kind of harnessed to the whole shebang—that's right, that's holy.

Later Casy develops the idea and translates it into action, ultimately even sacrificing himself for it. But at first he finds few hearers. At breakfast, Ma is the only one who seems to notice the unusual "prayer," and she watches Casy "as though he were suddenly a spirit, not human any more, a voice out of the ground." The other Joads listen to Casy, but they do not hear him for a long time.

CASY VIEWED AGAINST A BROAD BIBLICAL SWEEP

Casy's role is central to the structure of *The Grapes of Wrath*, for in him the narrative structure and the thematic structure are united. This role is best seen when set against the Biblical background which informs both types of structure in the novel. Peter Lisca has noted that the novel reflects the three-part division of the Old Testament exodus account (captivity, journey, promised land), but that the "parallel is not worked out in detail." Actually, the lack of detailed parallel seems to be deliberate, for Steinbeck is reflecting a broader background of which the exodus story is only a part.

Steinbeck makes the incidents in his novel suggest a wide range of Old and New Testament stories. As the twelve Joads (corresponding to the twelve tribes of Israel) embark on their journey (leaving the old order behind), they mount the truck in ark fashion, two by two:

> . . . the rest swarmed up on top of the load, Connie and Rose of Sharon, Pa and Uncle John, Ruthie and Winfield, Tom and the preacher. Noah stood on the ground looking up at the great load of them sitting on top of the truck.

Grampa (like Lot's wife) is unable to cope with the thought of a new life, and his wistful look at the past brings his death—a parallel emphasized by the scripture verse (quoting Lot) which Tom picks out to bury with Grampa. Uncle John (like Ananias) withholds money from the common fund, in order to satisfy his selfish desires. The list could be lengthened extensively,

THE TITLE, *THE GRAPES OF WRATH*

John Steinbeck's title The Grapes of Wrath *is a phrase used in earlier sources. Julia Ward Howe wrote in the "Battle Hymn of the Republic": "Mine eyes have seen the glory of the coming of the Lord/ He is trampling out the vintage where the grapes of wrath are stored." The reference dates back to the Old Testament of the Bible. In Isaiah 63, the author tells of a conversation with a man who comes from the distant Edom, a man who had trampled grapes in his wrath.*

1 "Who is this that comes from
         Edom,
     from Bozrah in garments
         stained crimson?
     Who is this so splendidly robed,
         marching in his great might?"
     "It is I, announcing vindication,
         mighty to save."
2 "Why are your robes red,
         and your garments like theirs
             who tread the wine press?"
3 "I have trodden the wine press
         alone,
     and from the peoples no one
         was with me;
     I trod them in my anger
         and trampled them in my
             wrath;
     their juice spattered on my
         garments,
     and stained all my robes.
4 For the day of vengeance was in
         my heart,
     and the year for my redeeming
         work had come.
5 I looked, but there was no helper;
     I stared, but there was no one
         to sustain me;
     so my own arm brought me
         victory,
     and my wrath sustained me.
6 I trampled down peoples in my
         anger,
     I crushed them in my wrath,
     and I poured out their lifeblood
         on the earth."

Bruce M. Metzger and Roland E. Murphy, eds., *The New Oxford Annotated Bible with the Apocryphal/Deuterocanonical Books.* New York: Oxford University Press, 1991.

and many allusions are as isolated and apparently unrelated to the context as the ones cited here. Looked at in one way, these allusions seem patternless, for they refer to widely separated sections of Biblical history. However, the frequency of allusion suggests the basic similarity between the plight of the Joads and that of the Hebrew people. Rather than paralleling a single section of Biblical history, the novel reflects the broader history of the chosen people from their physical bondage to their spiritual release by means of a messiah.

If the reader approaches *The Grapes of Wrath* searching for too exact a parallel, he will be disappointed, for just when it seems as if a one-to-one ratio exists, Steinbeck breaks the pattern. Tom, for example, is a Moses-type leader of his people as they journey toward the promised land. Like Moses, he has killed a man and has been away for a time before rejoining his people and becoming their leader. Like Moses, he has a younger brother (Aaron-Al) who serves as a vehicle for the leader (spokesman-truck driver). And shortly before reaching the destination, he hears and rejects the evil reports of those who have visited the land (Hebrew "spies"–Oklahomans going back). But soon the parallel ends. Carried out carefully at the beginning, it does not seem to exist once the journey is completed. Granma, not Tom, dies just before the new land is reached, and Tom remains the leader of the people until finally (and here a different parallel is suggested) he becomes a disciple of Casy's gospel. This, in the miniature of one character, is what continually happens in *The Grapes of Wrath*. The scene changes, the parallel breaks; and gradually the context shifts from a basically Old Testament one to a New Testament one.

STEINBECK'S SOLUTION TO THE PROBLEM OF TIME

Steinbeck makes his allusions suggestive, rather than exhaustive, and he implies certain parallels without calling for too rigid an allegorical reading.... In *The Grapes of Wrath*, the method gives Steinbeck the freedom to skirt the particularly vexing time problem, for in the background myth the changes in the Hebrew people take place over centuries, while similar ideological changes in Steinbeck's characters occur within one year. In effect, Steinbeck collapses several hundred years of Hebrew history into the single year of his story; the entire history of man (according to the Judeo-Christian tradition) is reflected in the long hungry summer of one persecuted family.

This span of centuries is focused in Casy, whose ideas bridge the gap from Old to New Testament (according to the

Christian concept of Biblical thought as developmental). Parallels between the life of Jim Casy and the messiah whose initials he bears are plentiful.... His conversion to a social gospel represents a movement from Old Testament to New Testament thought, an expanded horizon of responsibility. The annunciation of Casy's message and mission sets the ideological direction of the novel before the journey begins (just as the messiah concept influences Jewish thought for centuries before New Testament times), but only gradually does Casy make an impression upon a people (Jews-Joads) used to living under the old dispensation. Over Route 66 he rides quietly—a guest, a thirteenth—and only as time passes does the new idea blossom and the new order emerge; and the outsider—the thirteenth—becomes spiritual leader of a people to whom he had been a convention, a grace before meals.

PAINTING WITH A BROAD BRUSH

Steinbeck's canvas is, on the surface, a painting of broad modern strokes, but its scenes are sketched along the outlines of the Judeo-Christian myth, a sort of polyptych [having several variant forms] depicting man's sojourn in a hostile world. The background is often faded, sometimes erased, and occasionally distorted, but structurally and ideologically it provides depth for Steinbeck's modern microcosm. In *The Grapes of Wrath* the background ideology becomes secularized and transcendentalized, but the direction of thought is still recognizable: a widening of concern. After the dispersion, there is still a saving remnant whose compassion begins to extend beyond its own familial or tribal group.

Steinbeck's method is perhaps not uniformly successful, and in some work done in this manner (such as *East of Eden* and *Burning Bright*) the fusion of the particular and the mythic seems, if not less perfectly conceived, less carefully wrought. But in *The Grapes of Wrath* the modern and mythic are peculiarly at one, and the story of a family which, in the values of its contemporary society, is hardly worth a jot, is invested with meaning when viewed against a history of enduring significance. . . .

THE JOADS' LIMITED VIEW

Though the movement from "I" to "we" is imaged several times throughout *The Grapes of Wrath*, the Joads do not really commit themselves to the new mode of thought until very late in the novel. Before their belated commitment, they show their limited view in many ways. Al cannot understand the men's cooperation in job-hunting: "Wouldn' it be better," he asks, "if one fella went alone? Then if they was one piece of work a fella'd get it," and he is told:

> You ain't learned.... Takes gas to get roun' the country. Gas costs fifteen cents a gallon. Them four fellas can't take four cars. So each of 'em puts in a dime an' they get gas. You got to learn.

Rose of Sharon and Connie think only of themselves and of how they will break from the group, and when difficulties arise Connie wishes that he had stayed in Oklahoma to man a tractor driving the people from the land. Later, alone, Rose of Sharon complains of her plight and frets about the coming child, and instead of sharing the family responsibility she adds to family worries. Uncle John is similarly preoccupied with his guilt and his personal problems and is almost useless to the group, picking cotton at only half the rate of the other men. Both he and Al withhold money from the family treasury. Noah, thoughtless of the others, wanders away. Connie, leaving a pregnant wife, also deserts. Even the children show a teasing selfishness. Ruthie eats her crackerjacks slowly so that she can taunt the other children when theirs is gone, and at croquet she ignores the rules and tries to play by herself.

Even though Ma, Pa, and Tom are less individualistic than the others, their concern is limited to the family group. Ma's one aim is keeping the family together, and when she says "This here fambly's goin' under," she is lamenting the disintegration of her entire world. While not a dynamic leader, Pa does his best to fulfill his patriarchal responsibility. Tom shows that he values the family over himself by breaking parole to make the journey with them, and he frequently demonstrates his dedication to them. Once, Tom wishes he could act like Al, but he is unable to forget his responsibility. Ma describes him well: "Everything you do is more'n you," she says.

CONVERSION TO A WIDER VIEW

Conversion to a wider concern comes rapidly toward the end of *The Grapes of Wrath.* Tom is the first Joad to extend his vision. In wrath, he moves to commitment beside the broken body of Jim Casy. A few days later, when he meets Ma in the dark cave, his dedication is complete. By contrast with Muley Graves (whose womb-like cave is an escape, a place where he feels "like nobody can come at me,") Tom does not plan to stay in his refuge. He tells Ma of his meditations about Casy and recites a passage Casy had quoted from Ecclesiastes (The Preacher):

Two are better than one, because they have a good reward for
their labor. For if they fall, the one will lif' up his fellow, but woe
to him that is alone when he falleth, for he hath not another to
help him up. . . . Again, if two lie together, then they have heat;
but how can one be warm alone? And if one prevail against
him, two shall withstand him, and a three-fold cord is not
quickly broken.

Tom has to leave the family to protect them, but by now he also
has a more important reason. He has seen the folly of a narrow family devotion like that of tractor-driver Willy Feely
("Fust an' on'y thing I got to think about is my own folks. What
happens to other folks is their look-out.") and plans to work
for a cause transcending family lines:

"Tom," [Ma] said. "What you aimin' to do?"
He was quiet for a long time. . . .
"Tom," Ma repeated, "what you gonna do?"
"What Casy done," he said.

Ma does not fully comprehend Tom's intention, but she has
moved from a rigid defense of family unity during the journey
(refusing to allow the family to split into two parts: "All we got
is the family unbroke") to acceptance of new ideas in a new
order. And after she leaves Tom she is tempted to reach backward—she takes "three steps toward the mound of vines"—
but then quickly returns to the camp. Back in the boxcar, Pa
talks wistfully of the past times ("spen' all my time a thinkin'
how it use' ta be"), but Ma is acclimated to the difference now.
"This here's purtier—better lan'," says Ma. Women, she
observes, can adapt themselves to change. Earlier, before her
meeting with Tom, she had lamented the breakup of the family; now she has a broader perspective: "*People* is goin' on—
changin' a little maybe, but goin' right on." Later, she is even
more explicit. "Use ta be the fambly was fust. It ain't so now.
It's anybody."

At the time of the birth, the larger unity is demonstrated. Pa
(who had said earlier that he would work for twenty cents an
hour even if it cost someone else his job) suddenly becomes a
leader of men, conscious of the strength of organized effort:

"Water's risin'," he said. "How about if we threw up a bank?
We could do her if ever'body helped."

The dam is for the Joads, of course, but it is also for the others;
all the families face the same danger, and each can flee—
alone—or work together for their salvation, and they decide to
stay:

Over the men came a fury of work, a fury of battle. When one
man dropped his shovel, another took it up.

Uncle John, choosing between desertion and devotion, works so hard that Pa has to caution him: "You take it easy. You'll kill yaself." And later, asked to dispose of the baby's body, Uncle John hesitates, then accedes:

> "Why do I got to do it? Why don't you fellas? I don' like it." And then, "Sure. I'll do it. Sure, I will. Come on give it to me." His voice began to rise. "Come on! Give it to me."

Al, whose only concern had been a good time, also moves toward what is, for him, an acceptance of larger responsibility (marriage to Aggie). Even Ruthie, on a child level, shows a change. On the way to the barn, she refuses to share the petals of her flower with Winfield, and, commanded to share, cruelly jabs one petal on his nose; but in her childish way she also senses that times are different:

> Ruthie felt how the fun was gone. "Here," she said. "Here's some more. Stick some on your forehead."

And, then, in Rose of Sharon, the final change.

THE GRAPES RIPEN: A NEW ORDER IS AFFIRMED

Rose of Sharon's sacrificial act represents the final breakdown of old attitudes, and climaxes the novel's thematic movement. The final bastion of the old order, Rose of Sharon had been the most selfish of the remaining Joads; her concern had never extended beyond herself and her immediate family (Connie and the expected child). In giving life to the stranger (symbolically, she gives body and wine: Song of Songs 7:7—"Thy breasts [are like] to clusters of grapes"), she accepts the larger vision of Jim Casy, and her commitment fulfills the terms of salvation according to Casy's plan. In their hesitancy and confusion in the old times, the Joads had been powerless to change their fate. Unlike the turtle who dragged through the dust and planted the seeds of the future, they had drawn figures in the dust impotently with sticks. Now, however, they too are purposeful and share the secret of giving life.

The Biblical myth informs the final scene through a cluster of symbols which emphasize the change and affirm the new order. As the Joads hover in the one dry place in their world—a barn—the Bible's three major symbols of a purified order are suggested: the Old Testament deluge, the New Testament stable, and the continuing ritual of communion. In the fusion of the three, the novel's mythic background, ideological progression, and modern setting are brought together; Mt. Ararat, Bethlehem, and California are collapsed into a single unit of time, and life is affirmed in a massive symbol of regeneration.

The novel's final picture—a still life of Rose of Sharon holding the old man—combines the horror with the hope. Its imitation of the madonna and child (one face mysteriously smiling; the other wasted, and with wide, frightened eyes) is a grotesque one, for it reflects a grotesque world without painless answers, a world where men are hit by axe handles and children suffer from skitters. Steinbeck does not promise Paradise for the Joads. Their wildest dreams image not golden streets, but indoor plumbing. Dams will continue to break—babies will continue to be stillborn. But the people will go on: "this is the beginning—from 'I' to 'we.'" The grapes of wrath have ripened, and in trampling out the vintage the Dispossessed have committed themselves (like Casy) to die to make men free. In despair they learn the lesson; in wrath they share the rich red wine of hope.

Indestructible Women in *The Grapes of Wrath*

Mimi Reisel Gladstein

Mimi Reisel Gladstein analyzes John Steinbeck's treatment of women in *The Grapes of Wrath*. She argues that Steinbeck creates in Ma Joad both a symbolic and a realistic character and that Ma trains Rose of Sharon to carry on the indestructible qualities. As a symbol, Ma is the optimistic pioneer woman moving west with her family to find a better life. She is the earth mother, who nourishes her own family members as well as those outside. As the goddess, she commands respect and holds power over those she leads. But as a realistic woman, she makes mistakes, shows her fears, and exhibits pride. In both roles, she is the indestructible woman who passes on her qualities and her responsibilities to her daughter Rose of Sharon.

Most of the enduring women in Steinbeck derive their positive value from the fact that they act as the nurturing and reproductive machinery of the group. Their optimistic significance lies, not in their individual spiritual triumph, but in their function as perpetuators of the species. They are not judged by any biblical or traditional sense of morality. The [Ernest] Hemingway credo may maintain that immorality was what made you feel disgusted afterward; the Steinbeck credo reads that perhaps there is no such thing as sin, only how people are. Those people who act for the good of the group or the greatest number, in whatever manner, are those whose behavior is valued. A number of Steinbeck's indestructible women function within that ethical construct. . . .

Ma Joad is perhaps the most easily recognizable example of the type. Her characterization is so unabashedly representative of these writers' [William Faulkner's, Ernest Hemingway's, and John Steinbeck's] attitude toward the indestruc-

Excerpted from *The Indestructible Women in Faulkner, Hemingway, and Steinbeck* by Mimi Reisel Gladstein. Copyright 1974, 1986 by Mimi Reisel Gladstein. Ann Arbor, MI: UMI Research Press, 1986. Reprinted by permission of the author.

tibility of woman that were it not for the fact that she follows rather than precedes others of her type in their works, she might be called the archetype [typical, a model] of the breed in American fiction.

In terms of overwhelming odds, both physical and mental, none of the other characters covered in this study has quite as much to endure as Ma Joad. The novel begins with her being uprooted from her home, having her center of being capsized. When her son Tom comments on the resultant change in her character, she explains, "I never had my house pushed over. . . . I never had my fambly stuck out on the road. I never had to sell—ever'thing." Not only is her home destroyed, but she must, because of the limited space in the truck, burn her mementos, her relics of the past. This she does of her own accord, privately, and without letting the others see the pain it causes her.

After losing her home and the tokens of the past, Ma must endure a series of deaths and hardships. First Grandpa does not survive the uprooting. Ma's compassion is displayed during Grandma's illness as Ma strives to make her comfortable, fanning Grandma, tending to her. Then Grandma succumbs. Ma's behavior on the occasion of Grandma's death is illustrative of her great compassion and personal indomitability. Ma also acts to impart to Rose of Sharon the need for responsibility and sharing, encouraging her daughter to fan Grandma also during her final illness. Because Ma is aware of the family need for her as a citadel of strength, she cannot even openly display her anguish. "Rose of Sharon watched her secretly. And when she saw Ma fighting with her face, Rose of Sharon closed her eyes and pretended to be asleep." Ma is so thoroughly dedicated to the good of the greater number that she lies all night with Grandma's dead body in her arms until the group gets across the state border and the California desert. The toll of this deed shows: "Her face was stiff and putty-like, and her eyes seemed to have sunk deep into her head, and the rims were red with weariness.". . .

MA JOAD: PIONEER, EARTH MOTHER, AND GODDESS

Ma Joad stands out in Steinbeck's works as a complete and positive characterization of a woman. Few of his other women are so fully drawn. None of his other women functions on so many interpretive levels, all affirmative. Not only is Ma realistically characterized as a believable woman, but she is also the embodiment of the myth of the pioneer woman, the symbol for positive motherhood, and the earth goddess incarnate. In a writer whose works are criticized for their preponderance of misfits, aberrations, and cripples, the characterization of Ma Joad's strength and goodness is a positive statement about the quality possible in the female. . . .

THE INDESTRUCTIBLE TURTLE

In the third chapter of John Steinbeck's The Grapes of Wrath, *a turtle crosses the road and, unaware, carries seeds of oats to the opposite side, where the seeds fall into the dust. In the essay "The Fully Matured Art:* The Grapes of Wrath," *Howard Levant comments on the symbolism of the turtle and its connection to the Joads, particularly Rose of Sharon.*

Allegory is a credible and functional device in *The Grapes of Wrath.* The turtle episode in chapter 3 is justly famous. Objectively, we have a fully realized description of a land turtle's patient, difficult journey over dust fields, across a road and walled embankment, and on through the dust. The facts are the starting point; nature is not distorted or manipulated to yield allegorical meaning. The turtle seems awkward but it is able to survive, like the Joads, and like them it is moving southwest, out of the dry area. It can protect itself against a natural danger like the red ant it kills, as the Joads protect themselves by their unity. The turtle's eyes are "fierce, humorous," suggesting force that takes itself easily; the stronger Joads are a fierce, humorous people. When mismanaged human power attacks, as when a truck swerves to hit the turtle, luck is on the animal's side—it survives by luck. The Joads survive the mismanagement that produced the Dust Bowl and the brutalizing man-made conditions in California as much by luck as by design. The relation to the Joads of the life-bearing function of the turtle is more obscure, or perhaps overly ambitious. The factual starting point is that, unknowingly, the turtle carries an oat seed in its shell and unknowingly drops and plants the seed in the dust, where it will rest until water returns. The most obvious link in the Joad family is the pregnant Rose of Sharon, but her baby is born dead. Perhaps compassion is "born," as in Uncle John's thoughts as he floats the dead baby down the flooding river in its apple box coffin.

Howard Levant, "The Fully Matured Art: *The Grapes of Wrath*," in *John Steinbeck's* The Grapes of Wrath, edited by Harold Bloom. New York: Chelsea House, 1988.

Steinbeck, who explained in a letter to his editor Pascal Covici that the novel had five layers, acquaints readers with Ma's archetypal role very early in the story. His initial description of her stresses her superhuman qualities. She is called "the citadel of the family, the strong place that could not be taken." Her position as wise and healing goddess also makes her the family judge. Her reaction to all this distances her from the ordinary mortals in the family. She becomes an ideal; everyone looks to her for guidance. Her affirmative and indestructible qualities are accentuated:

> Her hazel eyes seemed to have experienced all possible tragedy and to have mounted pain and suffering like steps into a high calm and a superhuman understanding. She seemed to know, to accept, to welcome her position. ... And since old Tom and the children could not know hurt or fear unless she acknowledged hurt and fear, she had practised denying them in herself. And since, when a joyful thing happened, they looked to see whether joy was on her, it was her habit to build up laughter out of inadequate materials. But better than joy was the calm. Imperturbability could be depended upon. And from her great and humble position in the family she had taken dignity and a clean calm beauty. From her position as healer, her hands had grown sure and cool and quiet; from her position as arbiter she had become as remote and faultless in judgment as a goddess.

Ma knows that she is the foundation of the family; they stand or fall on the basis of her strength. Steinbeck makes that clear.

MA JOAD: A REALISTIC WOMAN

But Ma's characterization transcends the mythic, as mythic characters tend to be flat and static. Her characterization, both narrative and dramatic, is multidimensional. Her character rises from the pages of the book as much more than Mother Earth or serene and aloof goddess. She is both leader and follower, a wise yet ignorant woman, simple in many ways and still complex. Hers is a fully developed realistic portrait, notwithstanding those critics who think she is too good to be true. Her strengths as a person are enhanced because Steinbeck chooses to show us, along with those situations in which she behaves heroically, examples of her weaknesses and doubts. Although she behaves bravely, Ma also expresses her fears. Her bravery is not of the foolhardy kind where actions arise instinctually without forethought. Ma has the intelligence to be frightened, but to act in spite of her fears. ...

Steinbeck's fully rounded portrait of this indestructible woman includes instances of her ignorance, suspicion, and pride. Having never seen bathroom facilities such as those at the government camp, she inadvertently ends up in the men's room. Her country background and pride make her suspicious of strangers and wary. She rejects the camp manager's friendly overtures until she is sure of his purpose. She is not free of a little family pride, boasting of the Joad lineage, "We're Joads. We don't look up to nobody.". . .

Steinbeck creates a number of indestructible women who are active and assertive. Ma Joad is both. She displays a number of traditionally masculine qualities without losing her womanly image. Pa Joad recounts with pride the story of how Ma "beat the hell out of a tin peddler with a live chicken." The story is humorous, but it serves as a foreshadowing for Ma Joad's future situation. . . .

Another scene that emphasizes Ma's forceful qualities is when she challenges Pa with a jack handle. . . . In a number of Steinbeck's works women assume the authoritative role for the good of the group. Ma not only challenges patriarchal authority but she does it in a traditionally masculine way, by a challenge to one-to-one combat. When Pa and Tom have decided that the group should split up, Casy and Tom remaining with the Wilsons, Ma balks. "I ain't a-gonna go," she says as she balances the jack handle in her hand. . . . Ma's challenge is made to prevent the weakening of the group structure, not for personal power. The fact that she acts on instinct as an agent for group preservation is underlined by her surprise at what she has done. Once the group realizes that she has taken control, that she is the power, they decide not to try to fight her. Tom reasons that even if he and Pa and the whole group try to rush Ma, it wouldn't do any good and so he says, "You win, Ma.". . .

MA'S ROLE PASSED TO ROSE OF SHARON

Ma Joad is not the only indestructible woman in *The Grapes of Wrath*. . . . In his development of Ma Joad and her daughter Rose of Sharon, Steinbeck . . . plays on the theme of the endless renewal of the female principle. Though [critic Howard] Levant claims that the final scene of the novel is a disaster because, among other things, "there is no preparation for Rose of Sharon's transformation," all through the story Steinbeck shows us Ma instructing Rose of Sharon and teaching her through precept and example nourishing and reinforcing behavior patterns. Rose of Sharon, who prior to the beginning of the story had been "a plump, passionate hoyden," is changed by her pregnancy. As the child grows within her, and she prepares to convert her role from daughter to mother, she becomes "balanced, careful, wise." Her whole thought and action turn inward and she is consumed with her sense of self as potential mother, as a reproductive agent. . . .

Rose of Sharon prepares for this role in a number of ways. She aids Ma with the care of the dying Grandma. She helps not only with care of the dying but also with nourishing the living. Even when she is feeling very weak as a result of both malnutrition and pregnancy, she tries to help with the cooking and cleaning chores. "I oughta help Ma . . . I tried, but ever' time I stirred about I throwed up." Bedraggled and burdened, deserted by her husband, Rose of Sharon still drags herself out of bed to do her part in earning money for the support of the family. Sick and weak, she insists on participating in the cotton picking. Ma tries to dissuade her, but she is adamant.

> The girl set her jaw. "I'm a-goin'," she said.
> "Ma, I got to go."
> "Well, you got no cotton sack. You can't pull no sack."
> "I'll pick into your sack."
> "I wisht you wouldn'."
> "I'm a-goin'."

Rose of Sharon goes to pick cotton with the family in her weakened state and becomes even more worn out. Her eyes lose their luster. She shivers and her knees buckle, but she holds her head high.

Ma instructs Rose of Sharon about her responsibilities in the cycle of life. She explains the terror, the loneliness, and the joy of woman's lot. In Ma's philosophy the hurt and the pain do not matter because they are part of the continuity of the species. The eternal cycle of womanhood is represented in a scene where Grandma, Ma, and Rose of Sharon are together in a tent: Grandma is dying; Ma is caring for her; Rose of Sharon is pregnant. Ma uses the occasion to prepare Rose of Sharon for what being a woman entails:

> Ma raised her eyes to the girl's face. Ma's eyes were patient, but the lines of strain were on her forehead. . . . "When you're young, Rosasharn, ever'thing that happens is a thing all by itself. It's a lonely thing. I know, I 'member, Rosasharn." Her mouth loved the name of her daughter. "You gonna have a baby, Rosasharn, and that's somepin to you lonely and away. That's gonna hurt you, an' the hurt'll be lonely hurt, an' this tent is alone in the worl', Rosasharn."

But while Ma acknowledges the pain and the loneliness that are in store for Rose of Sharon, she also tries to share with her daughter her ability to transcend those experiences.

> And Ma went on, "They's a time of change, an' when that comes, dyin' is a piece of all dyin', and bearin' is a piece of all bearin', an' bearin' an' dyin' is two pieces of the same thing. An' then things ain't lonely any more, Rosasharn. I wisht I would tell you so you'd know, but I can't." And her voice was so soft,

so full of love, that tears crowded into Rose of Sharon's eyes, and flowed over her eyes and blinded her.

Rose of Sharon's tears show that she has been touched by Ma's explanation.

Steinbeck shows us Ma infusing Rose of Sharon with her own strength and indomitability. In two particularly meaningful scenes, Ma symbolically passes the torch to Rose of Sharon. In the first of these scenes, the torch is passed by means of an icon, earrings, an appropriately feminine symbol. . . . To force her out of her lethargy and coax her out of her pessimistic stance, Ma gives her a pair of small gold earrings that are one of the few things she has painfully salvaged from the past. In order to wear the earrings, however, Rose of Sharon must bear the pain of having her ears pierced. Symbolically, she must suffer to prove herself ready to assume Ma's responsibilities and position. Lest we miss the import of this scene, Steinbeck underlines it for us. Rose of Sharon asks, "Does it mean somepin?" Ma answers, "Why, 'course it does . . . 'Course it does."

The final scene in the book is the other significant indicator that Rose of Sharon will succeed Ma as enduring matriarch, indestructible woman. The scene has been problematic for critics. Steinbeck's editor, Pascal Covici, tried in his diplomatic manner to get Steinbeck to rethink it. "No one could fail to be moved by the incident of Rose of Sharon giving her breast to the dying man," wrote Covici, "yet, taken as the finale of such a book with all its vastness and surge, it struck us on reflection as being too abrupt." But Steinbeck would not be swayed. He wanted the scene as it was for a number of reasons: first, he saw the action as "a survival symbol not a love symbol"; second, he did not want the reader to come away from the story satisfied, for he had done his damndest "to rip a reader's nerves to rags." As for the genesis of the action, Steinbeck explained, "The incident of the earth mother feeding by the breast is older than literature.". . .

THE STRENGTH AND FLEXIBILITY OF WOMEN

Two things in the scene argue strongly for an interpretation that includes Rose of Sharon among Steinbeck's indestructible women. First, Rose of Sharon has become an extension of Ma. As in the Demeter/Persephone myth, the daughter has become the mother. Having experienced great pain, she has been forged as Ma has, through suffering. A parity between the two women has been established. Up until this point in the novel, Rose of Sharon is always referred to as a girl, but in the narrative description of this final scene, Steinbeck emphasizes the equal status of the pair: "and the two women looked deep into each other." In the bulk of the novel, Ma has been the nourisher, the one who sees to the feeding of family and strangers. In this scene, though Ma is the instigator, she cannot do the feeding. It must be Rose of Sharon. By giving her breast to the old man, Rose of Sharon takes her place with Ma as earth goddess. Her youth and fertility combine with her selfless act to signify continuity and hope.

The second idea that should be stressed here is the sex [gender] of Steinbeck's symbols of hope and fortitude, Ma Joad and Rose of Sharon. Throughout the novel Steinbeck emphasizes the special indestructibility of women. When the men are disheartened and defeated, the women bear up and take charge. Pa comments on this phenomenon twice. As the family is mired in the comfort of the Weedpatch camp, it is Ma who demands affirmative action. The relative comfort of the camp does not lull her into complacency. She knows that they cannot continue without adequate food or work. "We got to do somepin. . . . You're scairt to talk. An' the money is gone. You're scairt to talk it out. Ever' night you jes' eat, then you get wanderin' away. . . . Now don't none of you get up till we figger somepin out." When the men voice their discouragement, Ma remonstrates, "You ain't got the right to get discouraged. This here fambly's goin' under.". . .

In the scene where Ma forces the family out of their lethargy, Pa comments, "Time was when a man said what we'd do. Seems like women is tellin' now. Seems like it's purty near time to get out a stick." Ma's reaction to this speech illustrates her special kind of authority, an authority which meets the demands of the time:

> Times when they's food an' a place to set, then maybe you can use your stick an' keep your skin whole. But you ain't a-doin' your job, either a-thinkin' or a-workin'. If you was, why, you could use your stick, an' women folks'd sniffle their nose an' creep-mouse aroun'. But you just get out a stick now an' you ain't lickin' no woman you're a-fightin', cause I got a stick all laid out too.

In her response to Pa she speaks not only for herself but for all women. The implication of her statement is that women will be subservient in the good times when there is plenty and the men are providing, but that in times of deprivation, a woman's true character, a commanding one, will [come] out. In hard times, women are not only just as tough, but probably tougher than men. . . .

Why do these women survive when others succumb? Why are they able to command in times of crisis and then turn over the reins of authority to their men when the men can once again cope? . . .

Steinbeck . . . in both his narration and through his characters proffers generalizations about the differences in the sexes' abilities to cope with change and disaster. Ma, whose wisdom on most matters is respected by both her creator and her family, explains the reason that the women are more enduring than the men. "Woman can change better'n a man," she says. When Pa is ready to give up and sees no hope for the future, Ma articulates her conception of an essential difference between the way men and women handle rites of passage:

> Man, he lives in jerks—baby born an' a man dies, an' that's a jerk—gets a farm an' loses his farm, an' that's a jerk. Woman, it's all one flow, like a stream, little eddies, little waterfalls, but the river, it goes right on. Woman looks at it like that. We ain't gonna die out. People is goin' on—changin' a little, maybe, but goin' right on.

The analogy between woman and a river is an apt one for this self-characterization by an indestructible woman. Like the river, like the stream of life, she goes on. She is allied to the natural flow of things.

Steinbeck's controversial ending is in keeping with a theme he sounds throughout this novel and in others of his works. In *The Grapes of Wrath* Steinbeck chooses two women to act as his symbols for survival. The objects of their ministrations are two men. Ma Joad and Rose of Sharon in the midst of rain and flood behave in the manner described by Ma as woman's way—like a river, they go right on.

John Steinbeck's Call to Conversion in *The Grapes of Wrath*

Stephen Railton

According to Stephen Railton's analysis, John Steinbeck's *The Grapes of Wrath* is structured around the images of seeds, nature, and movement, and its purpose is to persuade the reader to reject the conditions that bring suffering and misery to the poor. By illustrating the conversions that occur within several members of the Joad family, Steinbeck clarifies the nature of change he wants enacted in the reader. This change involves an inner concern and love for others *and* action on their behalf. Both, not just one or the other, are what Steinbeck's kind of conversion requires.

The Grapes of Wrath is a novel about things that grow—corn, peaches, cotton, and grapes of wrath. From the start Steinbeck identifies his vision of human history with organic, biological processes. A recurrent image is established in the first chapter, when the drought and wind in Oklahoma combine to uproot and topple the stalks of corn. In Chapter 29, the last of Steinbeck's wide-angle interchapters, it is the rain and flooding in California that "cut out the roots of cottonwoods and [bring] down the trees." Tragically, even human lives are caught in this pattern of being pulled up from the soil. Farmers are made migrants. Forced to sell and burn all of their pasts that won't fit onto a homemade flatbed truck, they too are uprooted, torn from their identities. Right alongside this pattern, however, Steinbeck establishes a second one: that of seed being carried to new ground, new roots being put down. This image is announced in Chapter 3. The turtle who serves as the agent of movement in that chapter has attracted a lot of commentary from the novel's critics, but Steinbeck's

Abridged from "Pilgrims' Politics: Steinbeck's Art of Conversion" by Stephen Railton, in *New Essays on "The Grapes of Wrath,"* edited by David Wyatt. Copyright 1990 by Cambridge University Press. Reprinted with the permission of Cambridge University Press.

main interest is not in the turtle. Chapter 3 is organized around seeds, all "possessed of the anlage [a fundamental principle] of movement." The turtle simply continues on its way, but by involuntarily carrying one "wild oat head" across the road, and accidentally dragging dirt over the "three spearhead seeds" that drop from it and stick in the ground, the mere movement of the turtle becomes part of the process of change and growth.

THE THEME OF DEATH AND REBIRTH

The Grapes of Wrath is a novel about an old system dying, and a new one beginning to take root. Movement, to Steinbeck, including the movement of history, works like the "West Wind" in [British poet Percy Bysshe] Shelley's ode. It is "Destroyer and preserver" both; it scatters "the leaves dead" and carries forward "The winged seeds." The system that is dying we can call American capitalism, the roots of which had always been the promises of individual opportunity and of private property as the reward for taking risks and working hard. Steinbeck makes it more difficult to name the new system that is emerging from the violent ferment of the old system's decay. It is certainly socialistic, yet a goal of the novel is to suggest that a socialized democracy is as quintessentially American as the individualistic dream it will replace. "[American revolutionary Thomas] Paine, [German revolutionary Karl] Marx, [American president Thomas] Jefferson, [Russian revolutionary Vladimir] Lenin" he writes in Chapter 14—this list would confound a historian, but it is meant to reassure the American reader by linking socialism with our own revolutionary tradition. That was one reason for his enthusiasm about the title his wife found for the novel. He wanted the whole of Julia Ward Howe's fighting song ["Battle Hymn of the Republic," which contains the words "grapes of wrath"] printed as a sort of preface, because, he wrote his editor at Viking,

> The fascist crowd will try to sabotage this book because it is revolutionary. They try to give it the communist angle. However, The Battle Hymn is American and intensely so. . . . So if both words and music are there the book is keyed into the American scene from the beginning.

At the same time, by tying his novel of history to the rhythms and laws of nature, the growth of seeds, the fermenting of grapes, Steinbeck tries to suggest that this coming American revolution is inevitable, organically decreed. The western states sense "the beginning change" with the nervousness of "horses before a thunder storm"; on the road west, separate families "*grew to be* units of the camps" (my italics).

These repeated biological locutions allow the novelist to assume the role of a Darwinian prophet, reading the political future instead of the natural past. Revolution is made to seem as inexorably sure as evolution. The novel is simply recording the process. Yet this quasi-scientific stance, while it helps account for the authority with which Steinbeck's prose tells his story, belies the real engagement of the book. Critics have accused Steinbeck of being wrong, because the drastic social change he apparently predicted never took place. But he knew better than that. If he had himself believed the stance his narrative adopts, he would have written a much less brilliant book, for the novel owes its power to Steinbeck's urgent but painstaking intention to enact the revolution he apparently foresees. Even his assumption of change is part of his strategy for creating it. And Steinbeck knew what he was up against. Despite his desire to make his vision seem "American and intensely so," he undertakes the task of radically redefining the most fundamental values of American society. The novel uproots as much as the forces of either nature or capitalism do, though far more subtly. And, ultimately, there is hardly anything natural about the kind of change—"as in the whole universe only man can change"—that Steinbeck is anxious to work. *Supernatural* probably describes it more accurately. Nor is *change* the right word for it, although it's the one Steinbeck regularly uses. *The Grapes of Wrath* is a novel about conversion.

THE READER AS CONVERT

You and I, the novel's readers, are the converts whom he is after. Working a profound revolution in our sensibilities is his rhetorical task. His chief narrative task, however, is to recount the story of the Joads' conversions. Thematically, Route 66 and the various state highways in California that the Joads travel along all run parallel to the road to Damascus [where Saul was converted] that Saul takes in Acts, or to the Way taken by [British writer John] Bunyan's Christian in *Pilgrim's Progress*. The problem with the way most readers want to see that turtle in Chapter 3 as an emblem of the Joads is precisely that it denies their movement any inward significance. Steinbeck finds much to admire in the Joads and the class of "the people" whom they represent, including the fierce will to survive and keep going which they share with that turtle, but he explicitly makes the capacity for spiritual regeneration the essence of

---

VIOLENCE AGAINST MIGRANT WORKERS IN SALINAS

Trouble for migrant workers was common long before the influx of Okies. In a letter in the October 17, 1934, issue of the New Republic, *writer Ella Winter describes the violence toward Filipino migrants who went on strike for wages of forty cents an hour, a ten-cent increase in pay.*

Last week the Filipinos went on the picket line again. They had been off it for about three weeks. The first day, large details of deputy sheriffs and police were called and there was a fracas in which one Filipino wounded an officer in the forearm and another hit a deputy with a sugar beet. That night a machine gun was set up outside the Filipino union headquarters and fifteen officers entered, clubbing sleeping men to left and right. Sixty-nine were arrested for "inciting to riot." The next day both the local newspapers, The Monterey Peninsula Herald and The Salinas Index-Journal, received anonymous notices that "something would happen that night." It did. Four houses of Filipinos were burned to the ground, being fired with "tracer" bullets. Several shots were fired at gasoline tanks near by so that the gasoline would spray the bunk houses and they would burn more easily. At the same time a fire was started in the town so that the fire engines would be busy there and would be unable to come out to the camp some three miles out of Salinas. The next day the leader of the Filipino Labor Union, Rufo Canete—who had taken the place of the deposed leader Marcuelo who signed the arbitration agreement—was arrested and jailed. He is now out on $500 bail. The day after, the Filipinos called off their strike and went back to work in the fields at thirty cents.

One man, Barsatan, was not allowed medical aid for twenty days and has now been removed to an insane asylum. (The same thing happened to a young Chinese in Sacramento, who was beaten into a state of gibbering terror and then carted off to Stockton insane asylum. He wouldn't say he was foreign born. He wasn't.)

The Arbitration Board (Monterey County Industrial Relations Board) has been meeting spasmodically. The growers refused to allow the item from their books revealing the profits they made this year to be read into the record. Their profits are known to be enormous, on account of the drought in the Middle West.

Ella Winter, "More Trouble in Salinas," *The New Republic* 80, October 17, 1934.

---

humanity. That humans can redefine the meaning of our lives is what makes us "unlike any other thing organic or inorganic in the universe." Con-version—to turn around, to turn together—is a metaphysical movement. This is the route on which Steinbeck sets the Joads. For, as much as he finds to admire in them, he also knows that before American society can be saved from its sins, "the people" will have to change, too.

Thus there is a tension between the novel's rhetorical and its narrative tasks. Steinbeck is writing about the migrant families, not for them; their lives have no margin, either of income or leisure, for reading novels. He is writing for the vast middle class that forms the audience for best-selling fiction, and one of his goals is to educate those readers out of their prejudices against people like the Joads. As soon as they reach California, the Joads are confronted by the epithet "Okie," and the attitude that lies behind it. . . .

STEINBECK'S UNSENTIMENTALIZED PICTURE

Perhaps the truest thing about the novel is its refusal to sentimentalize the life in the Midwest from which the Joads and the other families they meet have been dispossessed. When their dream of a golden future out West is destroyed by the brutal realities of migrant life in California, the past they left at the other end of Route 66 appeals to them as the paradise they have been driven from. When the novel winds up at the Hooper Ranch, the place seems as infernal as Simon Legree's plantation in *Uncle Tom's Cabin* [written by Harriet Beecher Stowe]. The armed guards, the filthy conditions, the edge of outright starvation on which Hooper Ranches, Inc., is content to keep the pickers—Steinbeck does want to expose this as one of the darkest places of the earth. At no point in the novel do the Joads feel further from "home," but Steinbeck also wants us to see how much Hooper's farm in California has in common with the Joad farm in Oklahoma that Tom had been trying to get back to at the beginning. . . .

The westward journey of the Joads is a moving record of losses: their home and past, Grampa and Granma's deaths, Noah and Connie's desertions. The sufferings inflicted on the family bear witness not only to their strength of character, but also to the evils of the social and economic status quo. Their hapless pursuit of happiness indicts and exposes the America they move across. Steinbeck forces his reader to suffer even more steadily. Ma has a sudden moment of insight on the road west when she "seemed to know" that the family's great expectations were "all a dream," but, for the first half of the novel at least, the Joads are sustained by their dreams. The reader is denied any such imaginative freedom. While most narratives are organized around some kind of suspense about what will happen next, *The Grapes of Wrath* is structured as a series of inevitabilities. Each of the book's wide-angle chapters precedes the Joads, and in them we see the tenant farmers being tractored off before Tom comes home to an empty house, or the new proletariat being exploited before the Joads even begin to look for work, or the rain flooding the migrant camps before the Joads try to battle the rising water. Again and again what will happen next is made narratively inescapable. "I've done my damndest to rip a reader's nerves to rags," Steinbeck wrote about the novel. It is a good technique for a protest novel. The narrative enacts its own kind of oppression, and, by arousing in its readers a desire to fight this sense of inevitability, it works strategically to arouse us toward action to change the status quo.

THE IMPORTANCE OF INNER CHANGE

On the other hand, however, the journey of the Joads is also an inward one. And there the same pattern of losses is what converts their movement into a pilgrimage toward the prospect of a new consciousness. As in Bunyan's book, homelessness and suffering become the occasion of spiritual growth. In several of the interchapters Steinbeck describes this process: "The families, which had been units of which the boundaries were a house at night, a farm by day, changed their boundaries." They expand their boundaries. Having lost their land, the migrants' minds are no longer "bound with acres"; their new lives, their very losses, lead them toward the potentially redemptive discovery of their interrelatedness, their membership in a vastly extended family—the "we." In the novel's main narrative, Steinbeck dramatizes this process; near the very end, Ma sums up the new way she has learned to define her life: "Use' ta be the fambly was fust. It ain't so now. It's anybody."

As an interpretive gloss on the meaning of her pilgrimage, however, Ma's pronouncement is much too pat. Simply quoting it denies Steinbeck the credit he deserves as both a novelist and a visionary. Again as in Bunyan's book, Steinbeck's faith is neither simple nor naive. Ruthie and Winfield, the youngest Joads, remind us how innately selfish human nature is. In his representation of their naked, nagging need for place and power, Steinbeck looks unflinchingly at the fact that "mine" is always among the first words an infant speaks. Similarly, Grampa and Granma are too old to learn to redefine themselves. The disruptions, the losses by which the others' assumptions are broken up, in the same way that a field has to be broken before new seed can be put into it, kill them both. Even with the other Joads, Steinbeck admits a lot of skepticism about whether they can be converted. Although Pa has become a victim of the capitalist system, it seems unlikely that he could ever abandon the economics of self-interest. As Tom tells Casy on the other side of the fence around the Hooper Ranch, it wouldn't do any good to tell Pa about the strike Casy is trying to organize: "He'd say it wasn't none of his business. . . . Think Pa's gonna give up his meat on account a other fellas?"

Steinbeck here allows Tom, in his blunt vernacular voice, to ask the novel's most urgent question. The American Dream of individual opportunity has clearly betrayed "the people," but can they plant themselves on a different set of instincts? Can they redefine their boundaries? When he looks at the horrors of the migrants' plight, he knows that the answer is—They must. . . .

While he was writing *The Grapes of Wrath*, Steinbeck apparently needed to disguise even from himself how skillfully the novel works to convert rather than confront the sensibilities of his audience. "I am sure it will not be a popular book" he wrote, not long before it zoomed to the top of the best-seller lists. He was writing a "revolutionary" novel fueled by his own wrath at the moral and economic horrors of contemporary America; such a work had to be "an outrageous book." Yet his deeper need was to reach "the large numbers of readers" he expected to outrage. His very ambitions as a prophet of social change depended on being read by the widest possible audience. . . .

To recognize and act collectively in the interests of the group, it seems, is not enough. Indeed, since the men remain divided and bitter after the failure of their dam, [which the migrants built together,] it seems that collective action in itself is meaningless. Instead, what the novel presents as most meaningful are Casy's and Tom's conversions: the purpose and inner peace that each man finds, not in acting with others, but in "feeling" or "seeing" his oneness with all. . . .

THE IDEAL: INNER PEACE AND OUTWARD ACTION

The novel's very last scene tries to build a bridge between the realm of spirit, where individuals find their home, and the world of action, where men and women can help each other; it redresses the imbalance of Tom's story, where the emphasis had been almost entirely on faith, by adding to that a doctrine of works. Thematically, the novel's last scene is perfect. It is the moment of Rose of Sharon's conversion. Out of the violent loss of her baby (which she has "witnessed" with her whole body) comes a new, self-less sense of self. When she breastfeeds the starving stranger who would otherwise die, a new, boundary-less definition of family is born. Rose of Sharon's act is devoutly socialistic: from each according to ability, to each according to need. At the same time, the novel's last word on this scene, which is also the novel's last word, is "mysteriously"—a word that has no place in Marx's or Lenin's vocabulary. The scene's implications are as much religious as political. Iconographically, like Casy's death, this tableau of a man lying in a woman's lap both recalls and subverts the familiar imagery of Christianity. By calling our ultimate act of attention in the novel to the look of "mysterious" satisfaction on Rose of Sharon's face, Steinbeck keeps this scene in line with his focus on the private, inward, ineffable moment of conversion. Yet here we also see how that inner change can lead to redemptive action. The barn in which this scene takes place is not only "away in a manger"; it is also halfway between the social but bureaucratic world of the government camp and the spiritual but solitary state that Tom found while hiding out in the bushes. And what happens in this barn triumphantly completes the novel's most pervasive pattern: One family has been uprooted and destroyed; out of those ruins, another, a new one, takes root. Manself can change, and by change can triumph over the most devastating circumstances. . . .

In any case, whether the novel's last scene is esthetically successful is probably not the most important question to ask. Having seen the starving migrants in the valleys of California, and determined to write a novel in response to that human fact, Steinbeck was shocked out of his modern assumption that art mattered more than life. At the end of a letter from the winter of 1938, recording in horrified detail his own reaction as a witness to the sufferings of the migrant families, he wrote: "Funny how mean and little books become in the face of such tragedies." He wrote the novel in the belief to which the trauma of seeing the homeless, wretched families had converted him: that American society had to change, quickly and profoundly. This then leads to the largest question raised by the novel's several endings. Is conversion the same as revolution? Can the re-creation of society be achieved by an individual's private, inner, spiritual redefinition of the self?

THE AMERICAN BELIEF IN A DREAM

That Steinbeck believed it could is the most "intensely American" aspect of the novel. "Paine, Marx, Jefferson, Lenin"—those names are relevant to his vision, but the tradition to which *The Grapes of Wrath* belongs is best identified with a different list: [Governor John] Winthrop, [American theologian Johnathan] Edwards, [transcendentalist Ralph Waldo] Emerson, [and poet Walt] Whitman. Steinbeck's emphasis on inner change as the basis of social salvation has its roots in the Puritan belief that the New Jerusalem is identical with the congregation of converted saints, and in the Transcendentalists' credo that, as Emerson put it, "The problem of restoring to the world original and eternal beauty is solved by the redemption of the soul." Harriet Beecher Stowe, as the author of *Uncle Tom's Cabin*, has to occupy an especially prominent place on that list. Her great protest novel is also organized around movement as both a means to expose social evil and as the pilgrimage of the spirit toward home. And when Stowe, in her last chapter, sought to answer the many aroused readers who had written to ask her what they could *do* to solve the terrible problem of slavery, her response was, "they can see to it that *they feel right.*" It is in this ground that the seeds of Steinbeck's revolution must also grow. Tom and Rose of Sharon at last feel right when they have redefined themselves as one with the people around them. Steinbeck oppresses and exhorts, threatens and inspires, shocks and moves us to bring us each, individually, to the same point of communion.

Ultimately, of course, people's feelings are all that any novelist has to work with. Even if Steinbeck had gone on to specify exactly what Tom will do to realize the vision of human unity that he has attained, Tom could never act in the real world. He can only act on the reader, as Casy's example acted on him. Hiding out in the bushes or reading *The Grapes of Wrath* both occur in private. Any change that the novel might make in American society will have to happen first in the consciousness of its readers.

John Steinbeck Awarded the Nobel Prize in Literature

Carl E. Rallyson Jr.

John Steinbeck received the Nobel Prize in literature on December 10, 1962, in Stockholm, Sweden. The Swedish Academy selected Steinbeck primarily for his novels published before 1940, but cited two works published in the 1960s. Most of the major news and literary magazines gave little attention to the award or to Steinbeck's acceptance speech at the academy. A few commented on the academy's poor selection.

The Nobel Prize in Literature was presented to John Steinbeck on December 10, 1962, by Anders Österling, Permanent Secretary of the Swedish Academy. The presentation emphasized the novelist's concern with "the common man's everyday life," noting that his upbringing in a small town near the Salinas Valley put him "on equal terms with the workers' families in this rather diversified area."

Steinbeck's first great success, *Tortilla Flat* (1935), was composed of comic tales that concentrated on the lives of Mexican-Americans (*paisanos*). *Tortilla Flat* was reminiscent of the Arthurian legend, and it was a "welcome antidote to the gloom of the then prevailing depression." The depth of Steinbeck's social perception was revealed in his novel *In Dubious Battle* (1936), which dealt with labor strikes in California's fruit and cotton farms. *Of Mice and Men* (1937), his "little masterpiece," told the compelling story of Lennie, "the imbecile giant," who could not stop himself from squeezing the life out of every living creature put into his hands.

In the Swedish Academy's view, the stories in *The Long Valley* (1938) paved the way for Steinbeck's great epic chronicle, *The Grapes of Wrath* (1939). Of special importance in the latter work was his ability to take a "tragic episode in the social history of the United States" (the emigration of the people in dustbowl Oklahoma to California in search of a new home) and make the poignant story of one family enduring an "endless, heartbreaking journey."

The presentation did not discuss Steinbeck's writing of the 1940's and 1950's, which, it was noted, had not been well received by critics. Instead the Academy focused upon his last novel, *The Winter of Our Discontent* (1961), as a worthy successor to *The Grapes of Wrath*. In *The Winter of Our Discontent* the novelist had recovered his "vigorous and realistic verve" to explore values in a postwar world. That novel and his account of his tour of the United States, *Travels with Charley* (1962), impressed the Academy with their "forceful criticism of society."

NOBEL LECTURE

In his Nobel lecture, Steinbeck affirms the vitality of the artist. Literature comes out of life; it is "as old as speech." He refers to the fact that a previous Nobel laureate, William Faulkner, had commented on the "gray and desolate time of confusion" through which humanity was passing. In Steinbeck's view, writers can speak to the contemporary sense of fear. They are "delegated to declare and to celebrate man's proven capacity for greatness of heart and spirit." In his most affirmative and challenging statement, Steinbeck avows that "a writer who does not passionately believe in the perfectibility of man, has no dedication nor any membership in literature."

Steinbeck acknowledges that it is difficult in modern life to proceed with confidence, knowing that nuclear weapons, with their capacity for destruction, have been man's work. Yet in taking as his example the life of Alfred Nobel, whose inventions made possible the creation of enormously destructive explosives, Steinbeck suggests that Nobel kept his belief in the "human mind and the human spirit." In the very categories of the awards that Nobel established he acknowledged that human beings have the choice of perfecting their lives.

Man's power for good and evil is so awesome, Steinbeck contends, that he has "usurped many of the powers we once ascribed to God." Now it is in man's hands to determine the life and death of all living things. The choice is clearly man's. "The test of his perfectibility is at hand," Steinbeck concludes.

Except for a few fine phrases, Steinbeck's Nobel lecture has not invited much comment. He gives an honest summation of his principles and declines to strive for much rhetorical ornamentation. Indeed, what is perhaps most noteworthy about his lecture is that it is down-to-earth and colloquial, as befits a writer praised for his championing of the common man.

CRITICAL RECEPTION

Most of the response in newspapers and periodicals to Steinbeck's Nobel Prize was negative or indifferent. It was thought that his career had been in serious decline since World War II, and everyone—apparently including Steinbeck himself—was surprised by the award. There were very few articles in major publications about the prize. The *Saturday Review*, for example, did not even mention it. *Time* (November 2, 1962) and *Newsweek* (November 5, 1962) were not favorable to Steinbeck, with *Time* even going so far as to say that *The Grapes of Wrath* was a "limited" work of fiction that would scarcely be able to "survive its time and place." The *New Republic* (November 10, 1962) suggested how little esteem it held for Steinbeck's prize in noting that of the six American writers who had received Nobel awards, three were not even considered to be of the first rank. An editorial writer for the *New York Times* (December 11, 1962) questioned the process of selection, since a writer had been chosen who was not particularly close to recent developments in American writing.

The *New York Times Book Review* (December 9, 1962) was the only major publication to commission a critic to consider carefully the appropriateness of the award to Steinbeck. Arthur Mizener called Steinbeck a dated writer, for whom there was considerable affection but little respect. His sentimental books about the poor had given him a special place in the hearts of adults growing up in the Depression, but after *The Grapes of Wrath* serious readers of literature had ignored Steinbeck.

Mizener's comments were representative of how little value the literary and academic community saw in Steinbeck's later work. Other American Nobel laureates—Ernest Hemingway and Faulkner, for example—had been the subjects of many book-length studies and articles. Yet Steinbeck had not been entirely ignored by academics and other serious readers. Book-length studies, articles, meetings, and associations devoted to his work had begun to appear in the late 1950's and early 1960's. No critic took issue with the judgment that the quality of Steinbeck's work had declined, but critics such as Warren French argued that his best work had not been sufficiently appreciated.

A careful reading of the Academy's presentation suggests

that Steinbeck was given the prize primarily because of his writing in the 1930's, which the Academy considered to have already stood the test of time. Although his work of the early 1960's was praised, the tenor of the presentation clearly suggested that recognition of Steinbeck's earlier achievements was long overdue. In fact, he had been seriously considered for the prize in 1945 but was passed over in favor of Chilean poet Gabriela Mistral.

Quite aside from the professional evaluations of Steinbeck's work, the reading public continued to read him. The Nobel Prize stimulated large sales for his works, and if the writer was not honored with discussions of his work in major literary publications, he was treated by the press as a major public figure. As such, he was often in demand for interviews and was asked to contribute articles to several national magazines. Mizener's verdict on Steinbeck seems harsh, for the reading public still found stimulation in his work long after many of his contemporaries in the 1930's were forgotten and their work allowed to go out of print.

CHRONOLOGY

1902
John Steinbeck born February 27

1903
Wright brothers' airplane

1906
San Francisco earthquake and fire

1909
Steinbeck's sister Mary born; Model T Ford first mass produced

1914
World War I begins in Europe; Panama Canal opens

1917
United States enters World War I

1919
Treaty of Versailles ending World War I; Steinbeck graduates from Salinas High School and enters Stanford University

1925
Steinbeck goes to New York, working as a laborer and as a reporter for the *American* newspaper

1927
Charles Lindbergh's first solo transatlantic flight

1928
Talking pictures; first Mickey Mouse cartoon

1929
Stock market crash in America; Hoover becomes president; Steinbeck publishes *Cup of Gold*

1930
Steinbeck marries Carol Henning; meets Edward Ricketts in Pacific Grove, California

1932
America in Great Depression; Charles Lindbergh Jr. kidnapped and murdered; Steinbeck publishes *Pastures of Heaven*

1933

Franklin D. Roosevelt becomes president; Steinbeck publishes *To a God Unknown*

1934

Steinbeck wins O. Henry Prize for "The Murder"; mother dies

1935

Works Progress Administration, work relief for unemployed; Steinbeck publishes *Tortilla Flat*; wins Commonwealth Club of California Gold Medal; Pascal Covici becomes Steinbeck's publisher

1936

Steinbeck publishes *In Dubious Battle*; father dies; publishes articles on migrants in *San Francisco News*

1937

Steinbeck publishes *Of Mice and Men*; wins Drama Critics Circle Award; publishes *The Red Pony*, three parts

1938

Steinbeck publishes *The Long Valley* and *Their Blood Is Strong*, a pamphlet based on news articles about migrants

1939

World War II begins in Europe; Steinbeck publishes *The Grapes of Wrath*

1940

Steinbeck and Ricketts's research trip to the Sea of Cortez; Steinbeck wins Pulitzer Prize for *The Grapes of Wrath*; films "The Forgotten Village" in Mexico; film versions of *The Grapes of Wrath* and *Of Mice and Men*

1941

Japanese bomb Pearl Harbor; America enters World War II; Steinbeck publishes *Sea of Cortez* with Ricketts

1942

Steinbeck publishes *The Moon Is Down*; writes script for *Bombs Away;* Steinbeck and Carol Henning divorce; film version of *Tortilla Flat*

1943

Steinbeck marries Gwendolyn Conger; they move to New York; film version of *The Moon Is Down*

1944

D-Day invasion of Normandy; Steinbeck writes script for *Lifeboat* with Alfred Hitchcock; son Thomas born

1945

Franklin D. Roosevelt dies; Harry Truman becomes president; Americans drop first atomic bomb on Hiroshima; World War II ends; Steinbeck publishes *Cannery Row*; *The Red Pony*, four parts; "The Pearl of the World" in *Woman's Home Companion*

1946

First meeting of the United Nations; son John born

1947

Steinbeck publishes *The Wayward Bus* and *The Pearl*

1948

Berlin blockade and airlift; Steinbeck publishes *A Russian Journal*; elected to American Academy of Letters; film version of *The Pearl*; Edward Ricketts dies; Steinbeck and Gwendolyn Conger divorce

1949

Film version of *The Red Pony*

1950

America involved in Korean War; Steinbeck publishes *Burning Bright*, novel and play; writes script for *Viva Zapata!*; marries Elaine Scott

1951

Steinbeck publishes *Log from the Sea of Cortez*

1952

Steinbeck publishes *East of Eden*

1953

Dwight D. Eisenhower becomes president

1954

Steinbeck publishes *Sweet Thursday*

1955

Civil rights movement begins; film version of *East of Eden*

1957

Steinbeck publishes *The Short Reign of Pippin IV*; film version of *The Wayward Bus*

1958

Steinbeck publishes *Once There Was a War*

1959

Alaska admitted as forty-ninth state; Hawaii admitted as fiftieth

1960

Steinbeck tours America with dog Charley

1961

John F. Kennedy becomes president; Soviets put up Berlin Wall; first U.S.-manned suborbital flight; Steinbeck publishes *The Winter of Our Discontent*

1962

Cuban missile crisis; Steinbeck publishes *Travels with Charley in Search of America*; awarded Nobel Prize in literature

1963

John F. Kennedy assassinated; Lyndon Johnson becomes president

1964–1975

America involved in Vietnam War

1965

Steinbeck reports from Vietnam for *Newsday*

1966

Steinbeck publishes *America and Americans*

1968

Martin Luther King Jr. assassinated; televised versions of *Travels with Charley*, *Of Mice and Men*, and *The Grapes of Wrath*; Steinbeck dies on December 20; buried in Salinas

1969

Richard M. Nixon becomes president; publication of *Journal of a Novel: The* East of Eden *Letters*

1970

Opera version of *Of Mice and Men*

1975

Steinbeck: A Life in Letters, edited by Elaine Steinbeck and Robert Wallstein

WORKS BY JOHN STEINBECK

1929

Cup of Gold

1932

Pastures of Heaven

1933

To a God Unknown

1935

Tortilla Flat

1936

In Dubious Battle
"The Harvest Gypsies," published in *San Francisco News*
Saint Katie the Virgin

1937

Of Mice and Men
The Red Pony, three parts

1938

The Long Valley
Their Blood Is Strong, pamphlet of *San Francisco News* articles

1939

The Grapes of Wrath

1940

The Forgotten Village, a film
Film versions of *The Grapes of Wrath* and *Of Mice and Men*

1941

Sea of Cortez, with Edward F. Ricketts

1942

The Moon Is Down, novel and play
Bombs Away
Film version of *Tortilla Flat*

1943

Film version of *The Moon Is Down*

1944

Script for *Lifeboat*, a film

1945

Cannery Row
The Red Pony, four parts
"The Pearl of the World" in *Woman's Home Companion*

1947

The Wayward Bus
The Pearl

1948

A Russian Journal
Film version of *The Pearl*

1949

Film version of *The Red Pony*

1950

Burning Bright, novel and play
Script for *Viva Zapata!*, a film

1951

Log from the Sea of Cortez

1952

East of Eden

1954

Sweet Thursday

1955

Pipe Dream, a musical based on *Sweet Thursday*
Film version of *East of Eden*

1957

The Short Reign of Pippin IV
Film version of *The Wayward Bus*

1958

Once There Was a War

1961

The Winter of Our Discontent

1962

Travels with Charley in Search of America

1965

Newsday columns

1966

America and Americans

1968

Television versions of *Travels with Charley*, *Of Mice and Men*, and *The Grapes of Wrath*; "Here's Where I Belong," a musical

1969

Journal of a Novel: The East of Eden *Letters*

1970

Opera version of *Of Mice and Men*

1973

Steinbeck: A Life in Letters, edited by Elaine Steinbeck and Robert Wallstein

FOR FURTHER RESEARCH

ABOUT JOHN STEINBECK

Richard Astro and Tetsumaro Hayashi, eds. *Steinbeck: The Man and His Work*. Proceedings of the 1970 Steinbeck Conference, sponsored by Oregon State and Ball State Universities. Corvallis: Oregon State University Press, 1971.

Jackson J. Benson. *The True Adventures of John Steinbeck, Writer*. New York: The Viking Press, 1984.

Harold Bloom, ed. *John Steinbeck's* The Grapes of Wrath. New York: Chelsea House Publishers, 1988.

Robert Murray Davis, ed. *Steinbeck: A Collection of Critical Essays*. Englewood Cliffs, NJ: Prentice-Hall, 1942.

Warren French. *John Steinbeck*. New York: Twayne Publishers, 1961.

Maxwell Geismar. *Writers in Crisis: The American Novel, 1925–1945*. Boston: Houghton Mifflin, 1942.

Tetsumaro Hayashi, ed. *A Study Guide to John Steinbeck: A Handbook to His Major Works*. Metuchen, NJ: The Scarecrow Press, 1974.

Frederick J. Hoffman. *The Modern Novel in America*. Chicago: Henry Regnery, 1951.

Thomas Kiernan. *The Intricate Music: A Biography of John Steinbeck*. Boston: Little, Brown, 1979.

Howard Levant. *The Novels of John Steinbeck: A Critical Study*. Columbia: University of Missouri Press, 1974.

Peter Lisca. *The Wide World of John Steinbeck*. New Brunswick, NJ: Rutgers University Press, 1958.

Harry Thornton Moore. *The Novels of John Steinbeck: A First Critical Study*. Chicago: Normandie House, 1939.

E. W. Tedlock Jr. and C. V. Wicker, eds. *Steinbeck and His Critics: A Record of Twenty-five Years*. Albuquerque: University of New Mexico Press, 1957.

David Wyatt, ed. *New Essays on* The Grapes of Wrath. New York: Cambridge University Press, 1990.

HISTORICAL BACKGROUND FOR THE 1930s

Frederick Lewis Allen. *Since Yesterday: The Nineteen-Thirties in America, September 3, 1929–September 3, 1939.* New York: Harper & Brothers, 1940.

Fon Boardman Jr. *The Thirties: America and the Great Depression.* New York: Henry Z. Walck, 1967.

Matthew T. Downey et al., eds. *The Great Depression and World War II (1930–1945).* Vol. 3 of *The Twentieth Century.* New York: Macmillan, 1992.

William Dudley, ed. *The Great Depression: Opposing Viewpoints.* American History Series, edited by Teresa O'Neill. San Diego: Greenhaven Press, 1994.

John Kenneth Galbraith. *The Great Crash: 1929.* 1954. Reprint, Boston: Houghton Mifflin, 1961.

Robert Goldston. *The Great Depression: The United States in the Thirties.* Indianapolis: Bobbs-Merrill, 1968.

Milton Meltzer. *Brother, Can You Spare a Dime: The Great Depression, 1929–1933.* New York: Alfred A. Knopf, 1969.

Jerry Stanly. *Children of the Dust Bowl: The True Story of the School at Weedpatch Camp.* New York: Crown, 1992.

Studs Terkel. *Hard Times: An Oral History of the Great Depression.* New York: Pantheon Books, 1970.

T. H. Watkins. *The Great Depression: America in the 1930s.* Boston: Little, Brown, 1993.

INDEX

abnormal behavior, 120-21
Abrahamson, Ben, 122
Achilles, 84
Aesop, 94
agriculture, 78, 119-20, 126-129, 165
alcohol, 66, 67, 68, 71-72
allegory
  in "Flight," 73
  in *Grapes of Wrath*, 158
  in *Of Mice and Men*, 127, 129, 132
  in *The Pearl*, 93-99, 100, 101, 139
American Literature and the Dream (Carpenter), 140
animal fables, 48, 94
animal imagery, 94, 96, 115-16
animals
  in *Grapes of Wrath*, 124
  in *Of Mice and Men*, 38, 118, 120, 123-24
  in *The Red Pony*, 32-33, 77, 80-85
  in *Tortilla Flat*, 34, 36-37
anthropomorphism, 107
Arthurian themes, 28, 34, 65, 69-71, 84, 130-37, 174

Baker, Carlos, 127
"Bartleby the Scrivener" (Melville), 79
"Battle Hymn of the Republic" (Howe), 149, 166
Beach, Joseph Warren, 30, 127
Benson, Jackson J., 68
Beowulf, 84
biblical analogies, 45, 54-57, 62, 131, 138-44, 145-55
bildungsromans (genre of novel), 81
Billy Budd (Melville), 110
birth, 78, 81
blacks, 119, 128
Book-of-the-Month Club, 129, 133
Buddhism, 144

Bumppo, Natty, 84
Bunyan, John, 167, 170
Burgum, Edwin Berry, 117
Burning Bright, 151
Burns, Robert, 45, 127, 128, 132

California, as promised land, 45, 60, 139, 144, 146, 147
Cannery Row, 56, 59
  characters, 46-47, 137
  as a farce, 46, 47
  Mexican-Americans in, 65
  naturalism in, 40
  parable in, 48
  preface to, 100
  Steinbeck on, 27, 29
capitalism, 46, 118, 166-67, 171
Carpenter, Frederic I., 139-41
Chaucer, Geoffrey, 70
Chekhov, Anton, 33
childhood, end of, 73-76, 86, 88-92
children of the earth, 33, 37, 45
Christian symbolism, 54-56, 62, 80, 131, 138-44, 145-55, 167, 172
"The Chrysanthemums," 30-32, 36
cinema scripts, 40, 45
commitment, 50, 53-57, 95
common man, 174, 176
communism, 41-44, 53
Cooper, James Fenimore, 84
Covici, Pascal, 28, 59, 133, 158, 162
Cowley, Malcolm, 127
Cox, Martha Heasley, 109, 113
Crane, Stephen, 43, 132, 139
Cup of Gold, 50-51, 130
  Henry Morgan, 51, 131, 134
  James Flower, 51
  Merlin, 51

Dante Alighieri, 98
death
  effect on Steinbeck, 27-28, 133
  in "Flight," 73-75

in *Grapes of Wrath*, 63, 142,
148, 150, 152, 154, 157, 158,
166, 169
in *In Dubious Battle*, 55-56
in *Of Mice and Men*, 38, 55,
118, 120, 124, 128, 133, 134,
136
in *The Pearl*, 95, 99, 104-105,
107, 110-11
in *The Red Pony*, 61, 78, 80,
82, 83, 88-90
Death of a Salesman (Miller),
134
democracy, 29
DeMott, Robert, 133
Dewey, John, 140
Divine Comedy (Dante), 98
Drama Circle Critics' Award,
133, 145
dramatic conflict, 40, 42
Dreiser, Theodore, 43
Drury, John, 105

East of Eden, 64, 151
Eliot, T.S., 144
Emerson, Ralph Waldo, 62, 80,
138-42, 173
epic, 40, 45
escapism, 50-52
Everyman, 95

fables, 40, 48, 93, 96, 132
animal, 48, 94
farce, 40, 46
Farewell to Arms, A
(Hemingway), 81-82
fascism, 61, 166
fate, 125, 126
fathers, 33, 74-76, 79, 89, 90
Faulkner, William, 58, 61, 156,
175, 176
Fitzgerald, F. Scott, 136
Flaubert, Gustave, 43, 105
"Flight," 73-76
Foerster, Norman, 43, 74
folklore, 28, 29, 84, 94
Forgotten Village, The, 65
Francis of Assisi, Saint, 37, 38,
70, 84
free spirits, 41, 46

French, Warren, 86, 130, 176
Freudian symbols, 144

Gabilan Mountains, 78, 82
Galahad, Sir, 71, 131, 132
Geismar, Maxwell, 93
gender roles, 101, 106, 112, 115,
163-64
"The Gift," 80, 81, 86-87
Gladstein, Mimi Reisel, 156
Goldsmith, Arnold L., 80
good and evil, 44, 93, 95, 96, 99,
100, 107, 111
Grapes of Wrath, The, 33
Al, 150, 152, 154
allegory in, 158
animals in, 124
California as promised land,
38, 45, 60, 139, 144, 146, 147
commitment in, 55-56
Connie, 148, 152, 154, 169
death in, 142, 148, 150, 152,
154, 157, 158, 166, 169
as epic, 45-46, 174-75
family in, 101, 102, 152-53,
160, 170-71
final scene of, 46, 143, 146,
160, 162-63, 171-72
Floyd, 55
Granma, 150, 157, 161, 169, 170
Granpa, 148, 157, 169, 170
heroes in, 45, 50
Jim Casy, 45, 55-56, 62-64, 83,
138-44, 146-48, 150-55, 171
Joad family, 45, 62, 139, 142,
146-48, 150, 152, 167, 169
Judeo-Christian symbols in,
54-56, 62, 80, 131, 138-44,
145-55, 167, 172
Ma Joad, 140, 142, 143, 148,
152-53, 156-64, 169
Muhly Graves, 147-48, 152
narrative in, 102
Noah, 148, 152, 169
Pa, 148, 152, 153-54, 160, 171
parables in, 48
proletarian theme, 119
Rose of Sharon, 46, 143, 152,
154-55, 156, 157, 158, 160-64,
172, 173

Route 66, 147, 151, 167, 169
Ruthie, 148, 152, 154, 170
settings in, 123, 152
social protest theme, 39, 60-63
structure in, 148-55
Tom Joad, 40, 45, 48, 55-56, 62-63, 138, 140-41, 150, 152-53, 157, 160, 170-71, 173
turtle, 48, 124, 154, 158, 165-66, 167
Uncle John, 148, 152, 154, 158
weaknesses of, 58-62, 146, 176
Winfield, 148, 154, 170
women in, 144, 153, 156-64
Gray, James, 95
Great Gatsby, The (Fitzgerald), 136
"The Great Mountains," 79, 80-82, 84, 89, 90
group-man, 101-103
groves, 123

Hawthorne, Nathaniel, 61
Hemingway, Ernest, 70, 76, 80-82, 127, 156, 176
heroism, 45, 50, 61, 76, 106, 110-11, 130, 136-37
Holy Grail, 71
Homer, 84, 97
humor, 35-37, 61, 65, 174
Hunter, J.P., 145

Iliad (Homer), 84
In Dubious Battle, 125
   commitment in, 53-55
   Dick, 54
   Doc Burton, 42, 44, 54, 64, 136
   dramatic conflict in, 42, 47
   heroes in, 50
   Jim Nolan, 54, 56, 132
   Mac, 44, 54-55
   objectivity, 132
   political theme, 40-41, 62, 118, 119, 123, 127, 174
   Root, 54
   settings, 123
   superficiality of, 59, 61-62
"Indian Camp" (Hemingway), 82
Indians, 33, 66, 69

individualism, 30, 50, 63-64, 67, 140
innocence, 74, 75, 86, 88-89, 95, 123

James, William, 140
John the Baptist, 56

knight themes, 70-72, 90, 130-37
   see also Arthurian themes
Kronenberger, Louis, 60

labor organization, 42-44, 54, 55, 174
La Paz, Mexico, 93, 98, 99, 112, 113
"The Leader of the People," 80, 82-83, 90-91
Levant, Howard, 100, 158, 160
Lewis, R. W. B., 58
life-death cycles, 82-84, 90, 143, 166, 172
Lisca, Peter, 50, 73, 97, 122, 133, 148
Literary Guide to the Bible (Drury), 105
Long Valley, The, 30, 32, 65, 86, 87, 174
love, 31, 33, 37, 42, 46

Malory, Sir Thomas, 69, 72, 131
manhood, attaining, 28, 73-76, 92
Martin, Eddy, 68
materialism, 41-42, 45, 47, 67, 69, 97, 103-104
Maupassant, Guy de, 38
mechanism, 44
Melville, Herman, 64, 79
Metzger, Charles R., 65
Mexican-Americans, 65-72, 93
migrant workers, 38-39, 42, 131, 133, 161, 165, 168-72
Miller, Arthur, 134
Milton, John, 55, 98
Mizener, Arthur, 176-77
mob behavior, 120, 127, 133
Moby-Dick (Melville), 64, 135
mock epic, 40, 41
Monterey, California, 27, 28, 33, 41, 52, 66, 68, 73

Moon Is Down, The, 59
  escape and commitment in, 56
  group-man in, 101
  heroism in, 61
  Steinbeck on, 27, 29
Moore, Harry Thornton, 77, 78
morality, 41
Morris, Harry, 93
mothers, 74-76
Murphy, Roland E., 149
mysticism, 55-56, 62, 80-85
myth, 73, 76, 84, 162

Nation magazine, 60
Native Daughters of the Golden
  West, 69
naturalism, 40-49, 74
nature
  in *Grapes of Wrath*, 165-66, 171
  in *The Red Pony*, 33, 81, 83-84,
    88, 90-91
  in *The Pearl*, 94, 96, 102
New Republic, 168, 176
Newsweek, 176
New York Times, 176
New York Times Book Review,
  176
Nobel, Alfred, 175
Nobel Prize for Literature, 174-
  77
Norris, Frank, 43
North American Review, 28, 77
*Novels of John Steinbeck: A First
  Critical Study* (Moore), 78

Odyssey (Homer), 97
Of Mice and Men
  allegory in, 127, 129, 132, 135
  Candy, 126, 128, 129, 131, 135
  Carlson, 118, 136
  characterization in, 38-39, 79,
    117-19, 131
  as cinema script, 45
  as comedy, 135
  commitment in, 55, 56
  Crooks, 119, 126, 128, 131, 135
  Curley, 118, 128, 132, 135-36
  Curley's wife, 118, 120, 126,
    129, 131-32, 135-36
  death in, 38, 118, 120, 124, 128,
    133, 134, 136
  escape in, 55, 56
  fate, 58, 59, 61
  George Milton, 38-39, 45, 55,
    117-21, 123-24, 126-29, 131-36
  heroism in, 130, 136-37
  Lennie Small, 38-39, 45, 55,
    105, 117-21, 122-24, 126-29,
    131-36, 174
  motifs in, 123-26
  patterns in, 122-29
  poor in, 117-21
  Slim, 128, 135, 136-37
  Steinbeck on, 27, 28
  symbols in, 123-24, 126
Okies, 38, 40, 45, 168-69
oneness, 83-84
"The Open Boat" (Crane), 132
Origin of Species, The (Darwin),
  84
"Out of the Cradle Endlessly
  Rocking," 82
"The Oversoul" (Emerson), 142

paisanos
  definition of, 33, 65-66
  as knights, 70-72, 174
  living conditions, 66-69
  moral system of, 67, 69, 70-71
  Steinbeck's use of, 33, 35-37,
    41-42, 47, 52, 78
  see also Mexican-Americans
parable, 40, 47, 48, 96, 105
Paradise Lost (Milton), 55
Pastures of Heaven, The, 51, 65,
  100, 123
Paton, Alan, 138, 143
Pearl, The
  as allegory, 73, 93-99, 100, 101,
    139
  Coyotito, 95, 96, 99, 101, 103-
    107, 111, 115
  death in, 95, 99, 104-105, 107,
    110-11
  doctor, 95, 96, 99, 104, 110,
    114-15
  escape and commitment in,
    56, 57, 95
  family in, 101-102, 106, 110,
    112

heroism in, 50, 106, 110-11
Juana, 95, 99, 101, 104, 106,
  110-13, 115
Juan Thomas, 96, 98, 114
Kino, 47-48, 56, 57, 93-99, 100-
  108, 109-15
metaphor in, 101-102, 107, 115
Mexicans in, 65, 93
as parable, 47-48, 96, 100-108,
  113
pearl buyers, 114
scorpion, 95, 96, 104, 109, 110
settings, 123
Steinbeck on, 27, 29
symbolic creatures in, 109-16
symbolism in, 96-99, 101, 104,
  106, 115
true story of, 109, 113
Pilgrim's Progress (Bunyan),
  167, 170
Pope, Liston, 138, 143
poverty, 34, 41-42, 43, 53, 54, 60,
  117-21, 176
proletarian literature, 119
"The Promise," 80, 82, 83, 89-90
Pulitzer Prize, 145

"The Raid," 53
Railton, Stephen, 165
Rallyson, Carl E., Jr., 174
Ramirez, Eddie. *See Tortilla
  Flat*, Pilon
realism, 93-94, 96, 102
rebirth, 123, 166
Red Badge of Courage, The
  (Crane), 139
Red Pony, The, 58
  Billy Buck, 81, 83, 86, 88, 90
  characterizations in, 30, 32-33,
    79
  death in, 61, 78, 80, 82, 83, 88-
    90
  Galiban, 82
  "The Gift," 80, 81, 86-87
  Gitano, 79, 82, 84-85, 89
  grandfather, 81, 82-83, 87, 90-
    91
  "The Great Mountains," 79,
    80-82, 84, 89, 90
  Jody Tiflin, 33, 77-79, 80-85,

86-90
  "The Leader of the People," 80,
    82-83, 90-91
  mysticism in, 80-85
  Nellie, 82, 90
  "The Promise," 80, 82, 83, 89-
    90
  Steinbeck on, 27-28
  style in, 77-79, 130
religious symbols, 54-56, 62, 80,
  84
  see also Christian symbolism
Ricketts, Ed, 66, 113
rites of passage, 28, 73, 88-92
rituals, 73-74, 124, 127
Robin Hood themes, 34, 38
romanticism, 65, 67, 69-70

Salinas Valley, 30, 77, 78, 80, 81,
  132, 168, 174
Santa Lucia Mountains, 78
Saturday Review, 50, 138, 176
Schweitzer, Albert, 141
science, 41-43, 45-49, 65-66
Sea of Cortez, 53, 57, 80, 84, 95,
  113, 127
sexuality, 81, 120, 128, 129, 131,
  132
Shelley, Percy Bysshe, 167
Shockley, Martin, 138
Silone, Ignazio, 121
Slater, John F., 125
social change, 166-73
socialism, 166, 172
social protest, 42-44, 127, 168,
  174
"Some Thoughts on Juvenile
  Delinquency," 50
soul journey, 96-98
Steinbeck, John
  and animals, 28, 235
  autobiographical work of, 28,
    77, 131
  body of work, 65
  Drama Circle Critics' Award,
    133, 145
  failure of, 58-64, 145-46, 176
  on his novels, 27-29
  popular approval of, 177
  wins Nobel Prize, 174-77

wins Pulitzer Prize, 145
Stowe, Harriet Beecher, 169, 173
Study Guide to Steinbeck: A Handbook to His Major Works (Hayashi), 113, 125
Sun Also Rises, The (Hemingway), 70
Sweet Thursday, 59, 65, 67, 69
symbolism, 73-75, 96-98
   see also Christian symbolism; *individual works*

Tennyson, Alfred Lord, 132
Thoreau, Henry David, 67, 81
Time magazine, 176
To a God Unknown, 65, 77, 123
Tortilla Flat, 59, 77
   Angelica Cortez, 71
   Arabella Gross, 71
   Arthur Morales, 71
   Big Joe Portagee, 34, 67, 69
   Caporal, 71
   characterization in, 33-38, 118
   Cornelia Ruiz, 71
   Danny, 34-36, 41, 52-53, 67-71, 130
   escapism in, 52
   extraneous material in, 130
   family in, 72
   humor in, 35-37, 65, 174
   Jesus Maria Corcoran, 34, 71
   Mexican-Americans in, 65-72
   as mock epic, 41, 46, 47
   movie of, 28
   Mrs. Morales, 69, 70, 71
   Mrs. Pastanos, 69
   Mr. Torrelli, 71
   Pablo, 34, 70
   Peaches Ramirez, 69
   Pilon, 34, 53, 68, 70
   Pirate, 34, 36-37, 67, 70, 71, 138
   preface to, 100
   Steinbeck on, 27, 28, 29
   Sweets Ramirez, 35-71
   Tall Bob Smoke,
   Teresina Cortez, 70, 71
   Tito Ralph, 67
   women in, 69-71
transcendentalism, 41, 42, 44-46, 49, 138-40, 151, 173

Travels with a Donkey, 51
Travels with Charley, 175
Treasure Island (Stevenson), 51
True Adventures of John Steinbeck, Writer, The (Benson), 68

Uncle Tom's Cabin (Stowe), 169, 173
Unitarianism, 139-41
universal soul, 40, 45, 62-63, 55-56, 80, 140, 141

violence, 38, 43, 44, 76, 80-82, 100, 104
Viva Zapata!, 65
Vogel, Dan, 73

Walcutt, Charles Child, 40
war, 29, 44, 53, 81, 94
Wayne, Joseph, 63, 64
Wayward Bus, The
   Camille Oaks, 57
   Elliot Pritchard, 57
   escape and commitment in, 56, 57
   heroes in, 50, 137
   Juan Chicoy, 57, 67
   Mexican-Americans in, 65, 67
   settings in, 123
Whitman, Walt, 82, 138-41, 173
Wide World of John Steinbeck, The (Lisca), 73
Winter, Ella, 168
Winterich, John T., 119
Winter of Our Discontent, The, 175
women
   in *Grapes of Wrath*, 144, 153, 156-64
   as mothers, 74-76
   in *The Pearl*, 111, 112
   in *Tortilla Flat*, 69-71
Wordsworth, William, 76
Working Days: The Journals of "The Grapes of Wrath," 1938-1941, 33

Zola, Émile, 43